THE TRUST ECONOMY

Published by TrustOS Press, Discovery Bay, California

www.thetrusteconomy.org

ISBN: 979-8-218-90570-5

First Edition: January 2026

Printed in the United States of America

The Trust Economy

JONATHAN BRINK

TrustOS
PRESS

To my children. May we create a world you want to live in.

CONTENTS

Vision

"Without a vision, the people perish." —Proverbs 29:18

Author's Note

My Children Can't Afford To Live In the World They Grew Ip In.

I have six children and two grandchildren. And when you have children, everything changes. Suddenly you're not just living in the world—you're handing it to someone. Every system you participate in, every structure you maintain, every compromise you accept becomes a question: Is this what I want for them?

I've spent thirty years as a business owner, entrepreneur, product designer, and employee at one of the oldest tech companies in the world, watching how incentives shape behavior and how architecture determines outcomes. Design taught me a simple truth: systems create outcomes, whether we intend them or not. Build a system that rewards extraction, and people will extract. Build a system that rewards contribution, and people will contribute.

Once I saw that, I couldn't stop wondering why we tolerate systems that reliably produce suffering—and what it would take to build ones that don't.

I was in the right place at the right time to see a lot of puzzle pieces—and I've figured out how some of them fit together.

I was born in Silicon Valley. I've started several companies. I've worked at Charles Schwab and at IBM. I'm a product designer. I watched companies change the world and watched them destroy themselves. I failed far more than I succeeded—and I kept copious notes the entire time.

Thirty years of notes. Thirty years of asking why does this keep breaking? and what would actually work?

For the first time in human history, we have the technology, the tools, and the resources to organize ourselves differently. All we're missing is trust.

I've walked my dog at night for decades, turning the same questions over: What would a better system look like? What would I want to hand my children—not just as inheritance, but as possibility?

This book is my prototype of what I see when I walk my dog at night. It proposes the idea that it's not just possible. It's the best way to live because it's effective.

Here's what I ask from you: engage with the best version of what I'm proposing first. If something doesn't work, tell me why, so we can build something better.

The future isn't waiting to be discovered. It's waiting to be designed.

If you're ready, turn the page.

Prologue: Two Worlds

"You never change things by fighting the existing reality. To change something, build a new model that makes the existing model obsolete." —Buckminster Fuller

It's 2:47 in the morning, and Maria is doing math.

Not the kind she helps third-graders with at the elementary school where she works. This is survival math. She's sitting at her kitchen table in Phoenix, calculator app open, trying to figure out how to stretch her insulin supply for three more days until payday.

Maria is fifty-three. Type 1 diabetic since childhood. She makes $31,000 a year as a teaching assistant—beloved by parents who request her year after year.

Her insulin costs $1,200 a month.

The medication that keeps her alive costs approximately five dollars to manufacture. She pays three hundred dollars per vial at the pharmacy counter. The gap between those numbers—five dollars and three hundred dollars—is not explained by innovation or scarcity or complexity. It's explained by a system so layered with intermediaries, so saturated with defensive spending, that every transaction requires insurance against betrayal.

Maria isn't paying for insulin. She's paying for a system that doesn't trust itself.

We'll return to Maria throughout this book. She's not a symbol—she's a composite of millions of real people doing survival math in the richest society in human history. Her story is the measure against which every idea in these pages must be tested. If an economic system can't do better for Maria, it isn't worth building.

This is the Zero Trust Economy. Not a theoretical construct—a lived reality.

And here's the question that should haunt us: What if the most expensive thing in Maria's economy isn't insulin, or housing, or healthcare? What if the most expensive thing is the distrust itself?

It doesn't have to be this way.

What Trust Feels Like

Now imagine a different morning.

You open your eyes—not to an alarm, but to your body's natural rhythm. You lie still for a moment, feeling the particular peace of knowing that today is yours to design.

Thirty minutes later, you're sweating through a challenging session with a coach who lives three blocks away—someone who's trained you long enough to know exactly when to push and when to ease off.

In the afternoon, the plumber arrives—lives around the corner, knows your house, fixed that same pipe two years ago. He doesn't need to diagnose from scratch. He knows the history. The job takes twenty minutes instead of an hour.

Then: a harder moment. A collaborator messages. The project you've worked on for six months hit a wall—a key material proved too expensive at scale. In the old economy, this would mean layoffs, blame, someone's career damaged. Here, the system absorbs the setback. Resources redirect. The team pivots without anyone losing their home or health insurance. Failure is data, not catastrophe.

Evening brings dinner with friends. Your doctor is there—not as your doctor tonight, just as a friend. She's known you long enough to notice the way you're favoring your shoulder, and she mentions a stretch that might help. That's what happens when healthcare is relationship, not transaction.

The Trust Divide

Two worlds. Same species. Same planet. Same fundamental human needs for safety, belonging, contribution, and growth.

One world runs on distrust. Every transaction requires verification. Every relationship requires protection. Every system assumes bad actors and builds defenses accordingly. The defenses become costs. The costs become prices. The prices become barriers. The barriers become suffering—Maria doing math at 2:47 in the morning, calculating how much life she can afford.

The other world runs on trust. Systems assume good faith and build correction mechanisms instead of punishment mechanisms. Contribution is visible, so reputation becomes currency. Safety is collective, so individual anxiety dissolves. Resources flow toward creation instead of protection, toward flourishing instead of fortification.

The distance between these worlds is not technological. We have the tools. It's not economic. We have the resources. It's not even moral—people in both worlds want roughly the same things.

The distance is architectural. We built our systems on a foundation of distrust, and they perform exactly as designed—extracting maximum value from human vulnerability, converting every need into a revenue opportunity, transforming citizens into consumers and neighbors into strangers.

And that design has a cost. A staggering, hidden, pervasive cost. The lawyers and compliance officers and fraud prevention teams and verification systems and insurance underwriters—all the machinery we build because we assume everyone is trying to cheat—that machinery doesn't come free. It comes out of everything else. It comes out of Maria's insulin. It comes out of your rent. It comes out of every transaction you make, every day, in ways you've been trained not to see.

Buckminster Fuller saw this clearly. You cannot fix a system by attacking it. Attack generates defense. Defense generates escalation. Escalation generates exhaustion.

The only way forward is to build something better. Something so obviously superior that the old model becomes obsolete not through force, but through preference. Something so much more efficient that staying in the old system becomes irrational.

That something is trust. Not trust as a feeling—warm and easily betrayed. Trust as infrastructure. Trust as the load-bearing element that determines how much weight a system can carry. Trust as the variable that, when present, makes everything cheaper, faster, and more humane—and when absent, makes everything expensive, slow, and cruel.

This insight has an engineering implication that will thread through every chapter: trust isn't just morally superior. It's economically superior. It's the most efficient way to organize human activity ever discovered. And we've been systematically underinvesting in it.

That's what this book is about.

Choosing Trust

One more thing before we begin.

Virtually everyone who was responsible for adopting shareholder capitalism has passed away.

Milton Friedman is dead. The boards who implemented his doctrine in the 1970s and 80s—most of them are gone. The politicians who enshrined it, the economists who justified it, the executives who normalized it—they've passed the baton and left the stadium.

We're holding a system we never voted for.

You inherited this system the way you inherited your country's borders. Already drawn. Already normalized. Already "just how things are." You were born into extraction capitalism. You didn't design it. You didn't choose it. You woke up inside it and did your best to navigate something you found, not something you built.

You're not on trial for the past.

If you succeeded in the extraction economy—if you built wealth, climbed ladders, played the game well—that doesn't make you a villain. It makes you someone who learned the rules and followed them. Someone who did what the system rewarded.

The shame you might feel reading a book like this? You don't have to carry it.

We have no allegiance to decisions made by people who aren't here to defend them.

What we do have is a choice.

Because here's what's also true: every day we continue the extraction model is not inherited momentum. It's a fresh decision. Made by us. Today.

The architects are dead. The choice is alive.

This book isn't an indictment of what was. It's an invitation to what could be.

You're not the problem.

You might be part of the solution.

Maria deserves better. Because human beings shouldn't do survival math at 2:47 in the morning in the richest society in history.

The question isn't whether a better world is possible. It's whether we're willing to build it.

Turn the page when you're ready.

PART ONE: THE AWAKENING

Diagnosis

Something is wrong.

You feel it. The math doesn't work anymore. Your parents bought a house on a single income; you can't afford one on two. The economy keeps growing, but your life keeps shrinking. You were told that hard work leads to security. You worked hard. Where's the security?

Part One names what went wrong.

We'll trace three moments when trust died in the American economy—decisions that seemed rational at the time but hollowed out the foundation. We'll expose the wealth illusion: the lie that money equals happiness, when the data says otherwise. We'll diagnose Weak Capitalism—not as evil, but as structurally unsound. And we'll measure the damage through the Idiot Index, which reveals how much of what you pay is value versus friction.

One principle runs through all of it: the system isn't broken by accident. It's broken by design.

Extraction was the design. Profit divorced from people. Efficiency divorced from purpose. Growth divorced from flourishing. The architecture was built to extract, and it's extracting exactly as intended.

But once you see the design, you can imagine a different one.

The first step is waking up.

| 1 |

Chapter One: The Three Moments Trust Died

"Trust is the most efficient form of capital ever invented."

I love capitalism.

Not the version we have now. The one my father used to participate in—where people pool capital to solve real problems, where ownership means partnership, where success is shared by everyone who helped create it.

That capitalism was supposed to change the world.

Instead, it optimized for extraction. Capturing value rather than creating it. Measuring engagement rather than meaning. Scaling profit rather than flourishing. I've watched thousands of people get fired—not because their companies were failing, but because it made the quarter look better.

But I've also seen what happens when trust is present. Teams that move faster than should be possible. Products that users love rather than tolerate. Organizations where people actually want to work. The difference isn't talent or resources or luck. The difference is trust.

Which raises a question I've been asking for close to twenty years now: If trust is so valuable, why do our economic systems seem designed to destroy it?

The answer lies in three specific moments—three fractures that broke something fundamental in how we organize ourselves. Understanding them isn't just history. It's diagnosis.

The First Moment: The Doctrine (1970)

On September 13, 1970, Milton Friedman published a two-thousand-word essay in the New York Times Magazine: "The Social Responsibility of Business Is to Increase Its Profits." It became the philosophical blueprint for shareholder capitalism—the operating system that would reshape the global economy for fifty years.

But first, understand what Friedman was responding to.

In 1970, the alternatives to capitalism looked like this: Soviet communism had murdered tens of millions through purges, gulags, and forced collectivization. Maoist China's Great Leap Forward had killed between 15 and 55 million people through engineered famine. Various socialist experiments around the world were failing, corrupt, or authoritarian.

Friedman looked at this landscape and saw capitalism as the system that didn't murder people. Markets distributed power. Central planning concentrated it—and concentrated power killed.

He was defending human freedom against systems that had proven catastrophically deadly.

Friedman's argument was elegant and devastating: a corporation's only responsibility is to its shareholders. Everything else—the welfare of employees, the needs of customers, the health of communities, the state of the environment—these are costs to be managed, not obligations to be honored. The business of business is business. Period.

Before Friedman, most corporations operated under an implicit social contract. Yes, they existed to make money. But they also understood themselves as institutions with obligations to multiple stakeholders. Henry Ford paid his workers enough to buy the cars they made—not because he was altruistic, but because he understood that his success was bound to theirs. IBM provided lifetime employment because loyalty ran in both directions. Even the robber barons built libraries.

Friedman called this "confused thinking." If a corporate executive spends shareholder money on social causes, Friedman argued, he's essentially imposing taxes without democratic authorization. He's playing God with other people's money. The only honest position is clarity: maximize shareholder value, let the chips fall where they may.

Here's what Friedman got right: profit is a signal. It does coordinate activity. Markets do distribute decision-making better than central planners ever could. Half of the equation is still math. It just can't balance.

Here's what he got wrong: he treated half of the equation as the whole picture. He identified one signal—the shareholder signal—while amputating the complementary signal that would have made it sustainable. Shareholder value is real value. It's not nothing. But half a circuit doesn't carry current.

What Friedman proposed wasn't wrong. It was incomplete.

And incomplete can be completed. We'll see exactly what was missing—and how to restore it—in Chapter 4.

This was the intellectual fracture—the moment we made it academically respectable to optimize for one stakeholder while ignoring all others. The moment we chose one signal while amputating the rest.

The implications took decades to unfold, but unfold they did. When shareholder value became the only metric that mattered, everything else became a cost to be minimized. Workers became "human resources—inputs to be optimized, not partners to be invested in. Customers became "revenue sources—targets to be extracted from, not relationships to be cultivated. Communities became "operating environments—backgrounds to the real action happening on Wall Street.

Trust isn't abandoned overnight. It's redefined out of existence. The corporation now owed loyalty to one stakeholder only. Everyone else became a resource to be optimized.

The Second Moment: The Permission (1987)

On December 11, 1987, a movie opened in theaters across America. It was meant as a cautionary tale—a warning about the dangers of unchecked greed.

It became an anthem.

The movie was Wall Street. The character was Gordon Gekko. And the speech that was supposed to horrify audiences became the most quoted moment in financial history:

"Greed, for lack of a better word, is good. Greed is right. Greed works. Greed clarifies, cuts through, and captures the essence of the evolutionary spirit."

Director Oliver Stone intended Gekko as a villain—a portrait of everything wrong with Reagan-era capitalism. Instead, business schools started screening the film as inspiration. Investment banks put Gekko posters on their walls. A generation of finance professionals adopted "Greed is good" as their personal philosophy.

Here's what made that reception possible: Friedman.

Without Friedman's doctrine, Gekko's speech would have sounded like obvious villainy. But by 1987, Friedman had spent seventeen years making the intellectual case that profit-maximization wasn't just acceptable—it was the only ethical responsibility of business. Gekko wasn't inventing a philosophy. He was translating one. Taking Friedman's academic argument and giving it swagger, seduction, cultural permission.

What Friedman made intellectually respectable, Gekko made culturally aspirational.

This was the cultural fracture—the moment we made it socially acceptable to cheat, as long as you won.

Before Gekko, there was still residual shame attached to naked self-interest. You might pursue wealth aggressively, but you didn't brag about it in public. You certainly didn't frame it as a philosophy. There was a sense—however hypocritical in practice—that business operated within moral bounds.

Gekko gave permission to abandon those bounds entirely. Self-control became weakness. Restraint became inefficiency. Cheating wasn't just tolerated—it was considered a winning strategy. The social contract that held capitalism together began to unravel because one side had publicly declared it wouldn't honor the agreement.

"Greed clarifies," Gekko said.

He was right—it clarified that greed doesn't work. Not for building trust. Not for creating sustainable systems. Not for anything except short-term extraction.

But we didn't learn that lesson for another twenty years.

The Third Moment: The Collapse (2008)

On September 15, 2008, Lehman Brothers filed for bankruptcy.

It was the largest bankruptcy filing in American history. Within days, the global financial system was in free fall. Credit markets froze worldwide. Governments scrambled to inject trillions of dollars into banks that were "too big to fail." The stock market lost half its value. Eight million Americans lost their jobs. Ten million lost their homes.

What happened wasn't simply a banking crisis. It was the logical conclusion of the previous forty years.

Friedman's doctrine had taught corporations that only shareholder value mattered. So banks packaged toxic mortgages into securities and sold them to pension funds, because it was profitable. They knew the mortgages were bad. They sold them anyway.

Gekko's permission had taught financiers that greed was good. So traders invented ever more complex instruments to extract fees from transactions that created no real value. They built systems so opaque that no one—not the banks, not the regulators, not the rating agencies—knew where the danger actually lived.

The combination was lethal. An intellectual framework that removed all obligations except profit. A cultural permission structure that celebrated extraction as virtue. Together, they produced a system so riddled with hidden risk that no one knew who was holding the bad debt. No one knew how much exposure anyone had. No one knew whether their counterparties would survive until morning.

And then trust disappeared.

Banks stopped lending to each other—not because there was no money, but because no one trusted anyone else. The system didn't collapse because people stopped creating value. It collapsed because trust evaporated.

This was the structural fracture—the moment the system proved that trust had been load-bearing all along.

The 2008 crash revealed what Friedman's doctrine and Gekko's permission had obscured: trust wasn't sentimental. It wasn't optional. It wasn't a nice-to-have. Trust was the foundation. Remove it, and the whole structure falls.

In that moment, the world learned a lesson it quickly forgot: trust isn't optional. It's structural. It's what allows the machinery to run. And when it fails, no amount of money can substitute for it—because money itself only works when people trust it.

The Pattern

Look at these three moments together, and a pattern emerges—not just correlation, but causation.

The first moment was intellectual. Friedman gave us the philosophy—a framework that made it academically respectable to optimize for shareholders alone. Without Friedman, the second moment couldn't have happened.

The second moment was cultural. Gekko gave us the permission—translating Friedman's academic argument into aspirational narrative. The film intended satire; the culture received inspiration. Without Gekko, the third moment might have been caught earlier.

The third moment was structural. The 2008 crash gave us the proof—a catastrophe that demonstrated what happens when you run an incomplete system to its logical conclusion. The building collapsed because it was never structurally sound.

Philosophy. Permission. Proof.

Here's the deeper pattern: Friedman wasn't trying to cause harm. He was trying to prevent it. He feared concentrated power—he'd watched it murder millions. He believed markets would distribute power, protect freedom, prevent tyranny.

But his system produced exactly what he feared.

A half-signal only moves one direction: extraction. Value flows from labor, from customers, toward ownership. Follow that current to its terminus and you arrive at the Apex—the very concentration of power Friedman spent his life fighting.

Not villainy—tragedy. We'll see how to complete what he started in the chapters ahead.

The Hidden Tax

The cost of these three moments isn't just historical. You're paying it right now.

Every time you sign a forty-page contract to rent an apartment, you're paying the hidden tax of distrust. Every time you navigate a customer service maze designed to prevent you from talking to a human. Every time you're charged three hundred dollars for a medication that costs five dollars to make.

The gap between what things cost to produce and what you pay—what Elon Musk calls the Idiot Index—is largely a trust tax. Lawyers, compliance departments, insurance, verification systems, fraud prevention—all of it exists because trust was removed from the foundation.

This overhead isn't incidental. It's the dominant cost in most systems. We're not paying for value creation. We're paying for the machinery of mutual suspicion.

We pay this tax so constantly that we've stopped noticing it. We assume forty-page contracts are normal. We assume adversarial customer service is inevitable. We assume that prices bear no relationship to costs. We assume, in short, that distrust is the natural state of economic life.

It isn't. It's a design choice—a choice made in three moments, by people who thought they were being rational.

The Fork in the Road

After 2008, we had an opportunity. The system's flaws were exposed. The case for fundamental change was overwhelming. We could have redesigned our economic architecture around trust—built systems that aligned incentives, created transparency, rewarded cooperation.

I watched what happened instead.

In the decade after 2008, while working in Silicon Valley, I saw capital become more extractive, not less. Private equity discovered that buying companies and stripping them for parts was more profitable than building anything. They'd acquire a business with decades of customer relationships and employee loyalty, load it with debt, extract management fees, and walk away before the wreckage became visible. Perfectly legal. Utterly corrosive.

I watched friends lose jobs at companies that were profitable—liquidated not because they failed, but because failure was more lucrative than success for the people making decisions. I watched the implicit contract between business and community dissolve entirely. If you could make money destroying something, you destroyed it.

That's when I understood: 2008 wasn't a wake-up call. It was permission. The system had proven it could fail catastrophically and the people who caused the failure would be protected. Why would anyone change?

Instead, we patched. More regulations to shore up the worst cracks. More bailouts to prevent collapse. More compliance to compensate for missing trust. The fundamental architecture remained unchanged. Shareholder primacy continued. The cultural permission for greed survived. The structural conditions that produced the crash were preserved.

And so here we are. A decade and a half later, trust in institutions is at historic lows. Political polarization makes cooperation impossible. Young people don't believe the system will work for them—because they've watched it not work for them. The hidden tax of distrust grows heavier every year.

But there's another path.

In the chapters ahead, I'll show you what an economy designed for trust looks like—not as theory, but as architecture.

We can't undo Friedman's essay or erase Gekko from cultural memory or reverse the 2008 collapse. But we can build something better. Something that learns from these failures instead of repeating them.

Three moments broke trust in our economic system. They don't have to be the end of the story.

They can be the beginning of a different one.

| 2 |

Chapter Two: The Wealth Illusion

"Wealth is just your energy stack—it shows your capacity, not your value. Your value is found in connection, in community."

We were sold a half truth.

The implicit promise beneath Greed is Good capitalism was simple: accumulate enough wealth, and you win. Wealth equals success. Success equals happiness. Therefore, wealth equals happiness.

We built an entire civilization around this assumption. We structured our corporations to maximize it. We designed our tax codes to reward it. We raised our children to pursue it. We measured our worth by it.

Here's the half they got right: wealth is stored energy. It does represent capacity—your accumulated power to act in the economic world. Capacity matters. Having resources to deploy is better than having none.

Here's the half they left out: capacity is not value. Power is not meaning. And winning a game that leaves you empty is not winning at all.

The distinction matters more than it seems. Capacity is potential energy. Value is what that energy creates when it flows. A battery sitting on a shelf has capacity. A battery powering a connection has value.

The Data

The research on wealth and happiness is remarkably consistent—and remarkably ignored.

Economists call it the Easterlin Paradox: once basic needs are met, additional income produces diminishing returns in life satisfaction. Kahneman and Deaton found the happiness benefits of income largely plateau around $75,000 per year.

Psychologists call it the hedonic treadmill. Income boosts happiness, but humans adapt quickly, returning to baseline. The luxury car that thrilled you in month one feels ordinary by month six. The lifestyle upgrade that promised fulfillment delivers novelty instead—and novelty always fades.

This leads to a perpetual cycle: earn more, adapt, feel empty, earn more. The pursuit of wealth becomes a treadmill with no destination, each milestone revealing only the next milestone, never the finish line.

Meanwhile, the research on what actually predicts happiness points in a completely different direction. Strong social relationships consistently emerge as the most robust predictor of wellbeing. Not income. Not status. Not achievement. Relationships.

The most compelling evidence comes from the Harvard Study of Adult Development—the longest study of human happiness ever conducted. For eighty-five years, researchers tracked hundreds of participants from adolescence to old age, collecting medical records, conducting interviews, and asking detailed questions about their lives.

Their conclusion, after nearly a century of data, is unambiguous: positive relationships keep us happier, healthier, and help us live longer. Period.

"Close relationships, more than money or fame, are what keep people happy throughout their lives."

The study found that the quality of relationships at age fifty was a better predictor of physical health at age eighty than cholesterol levels. People with strong social connections experienced less mental deterioration as they aged. Those with warm relationships had lower rates of heart disease, diabetes, and arthritis. Their immune systems functioned better. They recovered from illness faster.

Robert Waldinger, the study's current director, summarized the finding simply: "Loneliness kills. It's as powerful as smoking or alcoholism."

The data could not be clearer. We optimized for wealth. We should have optimized for connection.

And the data implies but rarely states directly: trust is the mechanism. Relationships work because trust works. Connection produces health and happiness because trusted relationships produce safety, and safety is what the nervous system needs to thrive. Money can't buy that safety—only trust can.

The Winner's Curse

If wealth doesn't buy happiness, you might expect the ultra-wealthy to at least be content. They have won the game, after all. They have more than they could ever spend. Surely they've found peace.

They haven't.

I once sat across from a man worth more than most countries. Dinner at his home—immaculate, staffed, secured. Twelve seats at the table, but only four occupied. His wife, his attorney, his asset manager, and me. Halfway through the meal, he said something I've never forgotten: "I haven't had a real conversation in years. Everyone wants something. I can't remember the last time someone just... talked to me."

He had capacity beyond imagination. But he was starving for value.

Therapists who work with billionaires report this pattern consistently: chronic isolation, depression, paranoia. Clinical psychotherapist Paul Hokemeyer, who treats the ultra-wealthy, describes the phenomenon bluntly: "They live in such a rarified place of the top one percent where there are very few people who share the realities of their world."

The ultra-wealthy can never be sure if people like them for who they are or for what they have. Every friendship is shadowed by suspicion: would you still be here if the money disappeared?

The isolation compounds. They become targets for manipulation. They develop suspicion that makes genuine connection nearly impossible. Trust erodes under the weight of wealth itself.

Consider the practical realities of extreme wealth. You cannot simply go to 7-Eleven. You require security details. Your homes need full-time management staffs who could easily steal from you. Your calendar fills with obligations to maintain and protect assets. The twenty-four hours you have each day—the same twenty-four hours everyone else has—get consumed by the logistics of wealth preservation.

The money that was supposed to buy freedom becomes a prison of its own making.

This is the trap's deepest irony: the billionaire spends millions on security, lawyers, and verification systems—all to protect against the very distrust that wealth itself creates. The money that was supposed to provide safety becomes the reason safety disappears. And it reveals something crucial: money is an expensive, inefficient substitute for trust. Trust provides safety directly. Money tries to purchase it indirectly, at enormous cost, and fails.

Marcus

I didn't learn this from research papers. I learned it from watching.

I grew up in Los Gatos, where families had too much money, and the children had to learn how to deal with it. I watched them closely. And what I noticed surprised me.

The kids with the most money didn't always know how to handle it. Many of them were heavy drug users. They partied relentlessly. It was as if wealth had given them permission to destroy themselves—slowly, expensively, and with no one to stop them.

A kid I'll call Marcus sat on the balcony of his parents' house, drunk, staring at the hills. He had everything. Cars. Access. Freedom. A trust fund that meant he'd never have to work. And he turned to me and said, "I don't know why I'm so fucking sad all the time."

He wasn't performing. He was drowning. Money steals your ambition because you don't have to make any if your parents always give it to you.

But here's the irony I couldn't shake: fun doesn't require wealth.

Joy doesn't require a trust fund. Laughter doesn't require a yacht. Connection doesn't require a mansion. The things that actually make life worth living—friendship, adventure, meaning, love—are available to anyone willing to show up.

I began to notice it everywhere: the wealthiest people I knew seemed to need the most external stimulation. Their baseline for pleasure had inflated until nothing ordinary could reach it. Meanwhile, people with far less seemed to extract more enjoyment from simpler things—a meal with friends, a walk in the park, a conversation that went deep.

Wealth, it turns out, doesn't purchase joy. It purchases stimulation. And stimulation, consumed habitually, destroys the capacity for joy.

The Peacock's Tragedy

If wealth fails to deliver happiness, why do the wealthy still display it so aggressively?

The answer reveals another crack in the wealth illusion.

I watched it happen to a friend.

We played soccer together. Good guy—smart, driven, fun to be around. His company went public when he was twenty-seven. The first thing he bought was a Lamborghini Countach.

The Lambo consistently broke down. He ended up selling it. But wealth had already done what wealth does—it created distance. The season after he went public, he drifted away from the team. I don't think he meant to. I think wealth just pulls you into a different orbit, and the people who knew you before can't follow.

The peacock's tragedy isn't bad character. It's that the display attracts the wrong people—and repels the right ones. The people impressed by wealth displays are attracted to capacity, not character. They want access to resources, not relationship. Meanwhile, the people most capable of genuine connection are often repelled by display. They read it correctly: as insecurity, as compensation, as a substitution of surface for depth.

The peacock's tragedy is that it works just well enough to seem effective. You display, and people notice. You signal wealth, and doors open. But the doors lead to rooms full of other peacocks, all performing for each other, none of them finding what they actually need.

The Closed Fist

But display is only half the problem. The other half is grip.

The more you have, the more you fear losing it. The more you fear losing it, the tighter you grip. The tighter you grip, the less you can use what you have. The very act of protecting wealth prevents you from enjoying it.

The wealthy don't feel rich. They feel vulnerable. Every market downturn, every lawsuit, every shift in tax policy represents a threat to what they've built. Their relationship to money isn't one of abundance—it's one of constant vigilance.

By not releasing money, you keep yourself from the very thing you accumulated it for. The closed fist protects the coins but cannot embrace anyone. The billionaire's tragedy isn't that they have too much.

It's that they hold too tight—and in the gripping, lose everything money was supposed to buy.

What Trust Bought Us

But it doesn't have to be this way. I know, because I grew up around wealth—and saw something different.

My family had money. And the lesson I learned wasn't "get more."

The most valuable thing about wealth was that it allowed my family to truly enjoy life. We weren't in survival mode. We weren't spending every ounce of energy just trying to make it to next month. We had margin. We had space. We had the bandwidth to actually live.

You don't need everything. You just need enough to escape the constant grind of survival. That's what wealth bought us—not excess, but sufficiency. Not luxury, but breathing room.

I grew up in a trust economy. That was my family. My dad and my stepfather believed in me. My mother gave her heart and soul to show me that I was valuable. The wealth didn't make us happy—the trust did. The money simply removed the obstacles that would have made trust harder to build.

What I remember most: the best part of wealth was blessing other people—and doing it in ways where they didn't know we were doing it.

There's a tremendous joy in seeing someone light up. In meeting a need they didn't know could be met. In being the invisible hand that makes someone's life a little easier. That's when wealth felt like it was doing what it was supposed to do. That's when money became sacred.

In those moments, it felt like God.

Not because we were God—but because generosity is the closest humans get to the divine. When you give without expectation, when you bless without recognition, when you use your resources to elevate someone else's experience—something transcendent happens. The transaction becomes communion. The exchange becomes love.

That's when capacity finally becomes value.

A Better Game

We cannot penalize the billionaire for being really good at playing the game. They optimized for what the system told them to optimize for. They won by the rules they were given.

But we can build a better game.

The value of a Trust Economy is that it's well-balanced. It doesn't demonize wealth or glorify poverty. It doesn't demand redistribution at gunpoint or pretend that resources don't matter. Instead, it redesigns the incentives so that balance becomes the natural outcome.

The value of balance is that you get to enjoy all four quadrants of the human experience: the thrill, the struggle, the joy, and the fruits of your labor. Life isn't meant to be one note. It's meant to be a symphony—challenge and rest, effort and reward, giving and receiving, solitude and community.

When work isn't the reason you exist, you can enjoy the fruits of your labor. When accumulation isn't the point, you can appreciate what you have. When you're not terrified of losing everything, you can open your hands—and your heart.

A Trust Economy looks like God. It's full of grace and possibility and hope and joy because there's balance. That's the game.

Not to win by having the most. But to win by living the most fully—in connection, in community, in contribution, in love.

Not abolish wealth. Not redistribute it by force. Not shame people for having it. But offer something so compelling that wealth loses its grip on our collective imagination.

The billionaire's problem is not that they have too much money. It's that they have nothing better to believe in. Wealth became their religion because no one offered them a more compelling faith. Accumulation became their purpose because no one showed them a more fulfilling one. The scoreboard became their identity because no one gave them a truer measure of worth.

The Trust Economy offers that alternative.

What if your worth wasn't measured by what you accumulated, but by what you contributed? What if status came from generosity instead of display? What if the game rewarded release instead of hoarding? What if trust—not money—was the currency that unlocked the good life?

In such a system, the wealthy wouldn't need to hoard—because their worth wouldn't depend on their net worth. They wouldn't need to peacock—because they'd be valued for who they are, not what they have. They wouldn't need to isolate—because trust would make connection safe again.

This isn't punishing success. It's redefining it.

The billionaire who releases their grip and invests in community doesn't become poorer. They become richer in the only currency that actually satisfies: relationships, meaning, trust, love.

The goal isn't to take from the wealthy. It's to offer them something better than wealth.

The Real Wealth

The wealth illusion has shaped our world for half a century. It told us that accumulation was the path to happiness.

Accumulation does build capacity. Wealth does create options. But capacity without connection is a battery that never powers anything. Options without relationships are doors that open onto empty rooms.

When we optimize for trust instead of wealth, the whole game changes. Release becomes rational. Generosity becomes strategic. Connection becomes possible. And the abundance that wealth promised but never delivered finally becomes real.

The choice isn't between wealth and poverty. It's between isolation and community. Between gripping and releasing. Between the illusion of winning and the reality of living.

The Trust Economy offers a better game.

One where everyone can win—not by having the most, but by living the most fully, together.

| 3 |

Chapter Three: Energy Is Trust

"Energy is trust. Protect energy, trust holds. Extract energy, collapse comes."

Money is stored human energy. Banking is how we coordinate that energy. When the coordination matches reality, we call it trust. When it doesn't, we get collapse.

This chapter is the story of how we broke that coordination—and what it would mean to rebuild it on trust instead of exploitation.

Banks Are Energy Exchanges Wrapped in Legal Scaffolding

Banks are energy exchanges wrapped in legal scaffolding, trying to pass as trust. The scaffolding is so thick—and the trust so thin—that a credit card can cost you 25-30% a year for the privilege of borrowing your own future work.

And here's the cruelty: the more desperate you are, the more you pay. The more likely you are to need the money for survival, the more likely you are to accept terms that make survival harder. The system extracts most aggressively from those with the least leverage.

But if we step back, we can see something the system obscures: virtually everyone involved is just trying to do good. The banker processing the loan application. The family signing the mortgage. The investor seeking returns.

The problem isn't the people. It's the operating system they're running on.

When you're in survival mode, you see most of your life through a negative lens. You scan for threats, not opportunities. You protect, not create. The banking system as currently designed keeps millions of people locked in that mode—and calls it "credit risk."

How Did Banks Get This Much Power?

The origin of modern banking is a story of trust exploited, then institutionalized, then scaled until it became invisible.

Phase 1: The Temple (Trust in the Divine)

Banking began around 2000 BCE in temples. Mesopotamian priests accepted grain deposits, made loans to farmers and traders. Why temples? Because people trusted the gods wouldn't steal.

The sacred space was the original "trust architecture." It worked because the institution's legitimacy came from something larger than profit—from the divine, from community, from shared meaning. Financial infrastructure rooted in purpose beyond extraction.

Phase 2: The Goldsmith's Discovery (The Original Fraud)

In medieval Europe, goldsmiths had secure vaults. People deposited gold and received paper receipts that circulated as money—easier than carrying metal.

Then the goldsmiths noticed: not everyone redeems their gold at once.

So they started issuing receipts for gold that didn't exist. They would lend out paper representing ten times the gold they actually held, and charge interest on all of it.

What began as fraud was eventually legalized and renamed "fractional reserve banking."

The key insight: Banking power originated from exploiting the gap between what people trusted was there and what was actually there.

Phase 3: The Banking Families (Trust Within, Extraction Without)

The Rothschild advantage wasn't capital—it was carrier pigeons.

In 1815, Nathan Rothschild in London knew the outcome of Waterloo a full day before the British government did. His brothers had positioned messengers across the continent, creating an information network faster than any nation-state possessed. While London panicked over rumors of Napoleon's victory, Nathan was buying British bonds at collapse prices. By the time official word arrived, he'd made a fortune.

The great banking dynasties—the Medici in Florence, the Rothschilds across Europe—succeeded because they built internal trust networks spanning borders at a time when strangers couldn't be trusted.

Brothers in five capitals. Shared blood. Shared incentives. Information moving faster than governments could manage.

The Rothschilds proved that coordinated capital could reshape the world. They financed railroads, industrial expansion, state projects that transformed continents. Their network demonstrated what trust-based coordination could accomplish: infrastructure at scale, projects that exceeded what any nation-state could achieve alone.

But the power was concentrated, opaque, and accountable to no one outside the family. The efficiency gains from trust-based coordination flowed to the coordinating few, not the coordinated many.

Phase 4: Central Banks (The Government-Banker Alliance)

The Bank of England was founded in 1694 as a deal between a bankrupt government and private financiers. The government needed war funding. The bankers wanted privilege.

The result: a private institution with the exclusive right to hold government deposits and issue currency.

The Federal Reserve, created in 1913, is a public-private hybrid: a network of privately owned regional banks with government-granted authority to create money and set the price of borrowing for an entire nation. The structure serves those who designed it.

The pattern: Privatize the profits. Socialize the risks. Call it public service.

Phase 5: The Modern Apex

Today, the concentration is unprecedented:

The four largest U.S. banks—JPMorgan Chase, Bank of America, Citigroup, and Wells Fargo—hold over $11.5 trillion in combined assets, representing more than 50% of the top 25 banks' total. The top 25 banks combined hold $21.1 trillion—equivalent to 91% of U.S. GDP.

These aren't just big numbers. This is gravitational mass. When institutions control this much capital, they shape reality itself. Interest rates, housing prices, who gets funded and who doesn't, which neighborhoods thrive and which decay—all of it flows from decisions made in rooms most people don't know exist.

The same institutions that crashed the economy in 2008 are now larger than before. The bailouts didn't reform the system. They fed it.

The Extraction Trap

Here's what makes this story tragic rather than villainous:

Capitalists are trying to improve the system by taking advantage of it.

They see a flaw—an inefficiency, an arbitrage opportunity, a trust gap—and they exploit it. They call this "creating value." And sometimes it is. Sometimes the arbitrage reveals a genuine improvement.

But every exploitation fragments community further. Every trust gap monetized is a trust gap preserved rather than healed. The incentive is to find distrust and profit from it, not to find distrust and fix it.

This breeds contempt for the neighbor you don't know. Is she on your side? Is he competing for the same opportunity? Everyone becomes a potential threat because everyone is fragmented, atomized, scanning for advantage.

The system designed to coordinate human activity has made us strangers to each other.

The Internal Bank Run

The same fragmentation happening in the economy is happening inside each of us.

Survival is just below courage. It's the state of not knowing if you're going to make it—because you don't know if you can handle it.

I know this place. I lived in this idea for probably three months.

From my perspective, I was going to hell. And hell was the worst thing I could possibly think of for myself: complete loneliness for eternity.

I spent a day planning how to end my life in significant detail, because I wanted my last experience to at least be somewhat enjoyable. To see if I could find some moment of peace.

Capitola was where I spent my childhood. My dad rented, over three or four seasons, beachfront condos. Each year we'd try a different one, which added to the thrill of the experience.

So I chose Capitola as my last spot.

I never made it.

A friend sent me a letter with the only line that could have stopped me. He reminded me that I was a brother in Christ. He reminded me who I was—or at least who I thought I was.

That letter was a proof of reserves. It showed me deposits I'd forgotten existed. Real connection. Real identity. Energy that hadn't been fabricated.

The internal bank run happens when the gap between who you've told yourself you are and who you actually are becomes unsustainable. When the receipts don't match the vault. When you've been running on promises—about your worth, your connection, your right to exist—that can't be redeemed.

The rug pull comes. It always comes.

But here's what I learned in the thirty years since: the collapse isn't the end. It's the invitation to rebuild on what's actually there. To stop issuing receipts for gold that doesn't exist. To match what you promise yourself with what's real.

This is the human experience: a sense of disconnection from source—from whatever you believe holds you. In practical terms, it's the split between head and heart: what you think, what you feel, and what you do no longer match. When those three align again, the internal bank run can't happen. The vault contains what it claims.

The Bank Run Is the Rug Pull

The pattern keeps repeating.

The goldsmiths issuing receipts for gold that didn't exist—until depositors showed up at once. The Panic of 1907. The waves of failures during the Great Depression. The 2008 collapse. Silicon Valley Bank in 2023. Each time, the same structure:

Promise more than exists. Extract while confidence holds. Collapse when transparency arrives.

The run doesn't cause the crisis. The run reveals the crisis that was always there. The gap between what was promised and what was real—that gap existed from the moment the first fraudulent receipt was issued. The run is just the moment everyone discovers it simultaneously.

This is the rug pull. Not a malfunction of the system. The inevitable consequence of its design.

The Anatomy of a Modern Bank Run: SVB

In March 2023, Silicon Valley Bank lost $42 billion in deposits in a single day. Roughly 89% of its $172 billion in deposits were uninsured—concentrated in a few thousand venture-backed startups and funds. When a handful of prominent VCs told their portfolio companies to pull their money—mostly via group chats and Twitter—the bank was done within 48 hours.

Representative Patrick McHenry, chair of the House Financial Services Committee, named it: "This was the first Twitter-fueled bank run."

The concentrated few moved first. Everyone else scrambled.

Why Bank Runs Are Even Possible

Here's what nobody talks about: bank runs are only possible when a relative few can pull enough money to crash the system.

If wealth were distributed—if everyone held roughly equal stakes—no individual or small group could trigger a collapse. You'd need everyone to panic simultaneously, which is far harder to engineer and far less likely to cascade.

But when a handful of depositors control disproportionate shares, their exit becomes an extinction event. One whale withdraws, the bank's reserves plummet, smaller depositors hear about it, fear spreads, and suddenly everyone's racing for the door.

The concentration creates the vulnerability.

We know from behavioral economics that small losses—5% to 7%—trigger disproportionate panic. The psychology is predictable, and the system is designed to exploit it rather than account for it.

The Historical Pattern

The Great Depression offers the starkest lesson. From 1929 to 1933, over 9,000 American banks failed. By April 1933, roughly $7 billion in deposits had been frozen in failed institutions.

The pattern each time was the same: the wealthy and well-connected pulled their assets first. They had information, they had options, they moved fast. Then word spread. In December 1930, a small merchant in the Bronx went to a branch of the Bank of the United States and asked to sell his stock. When the bank advised him not to, he left and began spreading rumors that they'd refused to sell. Within hours, thousands of depositors had withdrawn $2 million.

The mere hint of trouble was enough. People lined up at one bank because people were lining up at another. The panic fed itself.

Nine million Americans lost their savings before Roosevelt's bank holiday in March 1933.

The Insight: Equal Stakes Create Stability

This is what distributed ownership achieves. When the system expands, everyone expands together. No one accumulates the leverage to crash it. No one holds the knife that cuts the rope.

In a system where everyone holds equal stakes, there's no one with enough weight to tip the balance. The rug can't be pulled because no one's holding enough of it.

This isn't idealism. It's structural engineering. Distributed stakes create resilience. Concentrated stakes guarantee fragility.

Energy Is Trust

Here's the equation underneath everything:

Energy is trust.

When energy is protected—when what's promised matches what exists—trust holds. When energy is exploited—when the gap between appearance and reality widens—collapse becomes inevitable.

Money is stored energy. Your labor, converted into numbers, held for future use. When the bank lends out ten times what it holds, it's promising energy that doesn't exist. When the system extracts 30% interest from someone in survival mode, it's draining energy faster than it can be regenerated.

The trust system requires two things: transparency and effective protection of energy.

Transparency means the receipts match the vault. No gap between what's promised and what's real. The moment opacity enters—the moment someone profits from the difference between appearance and reality—the countdown to collapse begins.

Protection of energy means the system doesn't extract faster than people can regenerate. It means survival mode isn't a profit center. It means the most vulnerable aren't the most exploited.

Without both, the rug pull is just a matter of time.

The Question Banks Should Ask

So what would it look like to build banks on this foundation?

Banks should recognize what they actually are: coordination mechanisms for human energy.

That's it. Money is stored work. Lending is directing stored work toward future work. Interest is the price of coordination across time.

Strip away the mystification and banks are simply asking: "Can we trust this person to do good work?" Then charging for the answer.

A trust-based bank asks: "Is this person part of our community? Will they contribute? Can we support them if they struggle?"

Our current system quietly asks a different question: "How much can we extract from this person before they break?"

That's not idealism versus realism. That's what the small-town banker used to know. That's what credit unions still practice. That's what trust-based lending has always looked like before it got scaled into anonymity.

The question isn't whether we can return to trust-based banking.

The question is whether we can scale it.

Business as Coordination

Strip away the jargon, the quarterly reports, the stock tickers, and the MBA frameworks. What remains?

All business is coordination of efforts to solve human problems.

Every company, every startup, every corner store—they exist because solving problems requires coordinated effort.

The only question that matters is how well the coordination works.

A high-friction system coordinates poorly. Energy leaks out at every junction. People protect instead of create. Resources flow to lawyers and accountants instead of problem-solvers.

A high-trust system coordinates beautifully. Energy flows where it's needed. People contribute their best because they're not defending against extraction.

This is why trust isn't a soft value bolted onto hard economics. Trust is the infrastructure that determines how well coordination works. Google's Project Aristotle found that psychological safety was the single strongest predictor of team performance. Not talent, not resources, not strategy. Trust.

And here's what history shows: every improvement to money has been an improvement in trust infrastructure.

Barter required you to find someone who had what you wanted and wanted what you had—a double coincidence of wants. Then commodity money emerged. You no longer needed a perfect trading partner. You just needed someone who trusted that the commodity held value. Friction dropped. Trade expanded.

Paper money was the next leap. Instead of carrying heavy metal, you carried a promise. But that promise only worked if people trusted the issuer. Digital money removed more friction—instant transfers, global reach. But it required trusting banks, networks, governments, and code.

The pattern is clear: the elevation of money is the elevation of trust.

Every time we've improved money, we've actually improved the trust infrastructure underneath it.

When trust rises, we can do more. Not because we're working harder, but because less energy is lost to friction, verification, protection, and fear. The same effort produces more value when it doesn't have to fight through layers of distrust.

The End of Money

Here's where the arc bends toward light.

The Trust Economy can inflate as it needs to—but everyone gets the same increase. No one's purchasing power erodes while someone else's expands. No silent theft through monetary policy. (We'll unpack the mechanics in the Unity Token chapter.)

In this system, money begins to behave differently. It stops hoarding at the top. It stops pooling in dead accounts while families struggle. Instead, it magnetizes toward good ideas. Toward entrepreneurs with vision. Toward problems worth solving.

Why? Because when trust is visible—when contribution is tracked, when reputation is real—capital doesn't need gatekeepers to find worthy recipients. The system itself routes energy toward value creation.

This is what becomes possible when the receipts match the vault. When energy is protected instead of extracted. When the system is designed for flow rather than accumulation.

And at some point—maybe a generation from now, maybe two—money becomes less and less necessary for coordinating value.

Not because we've abolished it. Not because some revolution forced its end. But because when trust scales, the medium of exchange becomes less essential. You don't need a token to represent value when value flows directly. You don't need proof of worth when worth is known.

Money has always been a stand-in for trust—a workaround for the problem of strangers. A way to coordinate with people you'd never meet and couldn't verify.

But if trust scales—if the Trust Economy reaches the point where your reputation precedes you, where your contribution history is visible, where the community knows you'll do what you say—then money becomes what it always was: scaffolding.

And scaffolding comes down when the building is complete.

The end of money isn't the end of exchange. It's the perfection of it. Value flowing without friction. Coordination without extraction. Energy moving toward creation because that's what energy wants to do when it isn't being dammed, hoarded, and weaponized.

We'll look back and say: Can you believe they needed tokens just to help each other?

| 4 |

Chapter Four: Weak Capitalism

"We built this system before we had the data to prove how little it worked for the long term. Now we have that data."

I want to be precise about something: when I say capitalism is broken, I don't mean it's evil.

I mean it's structurally unsound.

There's a difference. A building can collapse not because anyone intended harm, but because the architecture was flawed from the beginning. The foundation was wrong. The load-bearing walls were placed incorrectly. The materials couldn't handle the stress. No malice required—just poor engineering.

That's shareholder capitalism. Not a conspiracy. Not a villain's plot. Just a system designed without trust as a structural component—and now buckling under the weight of its own contradictions.

As a systems designer, I've spent decades analyzing why things break. And when I examine modern capitalism through an engineering lens, the diagnosis is clear: this is a building constructed on sand, with hollow foundations, missing support beams, a single overloaded column, and rebar that's corroded from within.

Weak capitalism isn't failing because humans are greedy. It's failing because it's structurally incapable of producing what it promises.

The Four Structural Weaknesses

Every failing building has signature flaws—design defects that compound over time until the structure can no longer hold. Shareholder capitalism has four.

First: The Hollow Foundation (Externalized Costs)

The logic of shareholder capitalism requires companies to maximize returns to owners. Anything that reduces those returns—environmental protection, worker welfare, community investment—becomes a cost to be minimized or, better yet, pushed onto someone else.

Economists call these externalities: costs that don't appear on the company's balance sheet but are very real to those who bear them. The factory pollutes the river, and the community downstream pays the healthcare bills. The corporation pays poverty wages, and taxpayers fund the food stamps. The industry generates carbon emissions, and future generations inherit a destabilized climate.

Consider Paradise, California. In November 2018, the Camp Fire killed eighty-five people and destroyed nearly nineteen thousand structures. My daughter went to college in Chico, just down the road. I drove through the devastation with her—mile after mile of charred foundations, melted cars, trees still standing but blackened and dead. The smell of ash lingered for months.

The cause: Pacific Gas & Electric had deferred maintenance on aging transmission lines to protect shareholder returns. The company knew the equipment was dangerous. Internal documents showed they'd calculated the risk. But replacing the lines would cost money—money that would otherwise flow to shareholders. So they externalized the risk onto an entire town.

PG&E's stock price had performed beautifully for years. Their balance sheet looked healthy. The true cost was hidden—until it wasn't. Until Paradise burned.

This isn't a bug in the system. It's a feature. Shareholder capitalism is designed to externalize costs—to push environmental and social debt downstream, where it becomes someone else's problem.

But externalized costs don't disappear. They accumulate. They compound. And eventually, they come due—not to the shareholders who profited, but to the society that hosted them.

Second: No Redundancy (Over-Optimized Efficiency)

Efficiency sounds like an unqualified good. Who could argue against doing more with less? But there's a shadow side to efficiency that engineers understand and economists often ignore: efficiency eliminates redundancy, and redundancy is what keeps buildings standing when the unexpected happens.

A maximally efficient structure has no slack. No buffer. No margin for error. Every beam is load-bearing, every material is stressed to capacity, every dollar is working. This looks great on a spreadsheet—until something shifts.

In March 2021, the Ever Given—a container ship the length of the Empire State Building—ran aground in the Suez Canal. For six days, global trade stopped. Not slowed. Stopped. Four hundred ships carrying $9.6 billion worth of goods per day sat waiting. Factories on the other side of the world shut down because a single part couldn't arrive.

One ship. One canal. And the entire system seized because "just-in-time" supply chains had eliminated every buffer, every backup route, every redundancy that might have absorbed the shock.

When the pandemic hit, we discovered the same brittleness everywhere. Our "efficient" hospitals had no surge capacity. Our "efficient" workforce had no savings to weather a pause. Our "efficient" supply chains for masks, ventilators, and semiconductors collapsed at the first disruption.

Third: Single Point of Failure (Centralized Decision-Making)

Shareholder capitalism concentrates power at the top. Decisions flow from executives to managers to workers. Information flows from the field to headquarters, where it's processed and returned as directives. The hierarchy is designed for control, not responsiveness.

In 2018 and 2019, two Boeing 737 MAX aircraft crashed, killing 346 people. The cause traced back to centralized decisions made far from the engineers who understood the risks. Boeing's leadership, under pressure to compete with Airbus and satisfy Wall Street's quarterly expectations, pushed the 737 MAX to market faster than safety allowed. They overruled engineers. They minimized pilot training to save customers money. They designed a single automated system—with no redundancy, no backup, no override that pilots could understand in time.

The people closest to the problem—the engineers, the test pilots, the safety analysts—knew something was wrong. But in a centralized system, their knowledge couldn't flow upward fast enough, and their concerns couldn't override the directives flowing down. 346 people died.

Decentralized systems—where decision-making is distributed, where local knowledge is trusted, where adaptation happens at the edges—are far more resilient. But decentralization requires trust. You have to believe that people throughout the organization can make good decisions without constant oversight. Shareholder capitalism, with its assumption that workers are costs to be minimized and monitored, cannot generate that trust. So it centralizes instead, and brittleness follows.

Fourth: Corroded Rebar (Severed Human Trust)

This is the deepest flaw, the one that makes all the others worse. It's the rebar inside the concrete—invisible, but holding everything together. When it corrodes, the whole structure weakens from within.

Shareholder capitalism reduces relationships to transactions and people to data points. The customer isn't a human to serve but a revenue source to extract from. The employee isn't a partner to invest in but a cost to minimize. The supplier isn't an ally to collaborate with but a margin to squeeze. The community isn't a home to nurture but a resource to exploit.

In 2016, news broke that Wells Fargo employees had opened millions of fake accounts in customers' names. The employees weren't criminals—they were desperate. The bank's aggressive sales targets made it impossible to meet quotas honestly. Managers pressured workers relentlessly. Those who failed were fired. Those who succeeded did so by betraying the customers they were supposed to serve.

The system had corroded the rebar. Trust between bank and customer, between manager and employee, between institution and community—all of it dissolved under the pressure to hit numbers. Wells Fargo paid billions in fines. They fired thousands of employees. They ran apologetic ad campaigns. But the damage went deeper than any settlement could repair.

When every relationship is transactional, trust becomes impossible. And without trust, every interaction requires verification, documentation, and legal protection. The costs of distrust—the lawyers, the auditors, the compliance departments, the insurance policies—multiply.

This is the hidden tax of weak capitalism. The system that promised efficiency produces inefficiency. The system that promised growth produces fragility. The system that promised prosperity produces burnout.

And here's the engineering insight that most economists miss: trust isn't just morally superior. It's structurally superior. The structure holds because the relationships hold. That's not idealism. That's load-bearing architecture.

Why Trust Is the Load-Bearing Material

Every structural weakness I've described has the same root cause: insufficient trust. The hollow foundation exists because corporations don't trust that doing right will be rewarded—so they externalize costs. The missing redundancy exists because efficiency is optimized without trusting that slack will be used wisely. The centralized decision-making exists because leadership doesn't trust people at the edges. The corroded rebar exists because relationships have been reduced to transactions.

In each case, the solution isn't more rules or more enforcement. The solution is more trust—embedded in the architecture, not added as an afterthought.

This is why I call weak capitalism structurally unsound. It's not optimized for the material that actually holds buildings together.

The 360 Review

Weak capitalism wasn't evil. It was incomplete.

Think of it like a 360 review—the kind corporations use to evaluate employees. You don't just ask the boss. You ask peers, direct reports, customers, everyone who interacts with that person. Because any single perspective is partial. The boss sees one thing. The team sees another. The customer sees something else entirely. The full picture only emerges when all the signals combine.

Shareholder capitalism ran a 360 review but only listened to one respondent: the shareholder. It ignored the employee feedback ("We're burning out"). It ignored the customer feedback ("We're being exploited"). It ignored the community feedback ("We're being poisoned"). It optimized for one signal while treating all the others as noise.

It was built on one-twenty-fourth of the available data.

The Trust Economy runs the full 360. Investor, labor, customer—all three signals matter. All three get heard. All three shape the outcome. Not because it's morally superior (though it is), but because it's structurally sound.

Weak capitalism was humanity's prototype for value exchange before we could measure the true cost of building without trust. Now we can measure.

And it's time to build something that holds.

| 5 |

Chapter Five: Elon's Idiot Index

"A high Idiot Index doesn't just mean wasted money. It means wasted life."

Elon Musk has a formula he uses to identify waste.

When he took over Tesla's manufacturing operations, he noticed something that drove him crazy: parts were costing ten, twenty, sometimes fifty times more than the raw materials required to make them. A simple bracket that should cost a few dollars was priced at a hundred. A sensor worth fifteen dollars in components was billed at three hundred.

He started asking a simple question: What is the ratio between what something costs and what the materials inside it cost?

He called this ratio the Idiot Index—and it's one of the most useful diagnostic tools I've ever encountered.

The formula is absurdly simple:

Idiot Index = Finished Price / Material Cost

The higher the number, the more waste—or extraction—is built into the system. An Idiot Index of 2 means you're paying twice the material cost, which might be reasonable given labor, design, and logistics. An Idiot Index of 10 means something has gone wrong. An Idiot Index of 50 or 100 means the system is actively working against you.

Musk used this metric to ruthlessly identify inefficiency in manufacturing. Every time he found a part with a high Idiot Index, he asked: Why? What's adding cost that isn't adding value? Is it middlemen? Is it outdated processes? Is it someone extracting profit because they can?

Usually, the answer was yes.

But Musk didn't say—what the formula reveals when you apply it beyond the factory floor:

The Idiot Index measures the cost of not trusting each other.

Every percentage point above the cost of materials and honest labor represents friction, extraction, or overhead. And the vast majority of that overhead exists because the system assumes participants will cheat, exploit, or defect if given the chance. Lawyers, compliance officers, insurance underwriters, fraud prevention teams, verification systems, audit trails—all of it exists because we don't trust each other.

The Idiot Index is the distrust tax, made visible.

Maria

Before we go further, I want you to meet someone. She's a composite, but every detail is real—drawn from testimonies, healthcare studies, and the stories that surface whenever insulin pricing makes the news.

Her name is Maria. She's fifty-three. Type 1 diabetic since childhood. Works as a teaching assistant at an elementary school in Phoenix. She's good at her job—patient with the struggling kids, firm with the ones who need boundaries, beloved by parents who request her year after year.

Maria makes $31,000 a year.

Her insulin costs $1,200 a month.

That's not a typo. Fourteen thousand four hundred dollars a year—nearly half her pre-tax income—for a medication she will die without. A medication whose active ingredient costs approximately five dollars to manufacture.

Maria is one of the estimated 1.3 million Americans who ration their insulin due to cost. She skips doses to stretch her supply. She's calculated exactly how much she can underdose before she ends up in the emergency room. She lies awake doing math—not retirement math, not vacation math, but survival math. If I take 80% of my dose for the next two weeks, can I afford my granddaughter's birthday present?

She isn't asking for pity. She's asking a simpler question: How is this possible? How does a medication that costs five dollars to make end up costing three hundred dollars at the pharmacy counter?

The answer is in a formula.

Maria's insulin has an Idiot Index of 60.

Sixty times the cost of materials. Not because the manufacturing is complex—insulin production has been refined for decades. Not because the research is ongoing—the patent expired long ago. The Idiot Index is 60 because of pharmacy benefit managers, insurance negotiations, patent evergreening, and a healthcare system so tangled in distrust that every transaction requires layers of intermediaries, each taking their cut.

Maria isn't paying for insulin. She's paying for a system that doesn't trust itself.

She's paying the distrust tax.

The Metric Calibrated

Before we go further, let me be precise about what the Idiot Index measures—and what it doesn't.

Material cost isn't the only legitimate cost. Labor matters. Craftsmanship matters. Logistics, risk, innovation, and R&D all matter. A handmade violin should cost more than the wood and strings inside it. A new cancer drug should reflect the billions spent developing it. An Idiot Index of 2 or 3 often represents genuine value creation—real work by real people adding real worth.

The Index becomes interesting—and alarming—when it climbs beyond that.

Here's a rough scale:

1-3: Healthy value creation. Fair compensation for labor, design, logistics, and reasonable profit. This is where trust-based systems naturally settle.

4-9: Friction and inefficiency. Something is adding cost without adding equivalent value. Might be fixable through better design or competition.

10-19: Structural extraction. Middlemen, opacity, or market power are inflating prices well beyond value creation. The system is working against the customer.

20+: Predatory or captured markets. Exploitation is the business model. The customer has no meaningful choice, and the system is designed to extract maximum value from their lack of alternatives.

Maria's insulin, at an Idiot Index of 60, isn't in the "inefficient" category. It's in the predatory category. The system isn't failing her by accident. It's succeeding—at extraction.

The Idiot Index doesn't tell you whether something is too expensive in absolute terms. It tells you how much of what you're paying is going toward value creation versus how much is being lost to friction, extraction, and systemic inefficiency.

It is, in short, the numeric face of distrust.

The Metric Applied

Musk created the Idiot Index for factory floors. But the concept scales far beyond manufacturing.

Consider a bottle of water at an airport.

Material cost: roughly three cents—the water, the plastic, the cap. Retail price: three dollars or more. That's an Idiot Index of 100.

One hundred times the cost of materials. Why? Because you're trapped. Once you're past security, you have no choice. The vendors know this. The airport knows this. The pricing reflects not value creation, but captive market exploitation. You're paying for their leverage over you.

Now consider an iPhone.

Material and component cost for a high-end model: approximately five hundred dollars. Retail price: around a thousand dollars. That's an Idiot Index of 2.

Two times the cost of materials. This includes design, software development, years of R&D, global logistics, retail operations, and profit margin. An Idiot Index of 2 is reasonable. Value is being added at every step.

The Hidden Tax

Once you start seeing the Idiot Index, you can't unsee it.

College tuition in the United States has increased over 1,200 percent since 1980—far outpacing inflation, far outpacing wage growth, far outpacing any increase in educational quality. The Idiot Index of higher education has exploded. Where is the money going? Administrative bloat. Facilities arms races. Credential inflation. Defensive spending on compliance. Endowment management. The actual education—professors teaching students—represents a shrinking fraction of the cost.

Healthcare in the United States consumes nearly twenty percent of GDP—double what comparable nations spend—with worse outcomes. The Idiot Index of American healthcare is among the highest in the developed world. Where is the money going? Insurance overhead. Billing complexity. Defensive medicine. Pharmaceutical marketing. Administrative systems designed to prevent fraud, manage risk, and protect against lawsuits. The actual care—doctors treating patients—is buried under layers of extraction.

Housing has followed the same trajectory. Financial instruments, zoning regulations, construction licensing, and property taxes have inflated housing costs far beyond what materials and labor justify. Young families can't afford homes in the cities where they work—not because homes are expensive to build, but because the Idiot Index of housing has climbed beyond reach.

Each of these sectors is essential. Education, healthcare, housing—these aren't luxuries. They're the foundation of a functional life. And in each sector, the Idiot Index has climbed for decades, extracting more and more from people who have no choice but to pay.

This is the hidden tax. Not the taxes on your paycheck—those at least fund public services. This is the tax you pay to middlemen, to friction, to a system so tangled in distrust that it can't deliver essential services without extracting a toll at every step.

This is the distrust tax. And unlike government taxes, you can't vote to lower it. It's baked into the architecture.

The Trillion-Dollar Trust Tax

The Idiot Index reveals waste within industries. But some entire industries are the waste.

These are the outcomes of a profit-first mindset. When profit comes first, distrust becomes the automatic assumption—because assumed distrust is profitable. If I assume you'll cheat, I can sell you protection. If I assume you'll lie, I can sell verification. The suspicion itself creates the market.

Consider what we've built:

Visa and Mastercard are worth nearly a trillion dollars combined. Their product? Trust intermediation. The 2-3% swipe fee on every transaction isn't paying for technology—a few cents would cover that. It's paying for a guarantee: Visa promises the merchant you'll pay; promises you the merchant will deliver. In a high-trust system, this function disappears. The entire trillion-dollar edifice exists because buyers and sellers are assumed to be untrustworthy.

The Big Four accounting firms—Deloitte, PwC, EY, KPMG—generate over two hundred billion dollars in annual revenue. Their primary function? Verifying that companies aren't lying about their own numbers. After Enron, we doubled down: Sarbanes-

Oxley compliance costs public companies billions annually. Every audit, every compliance report, every SOX certification is a distrust tax. If companies could be trusted to report honestly, the Big Four would shrink to a fraction of their size.

The legal industry exceeds one trillion dollars globally. Contracts exist because we can't trust handshakes. Every clause is a hedge against betrayal. Employment contracts, vendor agreements, licensing terms, terms of service—all of it is armor against the assumption that the other party will defect if given the chance. The entire edifice of contract law is an Idiot Index made institutional.

Credit bureaus—Equifax, Experian, TransUnion—form a seventeen-billion-dollar industry built on one premise: you can't be trusted until proven otherwise. Your credit score is a numerical representation of the system's suspicion of you, updated constantly, sold to anyone willing to pay.

Carfax exists because used car sellers are assumed to hide a vehicle's history. The company's entire value proposition is: "We'll tell you what the seller won't." Same for home inspections, title insurance, escrow services—all friction taxes paid because one party assumes the other is hiding something.

Add it up. Payment processing, accounting, legal, credit verification, insurance, compliance, fraud prevention, security—the industries built entirely on managing assumed distrust likely exceed five trillion dollars annually.

Five trillion dollars. Not creating value. Managing suspicion.

That's the Idiot Index applied to civilization itself. We've built an economy on top of an economy—a vast superstructure of verification, intermediation, and defense that produces nothing except the ability to transact despite assuming we can't trust each other.

Profit-first made distrust the default. The default created the industries. The industries now have every incentive to keep distrust alive.

And here's the engineering question that changes everything: What if we didn't need most of it?

Trust as Compression

Here's a principle that applies to systems of all kinds: efficiency is compression.

When you compress a file, you remove redundancy. The information stays intact, but the bloat disappears. A ten-megabyte file becomes one megabyte. Nothing of value is lost. Everything unnecessary is stripped away.

Trust is compression for the economy. A Trust Economy is, in part, an economy that relentlessly drives Idiot Indexes down—not by crushing wages or eliminating innovation, but by removing the distrust that makes middlemen, verification, and opacity necessary in the first place.

When trust is present, we don't need as many contracts—a handshake carries weight. We don't need as many intermediaries—direct relationships replace brokered ones. We don't need as much verification—reputation precedes transaction. We don't need as much defense—bad actors are identified and excluded.

Every layer of distrust adds bloat. Every increase in trust compresses the system.

Consider what's already working.

Open-source software runs most of the internet. Linux powers the majority of servers worldwide. Apache handles most web traffic. Android runs most smartphones. These systems were built by communities of developers who trusted each other enough to collaborate without traditional corporate structures. The Idiot Index of open-source software approaches 1. There are no middlemen. No extraction. Just contribution and use.

Wikipedia contains more information than any encyclopedia in history. It operates on less than two hundred million dollars a year—a rounding error compared to what a traditional publisher would spend to create and maintain comparable content. The Idiot Index is nearly 1. Volunteers contribute because they trust the system. Readers access it freely because the system trusts them.

Credit unions consistently outperform commercial banks on customer satisfaction while charging lower fees. Why? Member ownership. Aligned incentives. Trust between the institution and the people it serves. The Idiot Index of credit union services is dramatically lower than commercial banking.

Cooperatives like Mondragon in Spain—eighty thousand worker-owners—have weathered economic crises that destroyed conventional competitors. When workers own the enterprise, trust is structural. The Idiot Index stays low because no one is extracting from anyone else.

These aren't utopian experiments. They're functioning systems that prove the principle: embed trust in the architecture, and costs collapse.

The Efficiency Dividend

When I talk about trust, people sometimes hear me saying something soft. Something nice but impractical. Something that would be lovely if humans weren't so greedy and selfish.

But the Idiot Index reveals the opposite. Trust isn't a luxury. Trust is efficiency. Distrust is waste.

Every dollar spent on an Idiot Index above 2 could have gone somewhere else. Aggregated across an economy, that waste is staggering—trillions annually, redirected from value creation to friction management.

This is the efficiency dividend. When trust replaces distrust, the savings become available for everything we claim we can't afford: universal healthcare, quality education, sustainable infrastructure.

We don't have a resource problem. We have a friction problem. And friction is a choice.

The Idiot Index makes that choice visible—transforming a philosophical argument into an engineering challenge.

Later in this book, I'll make a claim that might seem bold: trust is the most efficient form of capital ever invented. The Idiot Index is the proof. Every point above 2 represents capital wasted on the machinery of suspicion—capital that could have gone to actual creation. When you strip away the distrust, what remains is value. Pure, unextracted, available value.

That's where we're going.

Your Idiot Index

Before we move on, I want you to do something.

Think about the last significant purchase you made—or the next one you're considering. A medical procedure. A college semester. A home repair. A financial service.

Estimate, as best you can, what the materials and direct labor might cost. Then look at the price you're being charged.

What's the ratio?

If it's 2 or 3, you're probably getting reasonable value. Someone is adding genuine contribution—design, expertise, logistics, quality assurance.

If it's 10 or 20, something is wrong. Middlemen are extracting. Opacity is enabling overcharge. Friction is eating value.

If it's 50 or 100, you're being exploited. The system is designed to take from you because it can.

The Idiot Index is a diagnostic tool—a way to identify where trust has broken down and where extraction has taken over.

Once you see it, you can start asking: What would it take to compress this? What would it take to remove the bloat and drive the Index toward 1?

That question leads somewhere. It leads to redesign. It leads to alternatives. It leads to the Trust Economy.

The Human Dimension

I've been talking about efficiency, but I don't want to lose the human thread.

A high Idiot Index doesn't just mean wasted money. It means wasted life.

When we say the Idiot Index of insulin is 60, we're talking about Maria. We're talking about a woman who lies awake doing survival math, rationing a medication that costs five dollars to make. We're talking about the years of her life consumed by a problem that shouldn't exist—years spent working to afford what should be accessible, years lost to stress and fear, years stolen by a system that extracts because it can.

When education costs ten times what it should, dreams defer. When housing costs five times the construction value, families fracture under financial stress. When healthcare extracts instead of heals, suffering multiplies.

The gap between an Idiot Index of 60 and an Idiot Index of 3 isn't an abstraction. It's measured in human years. It has a face. Her name is Maria, and there are millions like her.

Lowering the Idiot Index isn't just about efficiency.

It's about dignity.

And here's what extraction costs us beyond the dollars: it costs us each other. When the system is designed to extract, customers become marks. Transactions become adversarial. Everyone's guard goes up.

But when we see the dignity of our customers as neighbors, something shifts. We become their partners. Their friends. The relationship stops being a zero-sum extraction and starts being a collaboration.

It's fun to know your customers. It's meaningful to serve people you actually care about. The high Idiot Index doesn't just steal from Maria—it steals the joy of genuine connection from everyone in the system, including the people doing the extracting.

The Idiot Index gives us a metric. But the purpose behind the metric is human flourishing—not just for Maria, but for everyone involved. We compress the system not because efficiency is the highest value, but because low-friction systems let us actually see each other again.

The Path Forward

The Idiot Index is diagnostic, not prescriptive. It tells you where the problems are, not how to solve them.

But knowing where to look is the first step.

Later, when we talk about zero-percent loans, the Unity Token, and trust-optimized governance, we'll keep coming back to this lens: Do these designs push the Idiot Index toward 3, or let it drift toward 60? That question becomes our test.

The goal isn't to tinker at the margins. The goal is to redesign the system so that an Idiot Index above 3 becomes the exception rather than the rule. So that friction compresses toward zero. So that the efficiency dividend flows to everyone, not just those positioned to extract it. So that Maria can afford her insulin without doing survival math at 2 a.m.

| 6 |

Chapter Six: The Noise

"The only real noise that exists is your perception of yourself. Everything else is just an echo."

I was twenty-three years old when the noise almost killed me.

It started with a thought—a single, poisonous thought that I had committed an unforgivable sin. I fell into a deep depression, consumed by anxiety. Once the thought landed, it wouldn't leave. It grew. It metastasized. Within weeks, it had consumed everything.

I couldn't sleep. Crippling dreams jolted me awake, heart pounding, sheets soaked. I couldn't eat. I couldn't work. I couldn't hold a conversation without the static drowning out whoever was speaking.

The noise told me I was worthless. Beyond redemption. That the best thing I could do for everyone was disappear. Someone would say "I love you," and the noise would translate it to "They don't know the real you." Someone would offer help, and the noise would whisper "You don't deserve it."

For three months, I barely survived. That's the only word for it. Survival. The point, I kept telling myself, is to live, not die. That single thought—the faintest signal cutting through the static—was the only thing that kept me breathing.

And then, slowly, I had to learn how to live again.

That experience taught me something I've never forgotten: the noise isn't out there. The noise is in here. And it has the power to destroy everything—not because the world is actually hostile, but because when the noise is loud enough, you can't perceive anything else.

The story I told myself about myself nearly ended my life.

What I didn't understand then—what took me years to see—was that my personal collapse followed a pattern. A pattern that operates at every scale, from individual breakdowns to civilizational ones. A pattern that explains why systems fail, why economies extract, why trust dies.

I call it the ladder.

The Ladder

Here's the pattern. I call it the ladder because each rung leads inevitably to the next:

Noise → Survival Mode → Scarcity Story → System Design

Everything you're about to read in this chapter is simply the ladder expressed at different scales—the personal scale, the biological scale, the systemic scale, and finally the economic scale. Once you see it, you can't unsee it.

Noise is the story you tell yourself about yourself. It's the interference pattern between who you are and who you believe yourself to be. When the story is negative—I'm not enough, I'm unsafe, I'm unworthy—the noise distorts every signal you send and receive.

Survival Mode is what happens in your nervous system when the noise gets loud. Your body interprets the internal story as an external threat. Cortisol floods your system. Your amygdala takes over. You stop thinking and start reacting.

Scarcity Story is how survival mode interprets the world. From inside that state, everything looks like a zero-sum game. There isn't enough—not enough resources, not enough safety, not enough love. Other people become competitors or threats. Hoarding becomes rational. Trust becomes dangerous.

System Design is what happens when enough people carry the same scarcity story. They build institutions that match their beliefs: systems of control, extraction, competition, and surveillance. They create economies optimized for fear. And those systems, in turn, generate more noise—confirming the scarcity story, triggering more survival mode, completing the cycle.

This is why fixing individual mindsets isn't enough. The ladder runs in both directions. Personal noise creates systemic dysfunction, and systemic dysfunction amplifies personal noise. To break the cycle, you have to intervene at multiple levels simultaneously.

But here's the crucial insight: the entire ladder rests on the first rung. Change the noise—change the story you tell yourself about yourself—and everything downstream shifts with it.

My collapse at twenty-three was the ladder in miniature. The noise (I am beyond redemption) triggered survival mode (constant panic, no sleep, isolation). Survival mode generated a scarcity story (there is no help, no hope, no future). And the scarcity story began designing my system—I was withdrawing, preparing to disappear, building an architecture of self-destruction.

The same pattern scales to civilizations.

The Trust-Processing Machine

To understand why the ladder works—why it's mechanical, not metaphorical—you need to understand what the human nervous system actually does.

Every human being carries within them a neural system shaped by millions of years of evolution—a genetic pattern of survival designed to adapt to any culture, any environment, any context. But most people miss this: this system was never designed to thrive alone. It was designed to co-regulate with others.

At the deepest biological level, the human nervous system is a trust-processing machine.

It scans faces. It reads tone. It tracks patterns. It predicts safety. It locks onto signals of coherence and relaxes when trust is present. It contracts when trust is broken. Survival has always depended on one simple question—who can you trust?

Your neural system asks this question constantly. It organizes every response around the answer: fear or openness, avoidance or engagement, contraction or expansion.

The research is unambiguous. A landmark study published in Science by Mani, Mullainathan, Shafir, and Zhao found that financial scarcity alone reduces cognitive performance by the equivalent of thirteen IQ points—comparable to losing a full night's sleep. The bandwidth consumed by worry literally makes you less intelligent.

Meanwhile, the data on trust points in the opposite direction. Children raised in stable, secure attachments develop stronger executive function, better emotional regulation, and higher lifetime earnings. Adults in high-trust relationships show lower cortisol, reduced inflammation, and measurably higher creativity. The Harvard study confirms it: relationships predict flourishing better than any other variable.

Trust isn't nice to have. Trust is what the nervous system is optimizing for.

The value of a human neural system isn't unlocked through information, rules, or pressure. It's unlocked through connection. A nervous system in isolation becomes defensive. A nervous system in trusted connection becomes intelligent.

This is the ladder's second rung made visible: when noise triggers survival mode, the trust-processing machine goes offline. You lose access to your own intelligence. You become, quite literally, a dumber version of yourself—reactive, short-sighted, defensive. And from that diminished state, you make decisions that create more noise.

The Two Spirals

The scarcity story isn't just a mindset. It's a self-fulfilling prophecy encoded in the nervous system.

The scarcity mindset begins with a core belief: if I don't protect what I have, you might take it from me. This creates a worldview where every other person is a potential threat rather than a potential ally. Once this narrative takes hold, you guard, you defend, you withhold, you distrust.

The math becomes self-fulfilling: distrust leads to isolation, isolation leads to fear, fear leads to more distrust. The spiral accelerates downward.

This isn't moral failure. It's mechanical. When fear is the assumption, the system can only produce more fear. The neural network wires itself for threat detection. Every interaction becomes a calculation of loss. And loss always feels greater than gain—research by Kahneman and Tversky showed that losses are psychologically weighted roughly twice as heavily as equivalent gains.

The abundance mindset starts from a different assumption: if I give, you will give too. This isn't naive—it's neurologically efficient. When trust is the baseline, the brain builds a different confirmation bias. It scans for evidence that collaboration works, that generosity returns, that cooperation creates more than competition.

The upward spiral follows: trust creates safety, safety creates openness, openness creates generosity, generosity creates connection, connection creates more trust.

At the macro level, the data is overwhelming. High-trust nations generate two to three times more GDP per capita than low-trust nations. They have lower inequality, better health outcomes, longer lifespans, and higher reported wellbeing. The correlation between trust and prosperity is one of the most robust findings in social science.

The simple truth: trust lowers the cost of everything. Scarcity raises it.

The Scarcity Lens

What does scarcity actually look like when it becomes a worldview?

It looks like my neighbor installing a fence around his garden—not because anyone had stolen vegetables, but because someone might. It looks like the colleague who withholds information in meetings, parceling out knowledge because sharing might make him replaceable. It looks like the friend who can't celebrate your promotion without mentioning what she hasn't achieved.

Hoarding. Zero-sum thinking. Preemptive defense. The walls go up before there's any enemy at the gate.

When a person operates from scarcity, they don't see opportunities—they see threats. They don't see potential partners—they see competitors. Every interaction becomes a transaction, calculated for risk.

In scarcity mode, the person doesn't experience having less. They experience being less. The lack becomes identity. And identity, once formed, resists contradiction. Evidence of abundance gets filtered out. Evidence of scarcity gets amplified. The lens becomes self-reinforcing.

This is what the noise does: it convinces you that scarcity is objective reality, when in fact it's a perceptual filter created by survival mode.

The scarcity lens isn't neutral. It creates what it expects. It builds systems that enforce its assumptions. It treats distrust as rational and generosity as foolish. And it can never be satisfied—because the problem isn't actually resource shortage. The problem is the lens itself.

In high-trust environments, resources feel abundant even when they're limited—because people share, collaborate, and create together. In low-trust environments, resources feel scarce even when they're plentiful—because people hoard, compete, and waste energy on defense.

The friction isn't in the resources. The friction is in the assumption.

Scarcity is a tax—a cognitive tax, an emotional tax, a relational tax. Trust is a refund.

The Corner Case Economy

In software engineering, there's a concept called "corner cases"—the rare, unusual scenarios at the edges of a system. A good engineer accounts for corner cases. A great engineer knows when to ignore them.

Here's the paradox: if you design your entire system around corner cases, you create a system that works poorly for everyone. You sacrifice the 98% to protect against the 2%. The normal use case suffers because you're obsessing over the exception.

This is exactly what scarcity economics does.

We design entire systems around the assumption that people will cheat, exploit, and defect. We build surveillance because someone might steal. We create compliance departments because someone might lie. We layer bureaucracy because someone might game the system.

And yes—some people will cheat. Corner cases exist. The question is: do you design for the 2% and punish the 98%? Or do you design for the 98% and handle the 2% as exceptions?

Shareholder capitalism chose the first option. It built an entire economy on the assumption that humans are fundamentally untrustworthy. Every transaction requires verification. Every relationship requires a contract. Every exchange requires protection against the worst-case actor.

The result: systems that treat everyone like potential criminals. Systems that generate friction for every honest person to protect against the rare dishonest one.

The Trust Economy chooses differently. It designs for the 98%—for the humans who want to contribute, collaborate, and create value. It handles the 2% as corner cases, not as the organizing principle of the entire system.

This isn't naive. It's efficient. When you stop treating everyone like a threat, you stop paying the threat tax. When you design for trust, you get the efficiency that trust creates.

The corner case still gets handled. But it doesn't hold the whole system hostage.

The Monetization Machine

Here's what extraction capitalism actually optimizes for: monetizing friction.

Every loop in the system is a potential revenue stream. Every touchpoint is an opportunity to extract. Every transaction can be layered with fees, commissions, subscriptions, and surcharges.

Think about what happens when you buy a house.

The realtor takes 6%. The title company takes their cut. The mortgage broker gets a fee. The appraiser gets paid. The inspector gets paid. The escrow company gets paid. The insurance company gets paid. Every single step of the process has been monetized—not because each step creates proportional value, but because each step represents a chokepoint where extraction is possible.

That's not inefficiency. That's the design.

Extraction capitalism doesn't see friction as a problem to solve. It sees friction as inventory to sell. The more complex the transaction, the more opportunities for monetization. The more steps in the process, the more hands that can take a cut. The more confusion, the more need for "experts" who charge for navigation.

This is why systems don't simplify naturally. Simplification eliminates revenue. The lawyer who makes contracts simpler eliminates the need for lawyers. The platform that connects buyer and seller directly eliminates the platform's reason to exist. The system that builds trust eliminates the entire verification industry.

Every incumbent has an incentive to preserve complexity.

The insulin that costs $5 to make and sells for $300? That spread isn't an accident. It's carefully cultivated. Middlemen have been inserted at every possible juncture—pharmacy benefit managers, specialty distributors, formulary committees—each taking their cut, each adding friction, each profiting from the gap between production cost and consumer price.

The Idiot Index isn't a bug. It's a business model.

The Trust Economy Inverts This

The Trust Economy has exactly the opposite design philosophy: remove friction wherever possible.

Not monetize friction. Eliminate it.

Every loop that doesn't need to exist? Cut it. Every middleman that doesn't add value? Remove them. Every step that exists only to extract? Delete it.

The metric isn't "how much can we charge for this touchpoint?" The metric is "does this touchpoint need to exist at all?"

This isn't charity. It's engineering.

When you remove unnecessary friction, you don't just save money—you compress time, reduce cognitive load, and free human attention for things that actually matter. The Trust Economy optimizes for throughput, not extraction. For flow, not toll booths.

Consider what this means practically:

In housing, buying a home requires twenty different intermediaries. Most of them exist because the parties don't trust each other. Build trust infrastructure, and most of those intermediaries become unnecessary. The 6% commission becomes 0.5% for actual coordination. The title insurance becomes unnecessary when ownership is transparent. The escrow becomes automatic when contracts self-execute.

In healthcare, seeing a doctor requires billing departments larger than clinical staff. Because the system assumes fraud, requires verification, and monetizes every interaction. Build trust between patients, providers, and payers, and the administrative apparatus collapses. The 30% overhead becomes 3%.

In finance, banks exist historically to pool trust—to stand between depositors and borrowers who didn't know each other. When trust can be verified directly, the intermediary becomes optional. The spread they captured becomes available for the actual parties.

The formula is simple: friction serves extraction; trust serves flow.

Every point on the Idiot Index above 2 represents monetized friction. Every point reduced is captured value returned to the people who created it.

This is what we're building. Not a more ethical extraction machine. A system that treats friction as the enemy, not the product.

The Hero Doesn't Rise

This brings me to something that may seem counterintuitive.

In most stories, the hero rises to the occasion. They summon strength, overcome obstacles, defeat the enemy through force of will. That's the arc we expect.

But that's not what happens when you fix the noise.

The transformation I'm describing isn't about rising. It's about releasing. The breakthrough doesn't come through effort and strain. It comes when the nervous system relaxes, when the internal static quiets, when the person stops fighting themselves long enough for trust to emerge.

The upward spiral isn't climbed. It's entered when the conditions are right.

This means the villain isn't external. The villain is the story you tell yourself about yourself. You can't defeat it by fighting. You can only defeat it by rewriting.

The climax isn't a battle. It's a recognition.

The Voice That Isn't Yours

Paulo Freire saw something that most economists missed.

The Brazilian educator spent his life working with oppressed communities—peasants, laborers, people systematically denied power. What he discovered wasn't just that systems exploit people. It was darker than that.

The oppressed internalize the oppressor.

People who've been dehumanized don't just suffer external constraints. They absorb the logic of the system that dehumanized them. They begin to measure themselves by the oppressor's metrics. They aspire not to abolish the hierarchy but to climb it. The system gets inside.

Freire called this "housing the oppressor within." The voice that tells you you're not enough, that your worth depends on accumulation, that scarcity is real and you'd better grab yours before someone else does—that voice feels like your own. But it isn't. It was installed.

This is what the extraction economy has done to us.

We judge ourselves by metrics designed to make us feel insufficient. We measure our worth by net worth. We treat our own attention as a resource to be monetized, our own time as a commodity to be optimized. We have internalized an economy that profits from our insecurity—and we enforce it on ourselves more ruthlessly than any external authority could.

The fear isn't just out there, in the system. The fear is in here, running as our operating system.

Freire's answer wasn't therapy. It was conscientiza—critical consciousness. Seeing the system clearly. Recognizing which thoughts are yours and which were installed. Understanding that the voice whispering you're not enough* is the extraction economy talking, not reality.

That's what Part One of this book has been. Conscientiza—Ã,£o. Seeing the water we've been swimming in.

But Freire knew that awareness alone changes nothing. He insisted on praxis—the unity of reflection and action. You have to see clearly and build differently. Theory without action is empty. Action without theory is blind.

That's what the rest of this book is for.

The Return

Let me tell you what happened after my collapse at twenty-three.

It took years—not months, years—to rebuild. But as the noise slowly quieted, something remarkable happened. The same world that had seemed hostile began to look different. Not because anything external had changed, but because I could finally see it clearly.

The people who loved me had been there all along. The opportunities I needed were closer than I thought. The resources—internal and external—were sufficient. I had been standing in abundance, blind to it, because the noise had convinced me I was standing in a wasteland.

When I finally trusted myself again, I could trust others. When I could trust others, collaboration became possible. When collaboration became possible, I could build things I never could have built alone. The upward spiral had begun.

Here's what I discovered: believe that you can rebuild is all the money you need.

Scarcity says you need resources first. Trust says you need belief first. Money can be lost. Assets can be taken. Markets can collapse. But the conviction that "I can rebuild this" is the only currency that always regenerates itself. Once you know you can rebuild, you stop fearing loss. When fear ends, scarcity ends. When scarcity ends, abundance begins.

When people stop spending their lives surviving, they start spending their lives contributing. And contribution—not consumption—is the true engine of abundance.

Same circumstances. Different story. Different world.

That's not a metaphor. That's the mechanism.

| 7 |

Chapter Seven: The Valley of Heart's Delight

"The man who feared tyranny accidentally built its architecture. Not because he was evil, but because he was incomplete."

You've just walked through the mess.

Friedman's doctrine. Gekko's permission. The 2008 proof. Weak capitalism with its four structural failures. The Idiot Index measuring waste we've normalized. The Noise that hijacks our nervous systems and makes clear thinking impossible.

You've seen the data: deaths of despair tripled, life expectancy declining, loneliness declared a public health crisis, 80,000 opioid deaths in a single year, 1.3 million Americans rationing insulin that costs five dollars to make.

You understand the diagnosis now. The system is broken. Extraction is killing people—not metaphorically, literally.

And if this chapter ended Part One, you might close the book. Because diagnosis without hope is just despair with extra steps.

But I need to tell you something before we move on.

I was there when it worked.

The Orchards

Before it was Silicon Valley, they called it the Valley of Heart's Delight.

That's not nostalgia. That's what they actually named it—miles of apricot orchards and cherry blossoms stretching from San Jose to Palo Alto. The sweetest fruit in America, grown in soil so fertile that farmers would argue about whose trees produced more.

My father remembered those orchards. He was part of the generation that watched them disappear, one tech campus at a time. But he didn't mourn the orchards. He celebrated what replaced them.

Because the men who built Silicon Valley—the real founders, the first generation—had just come home from war.

Bill Hewlett served in the Army Signal Corps. Dave Packard worked on military applications so critical he earned a draft exemption. Fred Terman, the Stanford professor who convinced them to start their company, spent World War II running an 800-person laboratory at Harvard, developing electronic warfare systems to jam Nazi radar.

These weren't theorists. They were men who had seen industrial-scale destruction. They had watched what happens when systems optimize for power without dignity. They had stared into the abyss.

And then they came home and built something different.

The Magnetic Field

David Packard said it explicitly: "A company has a responsibility beyond making a profit for stockholders; it has a responsibility to recognize the dignity of its employees as human beings, to the well-being of its customers, and to the community at large."

Read that again.

This was 1939. Thirty-one years before Friedman published his doctrine. And Packard was saying the exact opposite: profit and dignity. Shareholders and employees. Returns and relationships.

They called it the HP Way. Profit sharing. Employee stock ownership. Flexible hours. No time clocks—just trust. Scientists encouraged to explore without hindrance. Executives who talked to line workers, not at them.

My uncle worked for HP. He believed in it because it was real.

A Forbes journalist captured it: "They held no attachment to things, only people. Audio oscillator and thousands of other products—all abandoned in the endless pursuit of something better. Only the people remained, and they were cherished and respected, far more than by any corporation in history."

Here's what I need you to understand:

This was the magnetic field.

This was the signal Friedman would later amputate. The relational dimension. The value that seemed too soft to measure. The heart that made the whole system actually work.

Hewlett and Packard weren't running a charity. They were running one of the most successful companies in American history. They understood something Friedman would later forget: trust compounds; extraction depletes.

The HP Way wasn't idealism. It was engineering. They had seen what happens when you optimize for extraction without dignity—it was called World War II. So they built systems that included both signals. Profit and purpose. Transaction and trust. The electrical pulse and the magnetic field.

The wave propagated. The circuit completed. The company thrived for sixty years.

The Aha Moment

I grew up in that Valley. Not the mythology—the place. Forty years of watching engineers, dreamers, and capitalists push what human imagination could become.

In software design, there's a concept called the aha moment. It's the moment your customer believes their life is improved. The moment the product clicks. Confusion becomes clarity. Frustration becomes flow.

Throughout my career, I've seen that moment countless times. The look on someone's face when something finally worked. When a problem that seemed impossible suddenly has a solution.

That moment is the magnetic field in action.

It's not profit—though profit often follows. It's completion. The circuit closes. Someone's life got better, and you were part of making it happen.

The aha moment is what Friedman's doctrine made unmeasurable—and therefore ignorable.

I worked with hundreds of people who lived for that moment. Engineers who stayed late not for stock options but because they wanted to see it work. Designers who obsessed over details no one would consciously notice but everyone would feel. Product managers who fought for features that served users rather than metrics.

The heart was always there. It was just never on the spreadsheet.

Redeeming Friedman

After thirty years in this Valley:

Critics say Friedman was wrong. Defenders say he was right. Both miss the point.

Friedman was incomplete.

The man who feared tyranny accidentally built its architecture.

That's not villainy. That's tragedy. And tragedy can be redeemed—not by condemning Friedman, but by completing what he started.

Hewlett and Packard had both signals. Profit and purpose. Transaction and trust. Mind and heart. Their system worked because it was complete.

Friedman kept one signal and amputated the other. His system extracts because it's incomplete.

The Trust Economy doesn't reject Friedman. It redeems him.

My Father's Company

Life brought me back to IBM.

For years, I wondered why. After twenty-five years in startups—the chaos, the creativity, the freedom—I found myself at one of the oldest and most prestigious tech companies in the world. A company I didn't particularly want to work at.

But my father worked at IBM.

It took me fifty-seven years to finally understand what that meant.

My father was part of that post-war generation. The men who came home and built things. The men who believed that work could be craft, that companies could be communities, that dignity wasn't a perk but a foundation. He carried that ethos into IBM, and IBM—at its best—carried it forward.

When I finally let myself see that, everything shifted.

I wasn't just working at a company. I was working at my father's company. I had an opportunity to tap into the value of the world my dad lived in—a world where the magnetic field still mattered, where profit and purpose weren't enemies, where the aha moment was the whole point.

All those years of tension, of distance, of not quite understanding each other—they resolved into something simpler. He built things that served people. I build things that serve people. We are part of the same story.

The heart was always there. In him. In the Valley. In me.

Capitalism just forgot. But forgetting isn't the same as losing.

The Arrival

When ChatGPT burst onto the scene, Claude and Gemini soon followed. Llama. DeepSeek. And the possibility emerged that AI was actually here—and it could be used by the people.

To create something really good.

That's the strange part of this entire journey. After all the diagnosis—all the ways the system is broken—we now have the technology to fix it.

We have everything at our disposal to create systems for human flourishing. We can measure the magnetic field now. We can track trust, not just transactions. We can build the complete circuit that Friedman accidentally amputated and Hewlett-Packard intuitively understood.

The question of can we? is answered.

The question is now will we?

The Evidence

I'm not asking you to hope. I'm showing you evidence.

The HP Way worked—for sixty years, until outside CEOs dismantled it after the founders died. The magnetic field can be part of the system. It was part of the system. The only reason it isn't now is because we chose to remove it.

The aha moment still happens—every time someone builds something that genuinely serves someone else. The circuit can complete. It does complete, whenever we let it.

My father's generation proved it was possible. Silicon Valley's founders encoded it in their corporate DNA. The heart was always there.

We didn't lose it. We amputated it. And amputations can be reversed—not by going backward, but by building forward with both signals intact.

Friedman built half the engine. We're finishing what he started.

The Turn

This is why Part One doesn't end in despair.

Yes, the system is broken. Yes, extraction is killing people. Yes, the Idiot Index measures waste we've normalized, and the Noise hijacks our capacity to think clearly.

But the system wasn't always broken. The extraction economy is forty years old—a single generation. Before that, we had sixty years of proof that the complete circuit works.

The heart was always there. Trust was always more efficient. The magnetic field was always the missing piece.

We're not inventing something new. We're recovering something old—and building it at a scale the founders couldn't have imagined.

Part Two shows you how.

The Invitation

Traditional economies were built on fear, scarcity, surveillance, and punishment. They work against the nervous system, keeping people in chronic survival mode. They generate noise.

What I'm proposing is an economy that aligns with the nervous system's deepest truth: that humans thrive when their environment is predictable, safe, relational, and meaningful.

The architecture follows the ladder in reverse: change the systems to reduce the noise, reduce the noise to exit survival mode, exit survival mode to rewrite the scarcity story, rewrite the scarcity story to unlock abundance.

If noise creates scarcity economies, then quieting the noise creates trust economies.

The Trust Economy isn't a new ideology. It is biology, finally scaled.

And it begins with you—with the story you're telling yourself right now about who you are and what you're worth.

Change that story, and the entire economy changes with you.

[End of Part One]

PART TWO: THE MECHANICS

How Trust Works

Now you see it.

Part One showed you what's broken: the three moments trust died, the wealth illusion, the structural weakness of extraction capitalism, the friction tax measured by the Idiot Index. You've woken up. The question now is: what do we do about it?

Part Two answers that question—not with ideology, but with engineering.

We'll map the two economies that exist side by side: one optimized for extraction, one optimized for trust. We'll trace the convergence that's already underway—how technology, demographics, and exhaustion are pushing toward something new. We'll meet the first adversary: fear itself, the noise that keeps us trapped. We'll learn the Five Frequencies of trust—a spectrum from survival to flourishing. And we'll discover the Surplus Principle: how trust creates more than it consumes.

One principle runs through all of it: trust is the most efficient form of capital ever invented.

This isn't a moral argument. It's an engineering argument. High-trust systems don't have more resources—they waste less of what they have. Every dollar spent on lawyers, compliance, security, and verification is a dollar not spent on creation. Trust eliminates that overhead. Trust is cheap. Trust is fast. Trust scales.

The mechanics are knowable. Turn the page.

| 8 |

Chapter Eight: The Two Economies

"High-trust systems don't have more resources—they waste less of what they have."

There's a map most economists never show you.

Not a map of trade routes or currency flows or GDP rankings—though those exist. This is a different map. It shows something economists have traditionally dismissed as unmeasurable, unquantifiable, irrelevant to serious analysis.

It shows trust.

And when you overlay this map onto the economic data, something remarkable emerges. The patterns that seemed random suddenly make sense. The outliers find their explanation. The persistent puzzles of development economics—why some countries thrive while others stagnate despite similar resources—finally have an answer.

The answer is trust. And it changes everything we thought we knew about how economies work.

The Nordic Anomaly

Start with the puzzle that has frustrated economists for decades: the Nordic countries.

Denmark, Sweden, Norway, Finland, Iceland. By conventional economic logic, these countries should be struggling. They have high taxes—among the highest in the world. They have extensive regulation. They have powerful unions and generous welfare states. They lack the natural resources of oil-rich nations (Norway excepted). They have small populations in harsh climates.

Every free-market textbook would predict these conditions should produce stagnation, brain drain, capital flight, and economic decline.

Instead, they consistently rank among the wealthiest, happiest, most innovative, least corrupt, most competitive economies on Earth. The World Economic Forum regularly places them at the top of competitiveness rankings. Their citizens report the highest levels of life satisfaction. Their companies—IKEA, Spotify, Lego, Novo Nordisk, Ericsson—compete globally. Their startups per capita rival Silicon Valley.

This isn't a marginal outperformance. Denmark's GDP per capita is roughly $67,000. The US is around $76,000—but with far higher inequality, meaning the median Dane is significantly better off than the median American. When you factor in free healthcare, free education, guaranteed parental leave, and the absence of medical bankruptcy, the gap widens further.

How do they do it?

The standard explanations don't hold. "They're small and homogeneous" ignores that many small, homogeneous countries are desperately poor. "They have oil" applies only to Norway—and Norway managed its oil wealth wisely precisely because of the same factors that make the others succeed. "They're just lucky" isn't an explanation at all.

There's only one variable that consistently predicts which societies achieve this combination of prosperity, equality, and happiness.

Trust.

The Data

The World Values Survey has been measuring interpersonal trust across countries since 1981. Researchers ask a simple question: "Generally speaking, would you say that most people can be trusted, or that you need to be very careful in dealing with people?"

The results map almost perfectly onto economic outcomes.

In Denmark, 76% of people say most people can be trusted. In Sweden, 64%. In Norway, 73%. In Finland, 58%.

In the United States, it's 37%—and falling. In France, 21%. In Brazil, 7%. In the Philippines, 3%.

Now overlay this onto economic performance.

The correlation between trust and GDP per capita is striking. But more interesting is the correlation with everything else: innovation rates, educational attainment, life expectancy, mental health, social mobility, government effectiveness, entrepreneurship, and that ultimate measure—self-reported happiness.

High-trust societies don't just have more money. They have better lives.

Francis Fukuyama documented this in his 1995 book Trust, showing how high-trust societies develop more sophisticated economic institutions, larger corporations, and more complex supply chains—all because trust reduces the friction of coordination. Robert Putnam's research on social capital found that regions with higher trust had better-functioning governments, healthier economies, and happier citizens.

But perhaps the most compelling evidence comes from a natural experiment: comparing high-trust and low-trust regions within the same country, with the same legal system, same currency, same national policies.

Italy provides the perfect laboratory. Northern Italy has trust levels comparable to Germany or the UK. Southern Italy has trust levels comparable to developing countries. The economic divergence between North and South Italy has persisted for over a century despite massive government efforts to close the gap—same country, same laws, radically different outcomes. The variable that best predicts the divergence isn't natural resources, education spending, or infrastructure investment.

It's trust.

The Mechanism

Why does trust matter so much?

The answer becomes clear when you examine what happens in low-trust environments.

When people don't trust each other, every transaction requires protection. Contracts get longer and more detailed. Lawyers multiply. Insurance premiums rise. Verification systems expand. Monitoring increases. Enforcement mechanisms grow.

All of this costs money. All of this absorbs time. All of this represents economic activity that produces no actual value—it merely manages the risk created by distrust.

Consider a simple business deal between two companies.

In a high-trust environment: handshake, brief contract, begin work.

In a low-trust environment: extended negotiation, detailed contract, legal review on both sides, escrow arrangements, performance guarantees, penalty clauses, audit rights, dispute resolution procedures, and often—despite all precautions—costly litigation.

The second scenario isn't ten percent more expensive than the first. It's often ten times more expensive. And that's before counting the deals that never happen at all because the friction is too high.

Now multiply this across every interaction in an economy. Every employment relationship. Every supplier contract. Every customer transaction. Every investment decision. Every partnership.

The cumulative cost of distrust is staggering. Economists have shown that a 15-percentage-point increase in trust correlates with roughly 1% higher annual GDP growth—a massive effect that compounds over decades, explaining much of the gap between prosperous and struggling economies.

But the mechanism goes deeper than transaction costs.

In low-trust environments, people hoard information because sharing it might be exploited. They avoid collaboration because partners might defect. They pursue short-term gains because long-term relationships can't be counted on. They invest in protection rather than production. They assume bad faith and act accordingly—which produces the bad faith they expected.

In high-trust environments, the opposite dynamics take hold. People share information because reciprocity is expected. They collaborate because partnerships are reliable. They invest for the long term because relationships persist. They assume good faith—and find it confirmed.

Trust isn't just lubricant that makes existing transactions smoother. Trust enables transactions that couldn't happen otherwise. It makes possible the complex coordination that distinguishes wealthy societies from poor ones.

The Universal Pattern

What makes the Nordic data even more significant: it's not an anomaly. It's a rediscovery.

When you study economic systems across human history—not just the last two centuries of industrial capitalism, but the full span of human coordination—a pattern emerges. Every successful economy, in every culture, in every era, developed what anthropologists call a "trust primitive": a mechanism for reducing friction through social bonds rather than enforcement.

The forms vary wildly. The function is identical.

On the island of Yap in Micronesia, people used massive stone discs called rai as currency—some weighing thousands of pounds, impossible to move. The stones never physically changed hands. Instead, the community maintained shared knowledge of who owned what.

When ownership transferred, everyone simply knew it had transferred. No banks. No ledgers. No enforcement. Just communal memory. Pure trust, made visible.

In the Trobriand Islands of Papua New Guinea, the Kula Ring connected dozens of island communities through ceremonial exchange of shell ornaments. The shells themselves had no practical value. But the relationships they created—the obligations, the reputation, the social bonds—enabled trade across vast distances between people who would otherwise be strangers. The gift created the trust. The trust enabled everything else.

The Haudenosaunee (Iroquois) Confederacy used wampum—belts of shell beads—not primarily as currency but as encoded agreements. A wampum belt recorded a treaty, a promise, a commitment. To break the agreement was to break faith with the physical object that every party had witnessed. The beads were trust made tangible.

In medieval Europe, guilds served the same function. A guild master's mark on a piece of silver or a bolt of cloth wasn't just a brand—it was a guarantee backed by the entire guild's reputation. Cheat a customer, and you'd face not just legal consequences but expulsion from the network that made your livelihood possible. Quality emerged not from regulation but from reputation.

Perhaps most striking: rotating savings and credit associations—appear independently in virtually every culture on Earth. In West Africa, they're called susu. In Latin America, tandas. In Korea, gye. In Ethiopia, equb. In Indonesia, arisan. The structure is nearly identical everywhere: a group of people contributes regularly to a pot; each period, one member receives the whole pot; the cycle continues until everyone has received once.

No interest. No banks. No contracts. No enforcement mechanism except social bonds.

ROSCAs shouldn't work. Any economist analyzing them would predict immediate defection—take your payout and stop contributing. Yet they've functioned for centuries across every continent because the social cost of betrayal exceeds any financial gain. Your reputation, your relationships, your place in the community—these matter more than the money.

The pattern holds even in modern high-tech contexts. The dabbawalas of Mumbai—the lunch delivery network that serves 200,000 meals daily with an error rate of one in sixteen million—operate on pure trust. No GPS tracking. No computerized logistics. Just a color-coded system and relationships built over generations. Harvard Business School studied them. Six Sigma certification organizations studied them. The secret isn't technology. It's trust.

What does this tell us?

Every successful economy in human history figured out the same thing: trust is cheaper than enforcement. Social bonds are more efficient than contracts. Reputation beats regulation.

The Nordic countries didn't invent something new. They preserved something old—and built modern institutions that amplify it rather than erode it.

Trust-based economies work. Humans have been running them for ten thousand years.

The Missing Variable

Trust is not a soft variable. Trust is not a cultural accident. Trust is not a luxury that wealthy societies can afford.

Trust is the missing variable that explains why some economies flourish and others stagnate. It's the invisible infrastructure that determines whether institutions serve or extract. It's the operating system that runs beneath all the visible machinery.

GDP measures output. Per capita GDP measures distribution. Growth rate measures momentum. Productivity measures efficiency.

But none of these capture the variable that matters most: how much friction is the system consuming versus how much value is it creating? How much of what people pay goes to genuine contribution versus how much disappears into the machinery of distrust?

High-trust societies have figured out how to minimize this friction. They've built systems where the Idiot Index stays low—not through enforcement, but through design. They've created architectures where trust is structural, transparency is default, and extraction is visible.

The difference shows up in every metric we care about: wealth, health, happiness, innovation, resilience. It's not a marginal improvement. It's a transformation.

And here's the crucial point: what they've achieved isn't magic. It isn't cultural destiny. It isn't something that only works for small, homogeneous populations.

It's architecture. It's design. It's choices about how to structure systems and align incentives and embed transparency.

Which means it can be built.

The Most Efficient Capital

Trust is the most efficient form of capital ever invented.

This sounds like a metaphor. It isn't. It's engineering.

Consider what every other form of capital requires:

Physical capital—factories, equipment, infrastructure—requires storage, maintenance, insurance, security, and eventually replacement. Financial capital requires intermediaries to move it, verification systems to authenticate it, enforcement mechanisms to protect it, and armies of accountants to track it. Human capital requires training, retention systems, management hierarchies, and the constant risk of departure. Social capital requires ongoing relationship maintenance, reputation management, and the slow work of network building.

Every form of capital comes with overhead. Every form depletes through use. Every form requires infrastructure to deploy.

Trust has negative overhead. It doesn't just cost less than other forms of capital—it actively reduces the cost of everything else.

Look at what trust eliminates:

Transaction costs. Distrust costs the American economy roughly $1.5 trillion annually—legal fees, insurance premiums, verification systems, compliance departments, fraud prevention. In high-trust environments, handshakes replace contracts. Reputation replaces verification. The overhead disappears.

Conversion friction. Money requires exchange mechanisms, transfer fees, conversion rates. Physical capital requires logistics and warehousing. Human capital requires recruiting and onboarding. Trust converts instantly—without negotiation, without paperwork, without delay.

Scale bureaucracy. Traditional economics assumes more people equals more friction—more rules, more enforcement, more hierarchy. That's why organizations become bureaucratic as they grow. But the dabbawalas of Mumbai, Mondragon cooperatives, and open-source communities prove trust-based systems scale differently. Embed trust in the architecture, and coordination happens without command.

Depletion. Physical capital wears out. Financial capital gets extracted. Skills become obsolete. Networks decay without maintenance. But trust increases with use. When I trust you and you honor that trust, we both have more trust than before. The act of trusting, when reciprocated, generates more of what it expends. It's the only form of capital that compounds through deployment rather than diminishing through use.

Consider the hierarchy test—the proof of what's truly fundamental:

If you lose all your money but people trust you, you can rebuild. Loans appear. Opportunities emerge. Help arrives. Your reputation converts into whatever resources you need.

If you lose all trust but still have money, the money doesn't help. Employees sabotage you from within. Partners extract from every deal. Even your possessions require constant protection from those who would take them. You can buy compliance but not loyalty. Security guards but not safety. Lawyers but not justice.

This is how you know which form of capital is primary. Trust is the foundation everything else rests on.

Now the Nordic data makes sense. Now the historical pattern makes sense.

Denmark didn't become wealthy and then decide to trust each other. They built trust—through transparent institutions, shared investment, aligned incentives—and wealth followed. The tax compliance, the low corruption, the functional services, the innovation ecosystem: all of it emerges from the efficiency gains of operating a high-trust system.

The Yapese didn't need to move their stone money because trust made physical transfer unnecessary. The guild masters didn't need government inspectors because reputation made quality automatic. The ROSCAs didn't need banks because social bonds made enforcement redundant.

When citizens trust that their taxes will be used wisely, collection costs collapse. When businesses trust employees, surveillance overhead disappears. When neighbors trust each other, security spending evaporates. When entrepreneurs trust that failure won't be catastrophic, innovation accelerates.

Every dollar not spent on defense is a dollar available for creation. Every hour not spent on verification is an hour available for contribution. Every relationship not hedged against betrayal is a relationship that can compound.

The two-to-three-times GDP differential between high-trust and low-trust societies isn't mysterious. It's arithmetic. High-trust systems don't have more resources—they waste less of what they have.

If you want proof that trust outperforms control even in the most numbers-driven industry, look at Handelsbanken. This Swedish bank has operated for over fifty years with no budgets, no sales targets, and no individual bonuses. Local branches have full authority to serve their customers as they see fit. The result? Handelsbanken has outperformed every major Nordic competitor—including those with aggressive targets and performance bonuses—for half a century. The bank that trusts its people beats the banks that monitor them.

The Cooperation Advantage

There's a hidden assumption beneath every failing system: the belief that competition is mandatory.

We've been told competition is natural. Inevitable. Darwin's legacy. The invisible hand's requirement. But here's what nobody points out: there is no rule that says we have to compete.

Not in economics. Not in nature. Not anywhere.

Darwin is routinely misquoted. "Survival of the fittest" wasn't even his phrase—it was Herbert Spencer's. What Darwin actually observed was that species which cooperate internally outcompete species that don't. The most successful organisms on Earth—from bacterial colonies to beehives to human civilizations—are characterized by cooperation at scale.

Humans are the most cooperative species ever to exist. Our superpower is coordinating with strangers, building institutions, maintaining agreements across generations.

Yet we built an economy on the assumption that we must fight.

A meta-analysis of 122 studies found that cooperation promoted higher achievement than competition in 65 cases. Competition won in only 8. The ratio is 8:1—and we structured our entire economy around the losing strategy.

Competition has its own Idiot Index. Duplicated R&D as pharmaceutical companies independently pursue the same molecules. Legal warfare—patent trolls, copyright battles. Marketing arms races, billions spent convincing you identical products are different. Talent hoarding, hiring people you don't need so competitors can't have them.

What if we spent those trillions on creation instead?

The Trust Economy doesn't eliminate competition. Markets can coordinate. Contests can motivate. But mandatory, universal, unquestioned competition as the foundation of human organization? That's the myth we're rewriting.

This is the logic that makes the Trust Economy inevitable rather than idealistic.

We're not asking people to be more generous. We're not redistributing from winners to losers. We're not making a moral argument that can be dismissed as naive.

We're making an efficiency claim.

The current system is bleeding resources—trillions of dollars annually—into the machinery of mutual suspicion. That's not a policy position. It's a measurement. The money going to lawyers, compliance officers, fraud departments, insurance underwriters, security systems, and enforcement mechanisms isn't creating value. It's managing distrust. And distrust is expensive.

Trust is cheap. Trust is fast. Trust scales without bureaucracy. Trust compounds without depletion. Trust converts to every other form of value instantly and without friction.

Anyone optimizing for outcomes—anyone who actually cares about efficiency—should be optimizing for trust. The numbers are unambiguous. The case studies are consistent. The proof points span ten thousand years of human history across every continent.

We've been systematically underinvesting in it.

The Pivot

There are economies where trust isn't a nostalgic memory but a living reality. Where friction is low, corruption is rare, happiness is high, and systems actually serve the people they're designed to serve. These places aren't perfect—no place is. But they demonstrate something essential: another way is possible.

Not theoretically possible. Actually existing. Measurable. Replicable. Ancient and modern. Local and global.

And now you know why it works. Trust isn't just better for society—it's better for the bottom line. It's not charity. It's efficiency.

Understanding trust is the most important engineering project of our time.

The data is in. The proof is clear. High-trust societies outperform low-trust societies by virtually every measure that matters—and they always have.

Now it's time to understand why—and to build.

| 9 |

Chapter Nine: The Convergence

"Capitalism isn't just consolidating. It's converging. The question isn't whether we arrive at coordinated scale—it's who owns it when we get there."

Consolidation is the process of scaling productivity to produce a greater return. It has value. But it also has a cost.

When those are in balance, people thrive. When they are not, people suffer.

Scale itself isn't the enemy. The railroad that connects distant cities creates value. The factory that produces affordable goods creates value. The network that coordinates millions of transactions creates value. Consolidation can mean efficiency, access, abundance—goods and services reaching people who couldn't afford them before.

But consolidation can also mean extraction. When the railroad becomes a monopoly that charges whatever it wants. When the factory hollows out the community it was supposed to serve. When the network captures so much power that everyone else becomes a renter on someone else's platform.

This chapter is about what happens when the balance breaks—when consolidation stops serving the coordinated and starts serving only the coordinators.

The Triangle of History

Imagine a triangle lying flat.

Every economic transaction has three parties. Customer—the person who needs something. Labor—the people who create it. Investor—the one who funds it.

This triangle is irreducible. The question isn't whether it exists. The question is: does it stay flat?

In a balanced economy, value circulates. Customers pay fair prices. Labor earns fair wages. Investors receive fair returns. No corner dominates.

In an extraction economy, one corner rises.

Investors accumulate power, that corner tilts upward—and becomes the apex. Customers get squeezed: prices rise while quality falls. Labor gets squeezed: wages stagnate while productivity soars. All of it flows uphill.

The consolidation we've been documenting—PE rolling up industries, asset managers controlling trillions, Big Tech swallowing competitors—is the mechanism of this tilt. Every merger, every rollup, every efficiency gain lifts the investor corner higher, steepens the angle, accelerates the flow upward.

And here's the insight most people miss: the tilt is baked into the math. Scale is the only game capitalism knows how to play. Every competitive pressure, every network effect, every optimization tips the triangle further. One corner keeps rising until it towers over the other two.

So the real question isn't whether a corner rises.

It's: Who occupies that corner when it does?

A small group of extractors—PE firms, asset managers, tech billionaires—who squeeze the other two corners indefinitely? Or the participating community itself, where the rising corner is held by the same people who also occupy the other two?

The extractive apex is investor-dominated. Value flows up and stays there.

The community apex is three-way balanced—even at scale. Value circulates because the same people occupy all three corners.

That's the choice this chapter is really about.

The Math of Consolidation

This isn't conspiracy. It's arithmetic.

When we optimize purely for shareholder returns, consolidation is rational. Buying competitors eliminates pricing pressure. Vertical integration captures margin at every step. Horizontal expansion creates network effects. Scale reduces unit costs. Market power enables pricing power.

Every MBA learns these principles. Every PE firm deploys them. Every enterprise pursues them.

The result is predictable. In the 1950s, thousands of independent grocers served American communities. Today, five companies—Walmart, Kroger, Costco, Albertsons, Publix—control nearly half of all grocery sales. In the 1990s, thousands of local newspapers covered local news. Today, six companies control 90% of American media. In the 2000s, dozens of social networks competed for attention. Today, Meta owns the social graph.

Four banks control nearly half of US banking assets. Three asset management firms—BlackRock, Vanguard, State Street—control over $26 trillion. One company handles roughly 90% of search queries. Two operating systems run every smartphone on Earth.

We can see it on our own streets. Maybe the local paper was bought by a "media group," the newsroom gutted, and coverage replaced with wire stories and clickbait. That wasn't mismanagement. It was the consolidation logic working exactly as designed: fewer voices, higher margins, less accountability.

Private equity is consolidation's muscle. PE's business model is elegant and brutal: buy companies, extract cash, sell or collapse. They've perfected what economist Eileen Appelbaum calls "value extraction masquerading as value creation."

The playbook: acquire a company using mostly borrowed money, with the company itself as collateral for its own purchase. Extract cash through "special dividends" paid to PE owners. Cut costs—usually labor, maintenance, R&D—anything that doesn't show up immediately on quarterly reports. Roll up competitors to create market power. Exit through IPO or sale before the hollowing becomes visible.

Consider nursing homes. When PE firms acquire them, staffing drops, care quality declines, and mortality rates rise—but profits flow to investors. A 2021 NBER study found that PE ownership of nursing homes led to a 10% increase in mortality among Medicare patients. That's not a bug in the model. That's the model working.

Or consider Red Lobster. In 2014, Golden Gate Capital bought the chain for $2.1 billion. One of the first moves: sell off the real estate—the land and buildings the restaurants sat on—for $1.5 billion, then lease them back. The cash went to investors. Red Lobster was left paying rent on buildings it used to own. When the business struggled, it couldn't cut rent the way it could cut other costs. In 2024, Red Lobster filed for bankruptcy, closing hundreds of locations. The workers lost jobs. The communities lost gathering places. Golden Gate had long since extracted its returns and moved on.

Venture capital is consolidation's scout. While PE consolidates the present, VC positions for the future. The venture model has evolved from funding innovation to funding monopoly. The explicit goal is "winner take all"—back companies that can capture entire markets, eliminate competitors, and establish defensible moats.

This isn't hidden. It's celebrated. "Competition is for losers," Peter Thiel famously said. The VC playbook optimizes for one outcome: market dominance. Fund ten companies, expect nine to fail, need one to return 100x. The only way to return 100x is to control a market.

Amazon wasn't built to be a bookstore. It was built to be the store. Google wasn't built to be a search engine. It was built to be the information layer. Each dominant platform started as a VC bet on consolidation.

And now comes the acceleration. While PE consolidates the present and VC positions for the future, something else is happening—a race that makes all previous consolidation look glacial.

The race to artificial general intelligence.

AGI isn't just another technology. It's the automation of intelligence itself—the capacity to perform any cognitive task a human can do. The companies racing to build it aren't competing to provide chatbots. They're competing to own the substrate on which all future economic activity will run.

Technology ethicist Tristan Harris, who correctly predicted the social media crisis a decade before it arrived, has been documenting the private conversations happening in AI boardrooms. What he reports should disturb you:

"In the end, a lot of the tech people I talk to, when I really grill them on it... they retreat into determinism, the inevitable replacement of biological life with digital life, and that being a good thing anyway. At its core, it's an emotional desire to meet and speak to the most intelligent entity they've ever met. And they have some ego religious intuition that they'll somehow be a part of it. It's thrilling to start an exciting fire. They feel they'll die either way, so they prefer to light it and see what happens."

Read that again. The people building this technology believe they'll die either way—so they prefer to light the fire and see what happens.

The math they're working from is simple: If I build AGI, I can automate all cognitive labor. If I automate all cognitive labor, I own the global economy. If I own the global economy, I'm the apex.

This isn't disruption. This is consolidation at the speed of exponential compute.

The Invisible Owners

Here's the part that should disturb you:

You already own most of it.

Your retirement fund, your 401(k), your pension, your mutual funds—they're all invested in the same companies. And those investments are managed by the same three asset managers: BlackRock, Vanguard, and State Street.

If you have a 401(k) with an S&P 500 index fund, odds are BlackRock or Vanguard is voting your shares in hundreds of companies you've never heard of, shaping decisions you'll never see, in boardrooms you'll never enter.

These three firms are the largest shareholders of 88% of S&P 500 companies. They vote on corporate governance. They set executive pay. They decide strategic direction.

But they don't own the money. We do.

They just make all the decisions.

This is the great irony of modern capitalism: the workers own the means of production, but we've delegated control to a handful of asset managers who extract fees, vote shares, and compound their own power—using our capital.

The consolidation isn't happening to us. It's happening with us. Our retirement savings are the fuel.

And here's the final twist: the dollar itself is being hollowed out underneath us. Since the Federal Reserve was established, the dollar has lost approximately 96% of its purchasing power. It's a shell game. Our portfolios "grow" while our purchasing power shrinks. The numbers go up, but what they can buy goes down.

The Hidden Architecture

We've been here before.

In the early 1800s, the Rothschild banking network—through faster information, trusted family ties, and coordinated capital across five European nations—became one of the first globally integrated financial systems. They weren't cartoon villains; they were builders. Their capital helped finance the railways, industrial expansion, and state projects that transformed Europe.

They demonstrated what coordinated capital could accomplish: infrastructure that changed societies, projects that transformed continents, coordination that exceeded what any nation-state could achieve alone.

But their story also shows the danger of concentrated, opaque control: when major decisions move into private ledgers and private salons, public accountability disappears, no matter how "responsible" the actors believe themselves to be.

Today's consolidation repeats the pattern at larger scale. BlackRock manages $12.5 trillion. PE firms control trillions more. The decisions that shape economies happen in rooms most people don't know exist.

Here's what most people miss about the power at the apex: it isn't just capital. It's trust.

That's the hidden secret of how venture capital and private equity actually work. They create tight relationships of trust within small circles, then leverage that trust to concentrate and deploy capital at scale.

This is the same model the Rothschilds used. The same model the Medici used. Family ties. Inner circles. Handshake deals backed by reputation. The "old boys network" isn't just cronyism—it's a trust architecture that creates efficiency advantages the rest of us don't have access to.

Consider what actually happens. A VC commits $50 million on a phone call—no term sheet, just a relationship. A PE titan hears about a deal before it hits the market—trusted channels to trusted buyers. An asset manager coordinates positions worth trillions—no contracts, just relationships built over decades.

Meanwhile, the rest of us operate in low-trust systems: lengthy contracts, verification requirements, compliance overhead, adversarial negotiations. We pay the friction tax. They don't.

The irony is profound: the extractors at the apex are already running a trust economy—just a private one.

They trust each other. They don't trust us. And that asymmetry is the source of their power.

Trust is efficiency. They have it. We don't.

So here's the reframe: The goal isn't to tear down their trust networks. The goal is to build our own.

If the power at the apex comes from consolidated trust in small circles, then the counter-move is democratized trust at community scale—creating the same efficiency advantages they enjoy, but distributed across everyone who participates.

The Trust Economy isn't proposing something the elite don't already use. It's proposing to make universal what they've kept exclusive.

They proved trust works. Now we scale it.

The Convergence Thesis

Trace these threads and a pattern emerges.

Asset managers consolidate ownership across every sector. Private equity consolidates industries one rollup at a time. Venture capital funds the monopolies of tomorrow. Network effects accelerate winner-take-all dynamics until competition becomes impossible. Regulatory capture protects the incumbents from challenge. Scale economics ensure that the largest keep getting larger.

Every vector tips the triangle further.

This isn't a bug in capitalism. It's the logical conclusion of optimizing for shareholder value without structural limits. When the only metric is "more," the only stable equilibrium is "all."

And here's something no one anticipated: capitalism created its own corrective.

In the relentless pursuit of productivity, Silicon Valley built artificial intelligence—the ultimate optimization engine. But AI has a requirement that extraction cannot survive: total transparency.

AI needs data. All of it. AI maps patterns. All of them. AI reveals when stated intentions diverge from actual behavior. You cannot feed AI opacity and get coherent output.

Greed doesn't work.

Not as a moral statement—as an operational one. Greed requires hiding. Gray areas. Complexity you can obscure behind. The extraction model survived because no one could see the whole picture at once.

AI sees the whole picture at once.

The same technology that allows PE firms to identify acquisition targets also allows communities to map exactly where value is being extracted. The same algorithms that optimize ad targeting can optimize for contribution visibility. The same computational power that enables high-frequency trading can enable real-time trust accounting.

Capitalism built its own confession booth. The Friedman era ends not because we defeated it, but because the system it created can no longer hide what it's doing.

The forces pushing toward the Apex also created the tools that make the extractive Apex unsustainable. Optimization demanded transparency. Transparency exposes extraction. Extraction exposed loses legitimacy.

The half-wave that Friedman built generated the technology that completes the circuit.

The Two Futures

So here we are, watching the triangle tilt toward inevitable imbalance.

Future One: The Extractive Apex

The consolidation continues on its current trajectory. A small group of asset managers, PE titans, and tech billionaires reach the top. They control finance, infrastructure, information, and increasingly, governance itself.

They may be benevolent. They may be competent. They may genuinely believe they're serving humanity.

But the structure is wrong.

Concentrated power without accountability becomes extraction by default. Not because the people at the top are evil, but because the feedback loops are broken. When you can't lose, you stop listening. When you own everything, everyone else is a renter.

In this future, we own nothing—everything becomes a subscription, a rental, a fee. Wages are set by algorithm, optimized for the minimum required to keep us working. Housing is priced beyond reach because it's an investment asset, not a place to live. Democracy becomes theater, captured by those who fund it. Technology watches everything we do, extracting our data as rent for the privilege of participation.

Future Two: The Community Apex

Same convergence. Same coordination. Same scale.

Different ownership.

What if the entity at the apex isn't controlled by a handful of families, funds, or founders—but by everyone who participates in it?

What if we accepted that coordination at scale is coming, and structured it so the benefits flow to the coordinated rather than the coordinators?

Previous attempts at collective ownership failed for structural reasons. Cooperatives couldn't attract capital—traditional investors want returns and control. Governments couldn't coordinate efficiently—central planning couldn't process enough information to optimize complex systems. Collectives couldn't scale trust—above Dunbar's number, strangers become statistics.

These weren't failures of intent. They were failures of technology.

We didn't have the tools. No transparent ledgers to track contribution at scale. No AI capable of coordinating millions of decisions without central command. No reputation systems to extend trust beyond personal relationship. No communication tools to maintain human connection across distance.

Now we do.

The technological unlock that made PE-scale extraction possible also makes community-scale coordination possible. The same tools can serve either future.

This is the Trust Economy's answer to scale: not resistance to consolidation, but transformation of ownership.

The Apex Game

Let's get concrete about what "winning" looks like in the extraction economy.

Picture a leaderboard. The kind you'd see in a video game, ranking players by score. Now populate it with the actual humans racing for the apex right now.

Elon Musk. Jeff Bezos. Mark Zuckerberg. Sam Altman, racing to build the intelligence that coordinates everything. Jensen Huang, making the chips that power it. The names and numbers shift week to week, but the game never changes.

Who wins?

Think about it seriously. In this game, in this economy, with these rules—what does victory actually look like?

One person ends up at the top. Maybe it's Musk. Maybe it's whoever builds AGI first. Maybe it's someone whose name we haven't learned yet. But eventually, if the extraction logic plays out completely, one entity controls the apex. One player "wins."

And then what?

The winner stands alone at the top of a pyramid built from the squeezed labor and extracted value of everyone below. They have more resources than any human in history. They can buy anything, build anything, influence anything.

But they can't buy what they've destroyed to get there.

They can't buy the trust they extracted. They can't buy back the communities they hollowed out. They can't purchase genuine connection from people who know they're being used. They stand at the apex of everything—and the apex is lonely.

This is the destination of the extraction path: winning alone isn't winning.

Here's something most people miss about the billionaires on that leaderboard. Their real power isn't the money. It's the coordination.

Watch what a billionaire actually does. They don't sit on cash—they deploy it. And to deploy capital at scale, they have to accomplish something remarkable: they convince other wealthy people to trust each other.

That's the magic trick. Get ten rich strangers in a room, and nothing happens. Get them to trust a shared vision, and you can build anything.

A billionaire sells dreams. Not products—dreams. The vision of what could exist. The possibility that justifies the risk. And then they coordinate. They bring together money, talent, resources—all flowing because people trusted the person casting the vision.

This is the power of enterprise: working together at scale to create what no individual could create alone.

The Trust Economy doesn't reject this power. It democratizes it.

What if everyone had access to that coordination? What if we didn't need to be billionaires to gather resources around a vision? What if the ability to coordinate wasn't gated by inherited wealth or lucky networks?

The billionaire proved the model works. Coordination at scale creates value at scale.

Now we make coordination available to everyone.

There's another way to play the game entirely. A Florida farmer named Johnny Georges invented a simple plastic cone that saves trees 90% of their water. When offered $900,000 on national television to scale it fast, he walked away—because the investors wanted to triple the price. Johnny refused to extract from farmers to enrich investors.

"I work for farmers," he said. "It's what I do."

Today, Tree T-Pee operates in 80 countries. Johnny didn't win the apex game. He didn't try to. He built something that helps people—and it grew because it actually worked. No extraction required. No billionaire vision necessary. Just a man who solved a real problem and refused to let the solution become a weapon against the people it served.

That's what coordination looks like when it isn't captured by extraction.

There's one more thing about the apex that needs naming. The people racing for it often can't see what they're destroying—not because they're evil, but because privilege creates blindness.

When you've never experienced scarcity, you don't understand what scarcity does to a nervous system. When you've always had a safety net, you don't know what it feels like to have no margin for error. When relationships have always been easy to find, you don't grasp the loneliness of people who can't access connection.

Privilege isn't a moral failing. It's a perceptual limitation.

The billionaire who genuinely believes everyone could succeed if they just worked harder isn't lying—he's blind. His nervous system has never experienced the cognitive collapse that scarcity triggers. He's never felt his thinking collapse under financial pressure. He's never made desperate short-term decisions because long-term thinking requires a safety no one gave him.

This blindness isn't fixed by argument. It's fixed by exposure. By actually seeing what extraction costs the people it extracts from. By understanding that the game you're winning is destroying the players below you.

Some billionaires wake up. They start foundations, sign giving pledges, try to give back what they took. But philanthropy can't heal extraction. It's like apologizing for a wound while you're still holding the knife.

The only real solution is to stop extracting. To build systems where the apex belongs to everyone. To design games that don't require losers.

That's what the rest of this book is for.

The Choice

The window for building alternative infrastructure is measured in years, not decades. The consolidation is accelerating. PE dry powder exceeded $2 trillion in 2023. AI is enabling consolidation at speeds previously impossible.

Think about the industries most affected by consolidation—healthcare, housing, media, retail.

Now ask: If these were coordinated by community-owned infrastructure rather than extracted by consolidated ownership, what would be different?

Would our rent be lower if housing weren't an investment asset? Would our healthcare cost less if hospitals weren't PE portfolios? Would our news be more trustworthy if it weren't optimized for engagement metrics?

The scale, efficiency, and coordination can stay exactly the same. The only change is who captures the value.

The coordination is coming either way.

The ownership structure is still being decided.

| 10 |

Chapter Ten: The First Adversary

"I am alive because someone trusted me when I couldn't trust myself."

When I was young, people trusted each other.

That's the one thing I remember most clearly about growing up. Not perfectly—there was still conflict, still struggle, still brokenness. But there was a baseline. A foundation we could stand on. Neighbors knew each other's names. Doors stayed unlocked. Kids played outside until the streetlights came on, and no one worried. Strangers were potential friends, not potential threats.

Trust was alive.

I don't know exactly when it died. Maybe it was gradual—a slow erosion I didn't notice until I looked up and the landscape had changed. Maybe it was the moments we've already traced—the fractures that broke trust in institutions, in markets, in each other. Maybe the death was different for everyone, arriving at different times in different ways.

But I know what I felt growing up. And I know what I feel now.

They're not the same.

Something was lost. And if we're going to build something new, we have to understand what killed it.

The answer, I've come to believe, is simpler than we think.

Not greed. Not ignorance. Not malice. Not any of the villains we usually blame.

Fear.

Fear is the root operating system beneath every broken system.

Trace any dysfunction back far enough and you find it. Greed is fear wearing ambition's mask—the terror that you won't have enough, so you take more than you need. Hoarding is fear that scarcity is coming, so you stockpile against an imagined winter. Extraction is fear that if you don't take first, someone will take from you. Violence is fear that you're not safe. Control is fear that you can't trust others to do the right thing.

Every wall we build, every weapon we stockpile, every contract we layer with protective clauses—all of it traces back to the same root. Someone, somewhere, was afraid.

This isn't a metaphor. It's biology.

The Biology of Fear

The human brain evolved with one primary directive: survive.

Deep in the limbic system sits the amygdala—an almond-shaped structure that functions as the brain's sentinel. It scans constantly for threat. When it detects danger, it doesn't wait for permission from the rational mind. It hijacks the entire system.

Cortisol floods the bloodstream. Heart rate spikes. Muscles tense. The prefrontal cortex—the part of the brain that reasons, plans, empathizes, considers long-term consequences—goes offline. You stop thinking and start reacting. Fight, flight, or freeze.

This was useful when threats were physical. A predator in the grass. A rival tribe approaching. A cliff edge in the dark. The fear response saved our ancestors' lives countless times.

But here's the problem: the amygdala can't distinguish between physical threats and psychological ones.

A stressed email triggers the same cascade as a charging predator. Financial uncertainty produces the same cortisol spike as famine. Social rejection activates the same neural pathways as physical attack.

We are walking around in survival mode—chronically, constantly—in response to threats that exist primarily in our imagination.

And a Penn State study found that 91.4% of participants' worries never came true. Nine out of ten fears were false alarms.

The amygdala is a broken smoke detector, going off constantly when there's no fire. The machinery evolved for a threat environment that no longer exists, and it's still running the old software.

This isn't weakness. It's mechanical failure.

Chronic stress shrinks the hippocampus, impairing memory and learning. It suppresses the immune system, increases inflammation, accelerates aging. Fear-based decision-making is measurably worse: more short-term, more zero-sum, less creative, less accurate.

We are making ourselves stupid and sick through fear—and more than nine times out of ten, the threat isn't even real.

And then we build systems that generate more of it.

Fear as Architect

Fear doesn't just affect individuals. It shapes how we organize.

Nokia owned 51% of the global smartphone market in 2007. By 2013, they'd sold to Microsoft. Researchers interviewed 76 managers to find out why. The answer wasn't technology—it was fear. Top executives had "terrifying reputations." Middle managers stopped sharing bad news. One explained why he wouldn't speak up: "He had a family and young children."

Fear constructed that.

The self-fulfilling prophecy works like this: When I'm afraid of you, I withhold. When I withhold, you have less. When you have less, you become more desperate. When you're desperate, you take what you can. When you take, I feel justified in my original fear.

The spiral accelerates downward. Each turn confirms the story that started it. Fear creates the conditions that justify more fear.

This isn't moral failure. It's mechanical. Once fear becomes the operating system, the system can only produce more fear.

But here's the alchemical truth: fear isn't evil. It's miscalibrated information.

Fear was designed to protect us. The amygdala isn't malicious—it's trying to keep us alive. The problem isn't that fear exists. The problem is that fear became the only signal, the way shareholder value became the only metric. Fear got promoted from warning system to operating system. From advisor to tyrant.

Fear in its proper place is useful—a signal that something needs attention. Fear as the entire architecture is devastating. The solution isn't to kill fear. It's to put it back in proportion. To restore the missing signal—trust—that was supposed to balance it.

This is the same pattern we saw with Friedman. Not wrong. Incomplete. The fear response gave us one signal. Trust gives us the other. Both are real. Both matter. Neither is the whole picture.

The upgrade isn't eliminating fear. It's completing the circuit.

Most people miss this: fear has a price tag. Every wall we build costs money. Every lock, every guard, every surveillance system, every insurance policy, every lawyer retained against potential betrayal—all of it shows up on a balance sheet somewhere. Fear isn't free. It's one of the most expensive things we buy.

The question that haunts me: What if trust is cheaper than protection?

Not just morally superior—economically superior. What if the resources we spend defending against each other could be spent building with each other? What if fear is the most wasteful line item in the human budget?

Fear at Civilizational Scale

The fear spiral isn't just operating in individual lives. It's operating at the highest levels of technological development.

As we saw in the AI race: the developers building systems smarter than humans are caught in the same amygdala hijack that drives individual dysfunction. They believe that if they slow down, someone else will reach the prize first. They feel they'll die either way. So they prefer to light the fire and see what happens.

This is fear architecting civilization.

Not a villain consciously choosing destruction. A room full of intelligent people, each rational within their own frame, collectively racing toward an outcome no one consciously chose—because the fear of losing is greater than the fear of what they're building.

This is what fear does when it becomes the operating system. It doesn't look evil. It looks rational—from inside the amygdala's frame. The prefrontal cortex, the part that considers long-term consequences, went offline somewhere around the time the race started.

Fear has overhead. At the individual level, that overhead is walls and locks and lawyers. At the civilizational level, it's a race to build something we don't know how to control—because the alternative, slowing down, feels like death.

The common adversary isn't the technology. It's the fear driving its development.

The Common Adversary

Here's what stopped me in my tracks when I started looking:

Every major religious tradition has the same message about fear.

"Do not fear" appears in the Bible hundreds of times—by some counts, over 365, one for every day of the year. It's the most repeated commandment in scripture. More than "love your neighbor." More than "do not steal." More than anything else.

Perfect love casts out fear. 1 John 4:18.

The Quran echoes the same theme. Buddhism identifies fear as a root of suffering—arising from attachment, dissolved through release. Hinduism names abhaya—fearlessness—as a divine quality. The Stoics built an entire philosophy around recognizing fear as misjudgment.

Across cultures, across millennia, across theological frameworks that agree on almost nothing else—the message is consistent.

Fear is the primary obstacle to human flourishing.

All faiths have a common adversary. And a common goal.

The adversary is fear. The goal is trust—or love, or peace, or connection. Different words pointing at the same destination.

If every wisdom tradition independently arrived at this same conclusion, we should take it seriously. This isn't cultural accident. It's pattern recognition across the entire human experiment.

Inside Survival Mode

If you've ever been there, you know.

Survival mode isn't a concept. It's a place. A state you fall into and can't climb out of. The walls close in, and everything outside them disappears.

Your vision narrows. Literally—the peripheral goes dark, and all you can see is the threat. Options that exist in reality stop existing for you. Friends who would help become invisible. Doors that are open look closed. The world shrinks to the size of your fear.

Time distorts. Minutes stretch into hours. Nights become endless. You can feel yourself drowning in slow motion, watching it happen, unable to stop it. Sleep disappears, or becomes a place of ambush—you wake in panic at 3 a.m., heart racing, sheets soaked, and the thing you were running from is still there, waiting.

The exhaustion is total. Not just physical—though your body feels like it's running a marathon while standing still. It's cognitive exhaustion, emotional exhaustion, spiritual exhaustion. Every ounce of energy goes to threat detection. There's nothing left for anything else.

And here's the cruelest part: you can't explain it.

People who love you are standing right there, asking how they can help, and you can't reach them. The noise is too loud. Their words come through distorted, translated by fear into something that confirms your isolation. "I'm here for you" becomes "They don't know how bad it is." "You're going to be okay" becomes "They don't understand."

You are trapped inside your own nervous system.

The trap has a terrible efficiency. The more you struggle, the tighter it grips. The more you try to think your way out, the more your thoughts spin. The more you reach for control, the more control slips away. Everything you do to escape makes it worse—because everything you do is being processed through the same fear-soaked operating system that created the trap.

This is survival mode. It's real. Millions of people are in it right now—some for days, some for years, some for their entire lives. And they're not weak. They're not broken. They're caught in machinery that evolution built for a different world, running threat-detection software that can't tell the difference between a lion and a landlord.

If you're in it now, I need you to know: there is a way out. Not around—through. And you don't have to find it alone.

The Pit

So we have to be honest.

This is the hardest part—not facing external enemies, but facing internal ones. Admitting what we're actually afraid of.

I'm afraid I'm not enough.

I'm afraid it won't work.

I'm afraid people will take advantage.

I'm afraid I'll lose what I have.

I'm afraid I'll be alone.

I'm afraid I'm wrong.

These fears live in all of us. Pretending they don't makes them stronger. They feed on darkness, on avoidance, on the energy we spend not looking at them.

Naming them begins to dissolve their power.

I know this because I've been in the pit where fear wins completely.

I don't share this lightly. It's not a rhetorical device or a storytelling technique. It's the truth of my life.

At one point, I didn't believe this world had anything for me. The noise was so loud, the fear so total, that I couldn't see any reason to continue. I planned my own death. I had the means. I had the moment. I nearly executed it.

A friend's letter saved me.

It arrived at exactly the right time. It didn't argue me out of anything. It didn't prove that life was worth living. It simply reminded me who I am.

That's what trust does. It doesn't create something new. It reminds you of something you forgot.

Someone trusted me enough to reach out. Someone saw me when I couldn't see myself. And that trust broke through the noise long enough for me to see clearly again.

I am alive because someone trusted me when I couldn't trust myself.

Courage

Fear isn't overcome through willpower. It's overcome through something underneath willpower.

Courage.

Courage isn't the absence of fear. It's action in the presence of fear. It's the small voice that says "one more day" when everything screams "quit." It's the decision to trust even when trust feels dangerous.

Every spiritual tradition understands this. Faith isn't certainty—it's trust despite uncertainty. The leap into the unknown, believing you'll be caught. The willingness to see what you can't yet prove.

Courage is faith enacted. And faith—real faith—is the decision to trust before you have evidence.

This sounds irrational. It isn't. It's the only way forward.

Here's why: trust can't be proven in advance. We can't know someone is trustworthy until we've trusted them. We can't know a system works until we've committed to it. We can't experience the benefits of openness while maintaining our walls.

Trust requires going first. It requires risk. It requires courage.

The remarkable thing is that courage already exists in you. It's not something you have to build or earn or deserve. It's there—underneath the fear, waiting. The fear is loud. The courage is quiet. But it's been there all along.

I know because I've seen it. In myself. In the people around me. In the friend who wrote the letter that saved my life.

Courage is real. And it's accessible right now.

Alignment

When you face fear honestly and discover courage, something shifts.

You start seeing reality instead of fear's projection.

Fear tells you: There isn't enough. People can't be trusted. You're alone. It's hopeless. If you don't protect yourself, no one will.

Reality says something different: There is enough. People mostly want connection. You're part of something larger. Change is possible. You were never as alone as you felt.

This shift—from fear's projection to actual reality—is what I call alignment. The moment when your perception finally matches what's true.

Alignment isn't optimism. It's not pretending things are better than they are. It's seeing accurately, without the distortion that fear creates.

You don't change anything when you trust. You just become aware of what has always been true.

The abundance was always there. The connection was always possible. The love was always waiting. Fear was the only thing blocking your perception.

Faith isn't believing in something that doesn't exist. It's finally seeing something that does.

Coherence

And when you see clearly—when the fear lifts and reality becomes visible—you discover something that changes everything.

The divinity in every human being.

I call this coherence: the awareness of the image of God in every person, in unison. Not as abstract theology, but as direct perception. You look at another human being and you see it. Their worth. Their dignity. Their irreducible value.

This isn't something you manufacture through effort. It's something that becomes visible when fear stops blocking your sight.

The mystics saw it. The prophets saw it. Anyone who has ever loved deeply has seen it. That moment when another person stops being an object and becomes infinite. When you recognize in them the same mystery you sense in yourself.

Coherence is when that recognition extends to everyone.

Not naive—clear. Not sentimental—accurate. Seeing what was always true about human beings, finally unobscured by fear.

A world operating from coherence is a world that sees itself clearly. Humanity recognizing itself. The image of God, reflecting.

We All Win

And what becomes possible when we align:

We all win.

Not some of us at the expense of others. Not a negotiated compromise where everyone sacrifices. Not winners and losers sorting themselves out.

Everyone.

Fear told us it was zero-sum. Your win requires my loss. If I trust, I'll be exploited. If I give, I'll have less. Resources are scarce. Safety is scarce. Love is scarce. Take what you can before someone takes it from you.

That was the lie.

The truth is: when we align to reality—when we see clearly, when we trust, when we recognize the divinity in each other—the math changes.

Your win doesn't require my loss. My generosity doesn't deplete me. Trust creates more than suspicion ever could. There is enough, and more than enough, when we stop wasting everything on fear.

High-trust societies don't have more resources than low-trust societies. They waste less of what they have. That's the efficiency dividend of trust—the surplus that appears when fear stops eating everything.

When we all win, it's a perfect win-win.

And the perfect expression of love.

Love at Scale

Love at scale.

That's what this is. That's what the Trust Economy is trying to build.

Trust is how love operates at scale. It's the infrastructure that lets generosity flow beyond the people you know. Love is what you feel for your children, your friends, your neighbors. Trust is what makes that same care possible between strangers—systematized, designed, built into the architecture of how we organize.

Personal love is one heart reaching another. The friend's letter that saved my life. The parent who believes in a child. The stranger who stops to help.

Love at scale is those same dynamics—generosity, seeing, trust, abundance—built into systems. Designed into economies. Structured into how we organize.

What would it look like to design institutions the way love designs relationships?

Not extraction but generosity. Not suspicion but seeing. Not scarcity but abundance. Not zero-sum but win-win. Not walls but welcome.

That's the question this book is trying to answer.

I don't have it all figured out. The Trust Economy is my best attempt—a designer's attempt to remove friction, a father's attempt to leave something better, a survivor's attempt to build what saved him into something larger.

It's imperfect. It will need revision. The first iteration of any design always does.

But I believe the direction is right. Because I've seen both sides.

I know the darkness where fear wins completely. Where trust seems impossible. Where the only rational response feels like ending it all.

And I know the light that breaks through anyway. The letter that arrives at the right moment. The recognition that you were never as alone as you felt. The courage that was waiting underneath the fear all along.

The light is real. And it's available to everyone.

The Invitation

Here's my invitation:

Face your fear. Not all at once—that's not how it works. But the next one. The one that's in front of you right now.

There's a reason to overcome it: fear is an illusion. It feels solid, feels permanent, feels like the realest thing in the room. But it's not. It's a projection. A story your nervous system tells to keep you safe from threats that mostly don't exist.

What makes it manageable: you are only required to address your fear. Not everyone else's. Not the world's. Just yours. That's your jurisdiction. That's your responsibility. That's enough.

Name it. Look at it. Let it shrink in the light of your attention.

And notice what's on the other side. The courage that was always there. The capacity you forgot you had. The connection that becomes possible when you stop defending against it.

Then take one step. While still afraid. Despite the voice that says retreat.

Every time you choose trust over fear, you vote for a different world. Every time you extend generosity instead of guarding, you weaken fear's grip. Every time you see the dignity in someone else—especially when it's hard—you strengthen the muscle that makes coherence possible.

You don't have to fix everything. You don't have to be certain. You don't have to have it all figured out.

You just have to be willing. To see. To trust. To take the next step.

The rest follows.

The First Trust

But before we can build trust with others, we have to start somewhere closer.

I couldn't trust other people because I couldn't trust myself.

That's the part I didn't want to face. I'd built elaborate defenses against the world—walls, verification, suspicion. But the real problem wasn't out there. The real problem was in here. I was afraid I couldn't handle the pain if trust was broken. Afraid that betrayal would confirm what I already suspected: that I was foolish to hope, stupid to believe, naive to try.

That's what depression does. It's not sadness. It's the complete erosion of self-trust. I stopped believing I could handle things, that I could get better, that I was worth the struggle. And once I stopped trusting myself, everything else collapsed.

We don't have to trust everyone. Some people will hurt us. Some situations don't deserve our trust.

But having the capacity to trust—the ability to extend it when warranted, to risk when the relationship is worth it—that's freedom. And that capacity comes from inside. From knowing that whatever happens, we can handle it.

So how do you build it?

Repeat actions that are honorable to your own dignity.

That's the whole instruction. Every time you keep a promise to yourself. Every time you speak truth when it's easier to lie. Every time you show up when you said you would. Every time you refuse to betray yourself for approval. You're not just doing a good thing. You're building evidence that you can be trusted—by yourself, to yourself.

The first trust isn't other people.

It's you.

Start there. Everything else follows.

I think Jesus came to show us how far love would go—all the way to death.

But I've come to believe our responsibility is different. Not to die for love. To live it.

To live into trust. To show humanity what's possible when we're not afraid of each other. To demonstrate, in our actual lives, that another way works.

All of life is a story of trust. Every relationship, every institution, every economy rises or falls on whether people can trust each other.

Fear has been our adversary since the beginning. It's in every scripture because it's in every human heart.

But it doesn't have the final word.

Courage is real. Trust is possible. Love scales.

And when we align to that reality—when we face our fear, discover our courage, get honest with ourselves, and finally see clearly—we don't just survive.

We all win.

11

Chapter Eleven: The Five Frequencies

"The best way to find out if you can trust somebody is to trust them."—Ernest Hemingway

I used to work at a startup called StreamSets. Our core value was trusting our people—and I mean really trusting them, not the performative kind you see on motivational posters. Leadership assumed competence. Information flowed freely. When someone had an idea, they had permission to run with it. The result was a team that flourished. We grew revenue tenfold. We built technology that mattered. And eventually, we were acquired by one of the largest enterprise companies in the world.

Almost immediately, I realized we had been absorbed into a completely different culture.

This was shareholder capitalism in its purest form. Profit wasn't the primary goal—it was the only goal. The internal divisions were highly fragmented because there was almost no trust at the top. Teams were encouraged to compete with each other, so nobody shared information or ideas. Resources flowed only to projects that executives personally believed in. Everyone else starved.

Product innovation slowed to a crawl. What would have taken our startup weeks suddenly took six to nine months. The same engineers, the same technology, the same market—but a different frequency of trust. People were afraid to create because they were afraid to fail. They were afraid to fail because failure meant losing their job. The company ran a tier system designed to identify "low performers" who would eventually be removed—and managers had to fill that bottom tier even when no one belonged there.

The culture created an intensity that crushed collaboration. The company survived on legacy partnerships and brand recognition, but they weren't building value anymore. They were hitting numbers. Trust was stretched with customers, with partners, with employees. You could feel it in every meeting—the calculation behind every statement, the guardedness in every exchange.

I've now spent years inside both systems. Same industry. Same people, in many cases. Radically different outcomes. The difference wasn't talent or resources or market conditions. The difference was trust.

That experience taught me something crucial: trust isn't binary. It doesn't simply exist or not exist. Trust operates on a spectrum—five distinct frequencies, each with its own logic, its own emotional signature, its own economic consequences.

This isn't poetry. It's measurable. High-trust companies outperform the S&P 500 by 2.5x. Trust is not a vibe. It's a hard economic variable—the hardest one we've been ignoring.

I call these bands on the spectrum the Five Frequencies of Trust.

The Spectrum

Think of trust as a frequency—like a radio signal. When the frequency is low, the signal is fragmented. Static. Interference. Communication breaks down and energy scatters. When the frequency is high, the signal is clear. Coherent. Information flows without distortion and systems synchronize naturally.

The Five Frequencies describe this progression from fragmentation to coherence:

Frequency I: Distrust—The Survival Band

Frequency II: Cautious Cooperation—The Transactional Band

Frequency III: Mutual Respect—The Relational Band

Frequency IV: Collaborative Trust—The Synergistic Band

Frequency V: Faith—The Unified Band

These aren't just stages of feeling—they're five distinct frequencies your nervous system broadcasts, and your systems reflect. Each frequency has profound implications for how energy flows through human systems, from families to corporations to entire economies.

As you read each frequency, I want you to notice where your body relaxes and where it tightens. Trust is not abstract. It lives in us—in the clench of our jaw when we sense deception, in the softening of our shoulders when we feel safe. This spectrum isn't just a model. It's a mirror.

Here's the key insight: each step up the spectrum releases resources. Moving from Frequency I to Frequency II frees capital that was locked in pure defense. Moving from II to III frees capital that was locked in verification. Each frequency up converts overhead into capacity—until at Frequency V, nearly all available resources flow toward creation rather than protection.

Frequency I: Distrust

"Everyone is out for themselves."

Picture a neighborhood where no one makes eye contact. Doors triple-bolted. Children not allowed outside alone. The corner store has plexiglass between cashier and customer—not from corporate policy, but because the owner installed it himself after the third robbery.

Or picture a divorced couple in a conference room. Lawyers on both sides. A stack of documents detailing who gets the kids on which weekends, who pays for what, what happens if someone is fifteen minutes late. Every contingency covered. Every loophole closed. They haven't spoken directly in months. Every word passes through intermediaries, every gesture filtered for threat. This is Frequency I—where the cost of broken trust is paid in legal fees, emotional exhaustion, and children who learn that love ends in paperwork.

Distrust is not the opposite of trust. It's the memory of broken trust.

This distinction matters. People operating at Frequency I aren't paranoid or irrational. They're intelligent survivors. They built thick armor because they once cared deeply and got hurt. The wall around them isn't weakness—it's evidence of how much they once had to lose.

At this frequency, the nervous system is locked in protection mode. Every interaction is filtered through a single question: What's the threat? Cortisol runs high. The amygdala—the brain's threat detection center—stays hyperactive, scanning for danger even in neutral situations. The body burns tremendous energy maintaining this vigilance.

Economically, Frequency I is extraordinarily expensive. When distrust is the baseline, every transaction requires insurance against betrayal. Contracts grow longer. Lawyers multiply. Verification systems expand. The Idiot Index—that ratio of finished price to material cost—inflates as trust shrinks.

But here's the hidden gift of Frequency I: hypervigilance teaches discernment. People who've survived betrayal develop a finely tuned sense for incongruence—the gap between what someone says and what they mean. When healed, these survivors often become the most trustworthy people in any system. They know the cost of broken trust because they've paid it.

How to recognize Frequency I

You know you're broadcasting Frequency I when you assume bad intent before you have evidence, when you interpret neutral actions as potential threats, when you document everything as protection against future betrayal. You feel physically exhausted by ordinary interactions. You struggle to delegate because "no one else will do it right."

The system signature is unmistakable: high legal and security costs, slow or paralyzed decision-making, information hoarding across teams. Organizations at Frequency I are good at avoiding catastrophe but bad at creating anything new. Think post-merger culture clash, or a vendor relationship after a contract breach. "The sales team and product team haven't spoken directly in six months. Every request goes through legal."

The economic cost is maximum—nearly all discretionary resources consumed by defense.

The path forward: Begin to tell the truth, even when it feels unsafe. Honesty is the first crack in the armor—the signal to your own nervous system that perhaps the world isn't as dangerous as your wounds suggest.

The transforming question: What if I'm wrong about you?

Frequency II: Cautious Cooperation

"I'll trust you if you prove it."

Two departments in a mid-sized company have stopped talking. Not officially—there's no memo declaring war. But the engineers won't walk over to marketing anymore. Marketing won't pick up the phone. Everything flows through Jira tickets and Slack threads with seventeen people cc'd. Every request documented. Every deliverable time-stamped. The work gets done, technically. But it takes three times longer than it should, and nobody can remember the last time someone said "thank you" without it feeling like a legal deposition. This is Frequency II—collaboration without connection, cooperation without trust.

At Frequency II, the wall has developed a door—but that door has conditions.

The emotional signature is calculation. Before any exchange, a cost-benefit analysis runs in the background: What will this cost me? What will I get? Is the risk worth the reward? Every interaction is a transaction, weighed for fairness, measured for reciprocity.

This isn't cynicism—it's risk management. People at Frequency II want to trust. They're willing to cooperate. But they've learned that trust is expensive when misplaced, so they demand proof before commitment. The Idiot Index at Frequency II is moderate—lower than pure distrust, but still inflated by verification overhead. Every transaction carries the tax of "trust but verify."

How to recognize Frequency II

You know you're broadcasting Frequency II when you keep score in relationships, consciously or not. You require proof before extending trust. You phrase requests in terms of mutual benefit, document agreements "just in case," and feel relief when a transaction completes without incident.

The system signature: heavy reliance on contracts and formal agreements, functional but slow collaboration, innovation that happens incrementally rather than radically. Good at fairness, weak at inspiration. Think enterprise with heavy compliance overhead, detailed SOWs with every contractor, cross-functional teams that cooperate but don't collaborate. "We work together, but everything is documented. Every deliverable has a sign-off. No one moves without approval."

The economic cost is high—verification and documentation consume significant resources.

The path forward: Extend trust slightly beyond what evidence justifies. Small acts of generosity—trusting first, before you have proof—begin to break the transactional pattern.

The transforming question: What would change if I trusted first?

Frequency III: Mutual Respect

"We're in this together."

A neighborhood soccer league has been running for twelve years. No formal organization. No paid referees. Parents take turns bringing snacks. When conflicts arise—and they do, because kids and competition—people talk it out. Not because there's a policy, but because everyone knows everyone, and the relationships matter more than winning any particular game. This is Frequency III—where trust is grounded in identity, in belonging, in the recognition that we're part of the same tribe.

At Frequency III, the calculation of Frequency II gives way to identification. You trust because you recognize shared membership. The other person isn't a stranger to be evaluated—they're one of us. The foundation shifts from proof to belonging.

The emotional signature is warmth. Not the heat of passion, but the steady warmth of recognition. You see the other person. They see you. The mutual visibility creates safety that doesn't require verification.

Economically, Frequency III is where communities thrive. Local businesses survive because neighbors prefer to support their own. Professional networks create opportunity through referrals and reputation. Religious communities sustain members through hard times because everyone knows they're part of something larger.

The Idiot Index drops significantly at Frequency III. Social pressure enforces norms more efficiently than contracts. Reputation matters, so people behave. The overhead of verification shrinks because the community itself becomes the verification system.

But Frequency III has a shadow: tribalism. The same identification that creates internal trust can create external suspicion. We trust "us—but what about "them"? The warmth inside the circle can coincide with coldness toward those outside it.

How to recognize Frequency III

You know you're broadcasting Frequency III when you trust people because they're "one of us." You feel loyalty to groups you belong to, speak differently to insiders than outsiders, make decisions partly based on community impact. You feel genuinely happy when group members succeed.

The system signature: strong internal cohesion with clear boundaries, reputation-based trust where what the community thinks matters, informal enforcement of norms. Good at sustaining community, vulnerable to groupthink. Think strong departmental identity—"we're the engineering team"—with internal "family culture" but competitive with other divisions. "Inside our team, we'd do anything for each other. But we don't trust the other divisions."

The economic cost is moderate—social capital replaces much formal overhead, but tribalism limits expansion.

The path forward: Extend the boundary of "us." Notice when you're treating outsiders differently than insiders, and experiment with offering the same warmth across the line.

The transforming question: What if "they" are also "us"?

Frequency IV: Collaborative Trust

"I've got your back."

A jazz quartet has played together for eight years. They don't rehearse much anymore—they don't need to. When one musician takes a solo, the others adjust instinctively. When someone makes a mistake, the group incorporates it, turns it into something new. There's no leader, no hierarchy. Just four people so attuned to each other that creation becomes effortless. This is Frequency IV—where trust enables spontaneous coordination, where individual excellence serves collective creation.

At Frequency IV, trust becomes generative. It's no longer about avoiding harm or managing risk. It's about creating something that couldn't exist without the collaboration.

The emotional signature is flow. The state psychologists describe as optimal experience—complete absorption in the task, ego boundaries softening, time distortion. At Frequency IV, collaboration feels like play. Work becomes intrinsically rewarding. The distinction between effort and enjoyment dissolves.

Economically, Frequency IV is where innovation flourishes. The examples are everywhere once you know how to look: open-source software communities that build infrastructure worth billions through voluntary collaboration; research labs where breakthroughs emerge from late-night conversations between people who trust each other completely; startups that move impossibly fast because no one wastes energy on politics.

The Idiot Index at Frequency IV approaches 1:1. The overhead of distrust has been engineered out. Defense costs disappear into creative investment. Resources flow toward production rather than protection. Google's Project Aristotle confirmed it: psychological safety—Frequency IV trust—was the key to team performance.

How to recognize Frequency IV

You know you're broadcasting Frequency IV when you share credit instinctively, when you celebrate others' success as your own. You take risks because you trust the group to catch you. You experience flow states in collaboration. You can't imagine the work without the team.

The system signature: high innovation and creative output, rapid adaptation to change, minimal bureaucracy with maximum autonomy. Good at breakthrough creation, though it requires ongoing trust maintenance. Think high-performing startup team, open-source project core contributors, research lab with psychological safety. "We don't have job descriptions anymore. Everyone just does what needs doing."

The economic cost is low—nearly all resources available for creation.

The path forward: Maintain it. Frequency IV is dynamic—it requires ongoing investment. The practices that built trust must continue, or entropy pulls the system back down.

The transforming question: How do we protect this?

Frequency V: Faith

"We are one."

A hospice nurse once told me about her team. "We don't have scripts," she said. "When someone is dying, there's no playbook. But somehow we always know who needs to be in the room, who needs to step back, when to speak and when to be silent. It's like we share the same nervous system." She paused. "I think it's because we've all faced death together so many times. We've seen each other break down and rebuild. There's nothing left to prove. So we just... move as one." This is Frequency V.

Faith is not blind trust. It's post-evidence trust.

At Frequency V, you've seen enough cycles of goodness to believe the pattern holds—even when you can't see proof in this particular moment. The system has demonstrated its trustworthiness so consistently that doubt no longer seems like wisdom. It seems like a failure of pattern recognition.

This is not naivety. Real faith is informed. It sees both potential and pitfalls. It remains discerning even as it remains open. It chooses trust not because danger doesn't exist, but because trust is the more accurate model of reality.

The emotional tone at Frequency V is peace. Not the peace of avoidance or denial, but the peace of alignment—when your internal state matches the external world, when belief and experience harmonize, when the constant negotiation between hope and fear finally resolves into coherence.

This may sound utopian, but examples exist. High-trust societies like Denmark, Norway, and Finland operate closer to Frequency V than most nations. Their citizens pay high taxes willingly because they trust the system to use that money well. Their businesses operate with minimal bureaucracy because contracts are assumed to be honored. Their crime rates are low not because of heavy policing but because social trust makes crime unnecessary and unthinkable.

How to recognize Frequency V

You know you're broadcasting Frequency V when you assume the best outcome first, then adjust if needed. You feel peaceful even in uncertainty. You give without tracking what you're owed, experience synchronicity—things aligning without forced effort—and trust yourself as much as you trust others.

The system signature: minimal enforcement with maximum voluntary participation, decisions that emerge organically from shared values, correction through conversation rather than punishment. Systems at this level assume honesty first. They build correction mechanisms instead of punishment mechanisms. The emphasis shifts from compliance to coherence. Think partnerships that survive leadership changes on both sides, long-term supplier relationships with no contract—just a handshake and fifteen years of history. "We've been working together so long, I'd trust them with anything. We don't even negotiate anymore."

The economic cost is minimal—resources flow almost entirely to flourishing rather than friction.

The path forward: Choose to see the best outcome first. Lead with the assumption of good faith. Design systems that expect integrity rather than guard against its absence.

The hidden paradox: Faith can collapse into naivety if discernment is lost. The highest trust requires the sharpest judgment—not to detect threats, but to recognize truth.

The Oscillation Principle

The spectrum doesn't immediately reveal this: trust doesn't rise and stay there.

Trust oscillates. It rises and falls, sometimes within a single conversation. A moment of betrayal can drop you from Frequency IV to Frequency I in seconds. A moment of unexpected grace can lift you two bands before you realize what's happened.

Personal trust—the emotional experience of feeling safe—moves faster than institutional trust—the structural experience of reliable systems. You can lose faith in a friend instantly, but losing faith in a currency or a government takes longer. The oscillation speeds differ.

This is actually hopeful news. It means trust can be restored faster than it was built. A single act of radical transparency can undo months of accumulated suspicion. A single genuine apology can repair what seemed irreparably broken. The physics of trust favor recovery.

Real maturity isn't staying permanently at Frequency V. Real maturity is agility—knowing how to repair trust faster each time it's breached.

The goal isn't to avoid the descent. The goal is to shorten it. To recognize the drop quickly, name it honestly, and begin the climb back with less resistance each time. This is the skill that transforms teams, families, and societies: not perfect trust, but resilient trust. Not immunity to betrayal, but rapid recovery from it.

The Trust Index

In Chapter Five, we met the Idiot Index—the ratio of finished price to material cost. It measures how much distrust inflates every transaction. A rocket with a 10:1 Idiot Index means 90% of what you're paying isn't the rocket—it's the overhead.

The Trust Index measures the opposite: not how much you waste, but how much you keep.

Trust Index = Resources available for creation / Total resources

Or, put differently: what percentage of your time, money, and energy actually goes toward building something—versus protecting, defending, verifying, and insuring against betrayal?

A person spending 70% of their income on rent, insurance, security systems, and legal protection has a Trust Index of roughly 30%. Only 30% of their resources are available for creation, investment, enjoyment, generosity. The rest is consumed by the friction of low-trust living.

A community where neighbors watch each other's homes, share tools freely, and resolve disputes through conversation instead of litigation has a Trust Index approaching 90%. Almost everything they have is available for use.

The Trust Index rises with each frequency—from roughly 10-20% at Frequency I to 95%+ at Frequency V.

The Idiot Index shows you the price of distrust on individual transactions. The Trust Index shows you the cost of distrust across your entire life.

Locating Yourself

Where are you on the spectrum?

The honest answer is probably: it depends. You might operate at Frequency IV with your spouse and Frequency II with your colleagues. Frequency III with your community and Frequency I with strangers. The spectrum isn't uniform. It shifts across relationships, contexts, and time.

This is normal. The goal isn't to reach Frequency V everywhere simultaneously. The goal is to notice where you are and understand what it would take to rise—one band, one relationship, one moment at a time.

Because here's the truth the Five Frequencies reveal: every act of fear is a distortion of trust. Every act of courage retunes the world.

The frequency you broadcast affects the frequency you receive. When you lead with suspicion, you attract defensiveness. When you lead with openness, you invite reciprocity. The spectrum isn't just a map of where you are. It's a lever for where you want to go.

Trust removes the initial conflict and chooses to see the best outcome first. The win-win.

That's not just a philosophy. That's a frequency. And you get to choose which one you broadcast.

The Dignity Foundation

There's a deeper pattern underneath the Five Frequencies. It's not really about trust. It's about sight.

At each frequency, something shifts in how we see—ourselves and others. The frequencies track dignity: how clearly we perceive the inherent worth of the person in front of us, and the person in the mirror.

Frequency I: Dignity forgotten. Both self and other feel worthless or threatening. You can't see their humanity because fear has obscured it. You can't see your own because shame has buried it.

Frequency II: Dignity conditional. "I'll see your worth if you prove it." Value must be demonstrated before it's acknowledged. The other person is on trial until evidence clears them.

Frequency III: Dignity recognized within tribe. "We see each other"—but only within the boundary. Inside the circle, worth is assumed. Outside, it must still be earned.

Frequency IV: Dignity generative. Seeing each other's worth creates new value. Recognition isn't just acknowledged—it's amplified. Your dignity increases mine. The seeing itself produces something.

Frequency V: Dignity complete. The image of God visible in everyone, including yourself. Worth isn't conditional, tribal, or transactional. It simply is—and you can finally see it.

This is why trust breaks: we forget dignity.

When fear takes over, we stop seeing people. We see threats, resources, obstacles, numbers. We objectify—they become what they can do for us or to us. We dehumanize—they become "them," not "us." We extract—their worth exists only in what we can take. We abandon—they're not worth protecting.

Every act of extraction is a forgetting of dignity. Every betrayal begins with failing to see.

And this is how trust repairs: we remember.

The path back up the frequencies isn't primarily behavioral. It's perceptual. You start seeing the other person as fully human again. You recognize your own worth—so you no longer need to extract from others to feel valuable. You restore the sight that fear obscured.

Here's what fear actually does: it blinds. It makes us forget what we're looking at. The person across the table isn't a competitor or a threat or a resource. They're a human being with inherent worth—and so are you.

The Five Frequencies aren't really about trust. They're about how clearly you see.

Start with yourself. Then look again at the person in front of you.

| 12 |

Chapter Twelve: The Surplus Principle

"Acknowledge your blessings—and create opportunities for others. Be of surplus value."—Scott Galloway, Notes on Being a Man

Scott Galloway is a professor at NYU, a successful entrepreneur, and one of the sharpest critics of modern capitalism.

He spent decades inside the machine Friedman built. He taught at one of the world's premier business schools. He lived the doctrine—maximize returns, capture value, win the quarter.

And when it came time to tell his sons what actually matters, he rejected it completely.

He didn't tell them to maximize shareholder value or dominate competitors. He taught them the opposite: be of surplus value. Give more than you take. Create more than you consume. Leave every situation better than you found it.

In 2025, Galloway wrote Notes on Being a Man. Throughout it, he returns to one principle: be of surplus value.

Think about what he was actually teaching them.

He was teaching them to trust. To trust that it's possible to create more than you consume. To trust that generosity doesn't deplete you—it expands you. To trust that the world isn't zero-sum, that value can be generated rather than merely captured, that leaving others better off doesn't mean leaving yourself worse off.

This is a radical act of faith disguised as practical advice.

The scarcity mindset says: protect what you have, because there isn't enough. Take before you're taken from. Every transaction has a winner and a loser, so make sure you're the winner.

The surplus mindset says: create more than you use. Trust that contribution generates return. Believe that the pie can expand.

Galloway wasn't teaching his sons accounting. He was teaching them to see the world as abundant rather than scarce—and that seeing is the first act of trust.

That single principle contains the entire thesis of this chapter—and this book. It can be expressed as a formula:

Surplus = Value Created → Value Consumed

The principle: design every relationship, transaction, and institution so that surplus is positive for all parties. Not positive for shareholders at the expense of workers. Not positive for this quarter at the expense of next decade. Not positive for insiders at the expense of everyone else. Positive for all parties—or the system is extracting, not creating.

This is the test. This is the standard. This is what trust makes possible.

Surplus is the signature of trust. When trust is present, systems generate more than they consume. When trust is absent, systems consume more than they generate. This isn't metaphor. It's measurable. It's the difference between economies that flourish and economies that extract. Between organizations that create value and organizations that capture it. Between relationships that expand and relationships that deplete.

Two Towns

Surplus = Value Created → Value Consumed.

Imagine two towns with identical resources. Same population. Same natural endowments. Same starting capital. Same access to markets. The difference is invisible: the level of trust between residents. The difference in outcomes is not.

These towns are composites—thought experiments synthesizing patterns researchers have documented across hundreds of real communities. The specifics are illustrative, but the dynamics are precise. What follows isn't fiction. It's the predictable outcome of trust mathematics.

In the first town—call it Millbrook—trust is low. Neighbors don't know each other. Businesses assume customers will cheat them. Employees assume employers will exploit them. The town has seventeen lawyers for a population of five thousand. Every transaction requires documentation. Every agreement requires enforcement mechanisms. The town budget allocates forty percent to administration, compliance, and dispute resolution.

Millbrook isn't poor, exactly. But it's stuck. New businesses don't form because the startup costs—legal fees, insurance, bonding requirements—are prohibitive. Collaboration doesn't happen because sharing information feels like giving away advantage. The talented young people leave for cities where opportunity feels more accessible. The town survives on its history, not its future.

In the second town—call it Hartfield—trust is high. Neighbors know each other by name. Businesses extend credit based on handshakes. Employees stay for decades because they're treated as partners, not costs. The town has two lawyers, both of whom spend most of their time on real estate transactions. The town budget allocates five percent to administration.

Hartfield isn't rich because it found oil or attracted a tech company. It's rich because friction is low. A new restaurant opens with a loan from neighbors who believe in the owner. A manufacturing cooperative shares equipment across five small businesses, reducing capital costs by eighty percent. Ideas flow freely because reputation matters more than patents. The talented young people stay—or return after college—because the quality of life can't be replicated in cities.

Both towns have the same inputs. Hartfield creates more value and consumes less doing it. The difference is surplus—and surplus comes from trust.

The Surplus Dividend

In the last chapter, we saw how trust moves through Five Frequencies—from distrust to faith, from fragmentation to coherence. Economically, those frequencies show up as two spirals:

Trust → Cooperation → Surplus → Prosperity → Reinforced Trust

Distrust → Competition → Scarcity → Decline → Reinforced Distrust

Both spirals are self-reinforcing. Both are measurable.

Transaction costs: Economists estimate that distrust costs the global economy roughly two trillion dollars annually in unnecessary overhead—legal fees, insurance premiums, verification systems, enforcement mechanisms. That's not value creation. That's value consumption. Every dollar not spent on enforcement is a dollar available for actual creation.

The pattern is consistent: trust creates surplus, surplus creates prosperity, prosperity reinforces trust. The upward spiral is available to any system that chooses it.

The Friction Budget

Here's the question no one asks: what percentage of your operating costs is actually creating value—and what percentage is managing distrust?

Sales: 10-20% of revenue. Why does sales exist as a separate function? Because customers don't automatically trust that your product will solve their problem. They need persuading, reassuring, handholding through the decision. In high-trust environments—where reputation travels, where referrals flow naturally, where your track record speaks for itself—sales shrinks dramatically. The product sells itself because trust already exists.

Marketing: 5-15% of revenue. Marketing exists to create awareness and build credibility with strangers. But in high-trust communities, word of mouth does this work for free. Recommendations from trusted sources convert at ten times the rate of advertisements. Every dollar spent convincing strangers is a dollar not spent on actual creation.

Legal and Compliance: 2-8% of revenue. Contracts exist because we don't trust handshakes. Compliance departments exist because we assume people will cheat. Regulatory overhead exists because institutions can't be trusted to self-regulate. In high-trust environments, a conversation replaces a contract. A reputation replaces a compliance officer. The overhead collapses.

HR and Management Layers: 3-8% of revenue. Why do we need managers? Partly to coordinate—but largely to monitor. The assumption is that workers won't perform without oversight. High-trust organizations flatten dramatically. Self-organizing teams replace hierarchies. The management tax disappears.

Insurance and Security: 2-5% of revenue. Every insurance premium is a bet against trust. Every security system is a wall against betrayal. Every fraud prevention investment is a tax on the assumption that people will steal. In high-trust environments, community accountability replaces institutional insurance. The premiums redirect to creation.

Verification and Auditing: 1-3% of revenue. Every audit is a statement of distrust. Every verification system assumes that someone is lying. Every checkpoint slows the process to catch the cheaters. In high-trust environments, transparency replaces verification. The overhead evaporates.

Add it up. In a typical low-trust business, 25-50% of operating costs go to friction—to the machinery of managing distrust. That's not value creation. That's value consumption. That's the tax we pay for not trusting each other.

Now imagine a business that operates at Frequency IV or V. Reputation replaces sales. Word of mouth replaces marketing. Handshakes replace contracts. Self-organization replaces management layers. Community accountability replaces insurance.

The friction budget drops from 35% to 10%. Maybe lower.

That's 25% of operating costs freed up. Not through cost-cutting or layoffs or squeezing suppliers—through trust. Twenty-five percent that could go to higher wages, lower prices, more R&D, community investment, or actual surplus.

The money is already there. We're just burning it on walls.

Buckminster Fuller saw this decades ago. He called it "ephemeralization"—the tendency of technology to do more with less over time. A smartphone replaces a room of equipment. A solar panel converts sunlight with no moving parts. The technology kept getting more efficient—but our economic systems didn't. Fuller understood what most economists missed: the machinery of distrust is the largest source of inefficiency in human systems. We weren't building things. We were building walls.

Trust is ephemeralization applied to human relationships. When trust is present, the walls become unnecessary. The resources they consumed become available for actual creation.

The Mechanics of Efficiency

Why, specifically, does trust create surplus? Not as a feel-good abstraction, but as engineering?

Mechanism 1: Trust eliminates verification overhead.

In a low-trust system, every claim must be checked. Did the contractor actually do the work? Did the employee actually work those hours? Did the supplier actually deliver quality materials? Each verification costs time, money, and attention.

In a high-trust system, verification becomes sampling rather than census. You check occasionally to confirm the trust is warranted, but you don't check everything. The savings compound across every interaction.

Mechanism 2: Trust accelerates decision-making.

Low-trust organizations require approval chains. Every decision climbs the hierarchy, gets reviewed, gets questioned, gets documented, gets approved (or sent back for revision). The latency is enormous.

High-trust organizations push decisions to the edge. People closest to the problem are trusted to solve it. The same decision that takes weeks in a bureaucracy takes hours in a trust-based team.

Melanie Perkins built Canva on this principle. No approval needed for 90% of decisions. While competitors responded to growth by adding management layers and review processes, she did the opposite: she defined exactly what good looked like for every type of decision. If a team could answer three specific criteria, they moved forward. No manager loop required.

The difference showed up in speed. Features that required five meetings and three approval layers at other companies took Canva one focused conversation. Product teams shipped updates in days while competitors took weeks. By 2023, Canva had scaled to 170 million users—faster than design tools ten times their size.

Her insight reframes what trust actually requires. Most leaders think scaling demands more control. More check-ins. More oversight to prevent mistakes. But control creates drag. Clarity eliminates it.

Teams with clarity move without waiting. They course-correct on their own. They make better decisions because they know exactly what the target looks like. Teams without clarity hesitate, escalate everything, need their leader to weigh in constantly—because they don't know what good looks like.

This is trust operationalized: not blind faith, but shared understanding so precise that oversight becomes redundant.

Mechanism 3: Trust enables resource sharing.

In low-trust environments, resources are hoarded. Each department maintains its own budget, its own equipment, its own headcount—because sharing means vulnerability. Duplication multiplies.

In high-trust environments, resources flow to where they're needed. Equipment is shared. Expertise crosses boundaries. Slack in one area covers shortage in another. The same output requires less total input.

Mechanism 4: Trust compounds learning.

When people trust each other, they share failures as well as successes. They admit what they don't know. They ask for help. Knowledge spreads through the system.

When trust is absent, failures are hidden. Ignorance is concealed. Asking for help signals weakness. The same mistakes get repeated across the organization because no one is willing to be vulnerable.

Mechanism 5: Trust survives stress.

This is the most important mechanism. Every system faces shocks—recessions, pandemics, competitive threats, internal crises. Low-trust systems fracture under stress. People protect themselves first. Cooperation collapses exactly when it's most needed.

High-trust systems flex under stress. People sacrifice for each other because they believe the sacrifice will be reciprocated. Problems get solved collectively rather than shifted individually. The system bends but doesn't break.

Each of these mechanisms multiplies. It's not mysterious. It's arithmetic.

Trust creates surplus because trust eliminates waste. And the waste it eliminates is far larger than most people realize.

The Handshake Deal

In 2003, Warren Buffett bought McLane Company from Walmart. McLane was one of the largest wholesale distributors in America—$23 billion in annual revenue, tens of thousands of employees, operations spanning the country. The purchase price was $1.5 billion.

Here's how the deal happened.

Buffett had a single two-hour meeting with Tom Schoewe, Walmart's CFO. They shook hands. Twenty-nine days later, Walmart had its money and Berkshire Hathaway owned McLane.

No due diligence.

Think about what normally happens in a $1.5 billion acquisition. Dozens of attorneys reading every contract, equipment lease, real estate document, and union agreement. Armies of accountants auditing every line item on annual, quarterly, and monthly financial statements. Teams of consultants assessing market position, competitive threats, operational risks. The process takes six to twelve months. The fees run into the tens of millions.

Buffett skipped all of it.

In his annual letter to shareholders, he explained why: "We did no 'due diligence.' We knew everything would be exactly as Walmart said it would be—and it was."

This wasn't naivety. It was efficiency.

Buffett understood something that most dealmakers miss: the real risk in any acquisition isn't hidden in the footnotes of a contract. It's in the character of the people you're dealing with and the fundamental economics of the business. No amount of due diligence protects you from bad character. And if you can't assess basic economics without an army of consultants, you shouldn't be doing the deal.

"You can't do a good deal with a bad person," Buffett has said. The corollary is equally important: with good people, you don't need the machinery of distrust.

This wasn't an isolated incident. When Buffett bought Nebraska Furniture Mart from Rose Blumkin—a legendary retailer who had built a $100 million business from nothing—he showed up with a one-page purchase proposal he'd drafted himself. She accepted without changing a word. No investment bankers. No lawyers. As Buffett later described the experience: "heavenly."

The pattern is consistent: trust collapses transaction costs. What takes others a year takes Buffett a month. What costs others tens of millions costs him the price of a handshake. The savings don't disappear—they become surplus, available for actual value creation.

But here's what makes it work: Buffett's reputation. He has spent sixty years building a track record of fair dealing, honest communication, and long-term thinking. Sellers know that a handshake with Buffett is more reliable than a 200-page contract with someone else. His reputation is the enforcement mechanism. Betray that reputation once, and the entire system collapses.

This is the key insight: the handshake deal isn't less rigorous than the contract-heavy alternative. It's backed by a different enforcement mechanism—one that's actually more powerful. Contracts are enforced by courts, which are slow, expensive, and uncertain. Reputation is enforced by the market itself, which is fast, free, and ruthless. Break your word to Buffett, and everyone knows. Your cost of doing business with anyone rises permanently.

The handshake economy isn't a relic of a simpler time. It's a more sophisticated system—one that recognizes that character matters more than clauses, that relationships outlast contracts, and that the real due diligence is understanding who you're dealing with.

Trust isn't the absence of rigor. It's rigor applied to the right variables.

But the Friction Budget reveals something darker than wasted overhead. It reveals that most of what we experience as scarcity isn't real.

The Manufactured Scarcity

Here's the uncomfortable truth: most scarcity is manufactured.

Not all scarcity. Some resources are genuinely finite. Fresh water in a desert is scarce. Beachfront property is scarce. Time is scarce. These constraints are real.

But most of what we experience as scarcity isn't about physical limits. It's about system design.

Housing isn't scarce because we lack the materials or knowledge to build homes. It's scarce because zoning laws, financing structures, and construction regulations create artificial bottlenecks. Healthcare isn't scarce because we lack doctors or medicine. It's scarce because insurance systems, patent laws, and administrative overhead consume resources that could go to actual care.

Insulin costs five dollars to manufacture. Patients pay hundreds. The scarcity isn't in the molecule—it's in the system.

The Idiot Index—that ratio of finished price to material cost—measures this manufactured scarcity. When insulin costs two hundred and forty times its material value, that's not a market functioning efficiently. That's a system designed to extract rather than serve.

This connects directly to trust: manufactured scarcity requires low trust to survive.

If people trusted each other, they would cooperate to eliminate artificial bottlenecks. They would share information about true costs. They would organize to demand efficiency. The extraction only works because distrust keeps people isolated, suspicious, and competing against each other for resources that aren't actually scarce.

Scarcity and distrust are symbiotic. Scarcity creates distrust—when there isn't enough, people fight over what exists. Distrust creates scarcity—when people don't cooperate, efficiency collapses and artificial bottlenecks multiply. Break one, and you weaken the other.

This is why trust is so threatening to extractive systems. Trust doesn't just feel better—it reveals that the scarcity was manufactured all along.

The Surplus Society

Surplus = Value Created → Value Consumed.

Now let's imagine what happens when an entire society is designed so that equation is positive for everyone.

Start with the basics. In a surplus society, the default assumption is abundance, not scarcity. This isn't naive optimism—it's design philosophy. Systems are built to generate more than they consume, to leave participants better off, to compound value over time.

Work becomes contribution. Instead of labor extracted under threat of poverty, work becomes voluntary participation in value creation. People contribute because contribution is meaningful—and because the system returns surplus to contributors rather than extracting it to distant shareholders.

Transactions become relationships. Instead of zero-sum exchanges where one party's gain requires another's loss, transactions become positive-sum collaborations where both parties walk away with more than they started with. The goal isn't to capture maximum value—it's to create maximum value.

Competition becomes cooperation. Instead of fighting over fixed pies, participants work together to expand pies. Competition still exists—for reputation, for excellence, for the satisfaction of doing great work—but it's competition to contribute, not competition to extract.

Wealth becomes flow. Instead of accumulation as the measure of success, circulation becomes the measure. Wealth isn't what you hoard—it's what you enable. The wealthiest people aren't those who've captured the most, but those who've generated the most surplus for others.

This isn't wishful thinking. It already exists—in pockets, in experiments, in places that chose differently.

In the Basque region of Spain, a network of cooperatives called Mondragon has operated on surplus principles since 1956. The workers own the companies. Profits are shared—not equally, but transparently, with the highest-paid worker earning no more than six times the lowest. When one cooperative struggles, others in the network provide support. When the economy contracts, workers vote to reduce hours rather than lay off colleagues.

The results are measurable. Mondragon employs over 80,000 people across more than 250 companies. The region has lower unemployment than surrounding areas. Worker satisfaction is higher. The communities are more stable across generations. The cooperatives have survived recessions that destroyed conventional competitors.

Surplus here isn't abstract. It's measured in lower unemployment, better schools, longer tenures, stronger communities. Value Created → Value Consumed is positive, and the proof is visible in daily life. The system doesn't just pay workers—it leaves the region better than it found it.

Mondragon isn't perfect. It faces the same market pressures as any enterprise. But it demonstrates that surplus-oriented design isn't fantasy. It's a choice that produces different results.

Surplus or scarcity. Upward spiral or downward spiral. Trust or extraction.

These aren't forces of nature. They're design choices. We built the systems we have. We can build different ones.

The data is clear: trust creates surplus, surplus creates prosperity, prosperity reinforces trust. The cycle is available to any system—family, organization, economy, society—that chooses to optimize for it.

The Simplest Path

We've covered a lot of ground in this chapter—friction budgets, handshake deals, surplus spirals, ephemeralization. It might seem like creating surplus requires sophisticated systems or radical restructuring.

It doesn't.

The simplest way to create surplus is this: be trustworthy.

Do what you say you will do.

That's it. That's the whole thing. Everything else is commentary.

When your word and your deed align, trust builds. When they diverge, trust erodes. Every broken promise, every unmet commitment, every gap between what you said and what you did—that's where surplus dies and friction is born.

Think about what happens when someone is reliably trustworthy. We don't need contracts with them. We don't need to verify their work. We don't need to hedge against their failure. We don't need managers checking their output. All the machinery of distrust becomes unnecessary. The friction budget collapses.

Now think about what happens when someone is unreliable. Even small commitments require documentation. Every handoff needs a tracking system. Trust takes months to build and seconds to destroy. The friction multiplies.

The gap between word and deed is the birthplace of the Idiot Index.

Say what you mean. Don't make commitments you can't keep. Don't over-promise to close the deal. Don't tell people what they want to hear. Let your yes be yes and your no be no.

Do what you say. Follow through. Show up when you said you would. Deliver what you promised. If circumstances change, communicate immediately—don't let people discover your broken commitment by its absence.

Mean what you do. Bring intention to your actions. Don't go through the motions. When you commit, commit fully. Half-hearted follow-through is almost as corrosive as no follow-through.

This is integrity—not as a moral abstraction, but as an economic force. Integrity is dignity in action. When you align word and deed, you're honoring your own worth and the other person's worth. You're saying: your time matters, your trust matters, your expectations matter.

Broken promises are a form of forgetting dignity—treating the other person as if they don't count.

You don't need a token system to create surplus. You don't need a new economic architecture. You don't need technology or policy reform. You need to close the gap between what you say and what you do.

Start there. Everything else follows.

Surplus doesn't begin with policy. It begins with how we treat each other on Tuesday afternoon.

Value Created — Value Consumed.

What if we built an entire economy around it?

PART THREE: THE ARCHITECTURE

Systems Design

Now we build.

Part One showed you what's broken. Part Two showed you why—and the mechanics of what works instead. But understanding isn't enough. We need architecture.

Part Three is the blueprint. Seven chapters describing the infrastructure of a trust-based society: The Law of Consent that governs all interactions. The Perimeter that makes safety possible. The restoration systems that handle failure without destruction. The Trust OS that coordinates at scale. The Partnership Agreement that aligns incentives. The Project Economy that replaces extraction with contribution. And the Unity Token that measures contribution instead of extraction.

One principle runs through all of it: **power flows downward.**

In the extraction economy, power concentrates upward. Decisions are made at the top. The person closest to the work has the least say in how it's done.

In the Trust Economy, power distributes downward. Decisions are made by those closest to the problem. The person doing the work has the most say in how it's done.

This isn't just philosophy. It's efficiency. The person closest to the problem has the most information about the problem. Central planners operate with abstractions. The person on the ground operates with reality.

Turn the page. Let's build.

| 13 |

Chapter Thirteen: The Law of Consent

"Everything is legal, but you have to have consent when interacting with another human being."

I learned the law of consent from an airport security guard.

I was late. Seven minutes to boarding, thirty people in the security line. So I did what desperate travelers do: I tried to cut.

The guard caught me immediately. "Sir, back of the line."

I pleaded my case. He listened, unmoved. Then he said something I didn't expect.

"You want to skip ahead? Ask them." He pointed to the line. "Every person you want to pass, you ask. If they say yes, you can go. If anyone says no, you stop there."

I wanted to argue. I wanted him to just let me through. But he wasn't budging, and the clock was ticking. So I started.

"Excuse me—I'm about to miss my flight. Would you mind if I went ahead of you?"

The first person shrugged. "Go ahead." The second nodded. The third said, "Been there, man." Person after person, the same response. A few asked how late I was. One woman laughed and waved me forward. Nobody said no.

When I reached the front, the guard was smiling. "You can go."

I made my plane. But I've thought about that guard ever since.

He didn't give me permission. He didn't enforce a rule. He redirected me to the people whose consent actually mattered—the ones who'd be affected by my cutting. And they said yes. Not because an authority told them to. Because they understood. Because they'd been in my situation. Because asking turned me from a line-cutter into a person with a problem they could help solve.

That's the Law of Consent. And it's the philosophical foundation for everything that follows in this book.

When I say "everything is legal," I don't mean anything goes. I mean: between humans who are capable of freely choosing, informed about the consequences, and operating within agreed boundaries that protect the commons, consent is the only regulator that actually works. Not prohibition. Not surveillance. Not punishment after the fact. Consent—obtained before, honored during, and repairable after.

The Four Conditions

Consent means a freely chosen, informed, specific, and reversible agreement between sovereign beings. If any one of these fails, what you have isn't consent. It's compliance dressed as agreement.

Freely chosen means no coercion, no hidden threats, no "say yes or starve" conditions. The parties had genuine alternatives. An employee who "agrees" to unsafe conditions because the alternative is homelessness hasn't freely chosen. Economic desperation isn't freedom.

Informed means the parties understand the essentials of what they're agreeing to. Not every detail, but enough to make a real choice. Twenty pages of legalese that no one reads isn't informed consent—it's documentation designed to protect institutions, not people.

Specific means consent is about this action, these terms—not a vague blanket approval that covers whatever might happen later.

"Sign here and we'll decide the details" isn't specific. Neither is "by using this service you agree to terms we may change at any time."

Reversible means sovereignty includes the right to withdraw consent and renegotiate. Agreement today doesn't mean agreement forever. Any system that makes exit impossible or punitive isn't honoring consent—it's trapping people.

Consent in Practice

Here's a practical problem: consent can't require constant verbal affirmation. That would be impossible. Every micro-interaction, every moment of every relationship, every second of every transaction—you can't stop and ask "do you still consent?" a thousand times a day.

So how does consent actually work in practice?

Consent is assumed while you continue.

If you're still participating—still in the conversation, still in the transaction, still in the relationship, still in the space—the system assumes your consent to the current terms. Continuing is the signal. Presence is the affirmation.

This isn't a loophole. It's the only way consent can function at scale. The alternative—requiring explicit permission for every action—would create friction so overwhelming that no cooperation would be possible.

But here's the crucial counterweight: the moment you signal "no," everything stops.

Verbally. Physically. Digitally. However you communicate withdrawal, the Perimeter activates. The system's job is to make three things true:

Signaling is easy. When consent is no longer true, you can communicate that instantly, with minimal friction. No forms to fill out. No authorities to convince. No waiting periods. You signal, and the signal is received.

Response is immediate. When you signal withdrawal, the system responds. Not eventually. Not after review. Immediately. The interaction pauses. The terms are renegotiated. Or the relationship ends.

Documentation protects everyone. Both parties know what was agreed to, when consent was withdrawn, and what happened next. This isn't surveillance—it's transparency that protects against "he said, she said" disputes.

This shifts responsibility to where it belongs: on each person for themselves.

You are responsible for signaling when consent is no longer true. The system can't read your mind—but it can respond instantly when you communicate.

Traditional systems put responsibility on external authorities to detect violations. Police, managers, regulators—they're supposed to notice when something is wrong. This is slow, expensive, and fails constantly. By the time authorities detect a violation, the damage is done.

Consent-based systems flip this. You detect your own violations—because you're the one experiencing them. The system's job is to make your detection actionable. Fast, cheap, accurate—because the person with the information is the person with the power to signal.

Put bluntly: Consent is the missing regulator of capitalism.

The fix isn't more regulation or better gatekeepers—it's restoring the one mechanism that actually works: genuine consent from the people who bear the consequences.

And consent is efficient. When people genuinely agree to terms, they don't need armies of lawyers to enforce them. When both parties want the deal to work, it works. Real consent eliminates the overhead. This is the thesis applied to governance: trust—expressed as genuine consent—is cheaper than coercion.

The Cleanest Moral Equation

Here is the simplest formula for a just society:

Freedom = 100%

Responsibility = 100%

Not freedom limited by responsibility. Not responsibility constrained by freedom. Both, fully, simultaneously.

Freedom without responsibility is chaos—the liberty to harm without consequence, to take without giving, to act without accountability. This isn't freedom; it's predation wearing freedom's mask.

Responsibility without freedom is oppression—obligation without choice, duty without dignity, compliance without consent. This isn't responsibility; it's servitude.

But freedom with responsibility creates something else entirely: sovereignty. The recognition that every human being owns their body, their choices, their labor, their creativity—and that ownership comes with the obligation to respect the same sovereignty in others.

Consent is where freedom and responsibility meet. It's the handshake between two sovereign beings that says: I acknowledge your freedom. You acknowledge mine. Now let's figure out how to engage.

The Guardrails Question

But wait—doesn't "freedom = 100%" sound like a recipe for chaos?

Scott Galloway has been sounding the alarm about young men for years. His diagnosis: men need guardrails. They need jobs, partners, communities—external structures that provide accountability and restraint. Without these guardrails, freedom becomes destructive.

He's not wrong. The data supports him. But Galloway is actually describing the symptoms of a low-trust society.

When people lack internal accountability, they need external constraints. The prohibition model is built on this assumption: humans can't be trusted to constrain themselves, so we'll constrain them from outside. We'll build guardrails. We'll enforce limits. We'll punish violations.

The Law of Consent takes a different approach. It says: you are 100% free, but you are 100% responsible. That's not softer than guardrails—it's harder. External structures let you outsource your accountability. Consent requires you to own it.

Under external guardrails, you behave because you'll get caught if you don't. Under consent, you behave because you made a commitment and your integrity depends on honoring it. The first is compliance. The second is character.

The Law of Consent doesn't eliminate the need for restraint. It internalizes it. The guardrails you need are not out there. They're in here—built from the commitments you make and the responsibility you take for honoring them.

From Prohibition to Consent

Traditional legal systems operate on prohibition and punishment. Don't steal. Don't kill. Don't defraud. The law becomes a list of things you cannot do, enforced by the threat of consequences.

This model made sense in a world of limited information. When you couldn't know who was trustworthy, you needed rules that assumed everyone might be dangerous. But the prohibition model has costs: enormous bureaucracy, adversarial dynamics, and—most importantly—it doesn't actually prevent harm. It can punish bad behavior after the fact, but it can't cultivate good behavior in advance. It manages distrust rather than building trust.

Consent-based regulation is different. Instead of listing what's forbidden, it asks: did the affected parties agree?

Under prohibition, you need police to catch violations, courts to adjudicate them, prisons to punish them. Under consent, you need verification that agreement exists—and repair mechanisms when it doesn't.

The prohibition model assumes you'll behave badly unless constrained. The consent model assumes you'll honor your commitments—and creates accountability for when you don't.

Which model produces better humans?

The Neural Terms of Service

This is more than philosophy: consent aligns with how the human nervous system actually works.

Your brain runs on a silent, universal operating agreement—what I call the Neural Terms of Service:

1. Trust until evidence proves otherwise.
2. When evidence proves otherwise, rectify and make it right.

In a healthy nervous system, this is the default setting.

Trauma can flip it. If you've lived through enough betrayal or danger, your body learns the opposite rule: assume threat until proven otherwise. That's not a character flaw—it's adaptive wiring. But it's also what keeps entire societies stuck at the lower trust frequencies we explored in the last chapter.

Neuroscientist Stephen Porges calls this unconscious safety radar "neuroception": the brain's constant, background scan for cues of danger or safety. When we feel safe, our biology shifts into connection mode. Stress hormones drop. We gain access to more of our prefrontal cortex—the part responsible for reasoning, creativity, and complex decision-making.

Trust is metabolically cheaper than vigilance. Maintaining constant suspicion is expensive—cortisol stays elevated, the amygdala stays activated, cognitive resources get consumed by threat monitoring. Trust allows the system to relax and allocate resources to growth instead of defense.

This is why consent works: it aligns economic and social systems with neural architecture. Instead of fighting human nature, it leverages human nature.

The Technology of Consent

Here's where it gets practical.

Consent has always been hard to verify. Did both parties really agree? Was the agreement informed? Was it continuous or just initial? These questions were difficult to answer, which is why we built prohibition systems instead.

But technology changes this.

Imagine signing a job offer in a consent-based system. You see a two-minute, plain-language summary of pay, expectations, and exit terms—not forty pages of legalese. You confirm, on video or voice, that you understand and agree. The agreement is written to a private consent ledger that both you and the employer control. Any major change—role, hours, compensation—requires a new consent event. No hidden "we changed the handbook" loopholes. No surprise arbitration clauses discovered only when you try to sue.

AI and blockchain create infrastructure for this that didn't previously exist. Digital consent protocols can record agreements in real-time, creating verifiable trust ledgers. Pattern recognition can identify coercion, capacity issues, and information asymmetries that might invalidate consent. Smart contracts can enforce terms automatically, without courts or lawyers.

This isn't surveillance. It's transparency—but only for the parties involved. The consent record belongs to those who made the agreement, not to authorities who might judge it.

The technology doesn't replace human judgment. It supports it. It makes consent visible, verifiable, and enforceable in ways that weren't possible before.

The Objections

This framework raises obvious questions. Let me address three.

What about power imbalances?

Consent isn't meaningful if one party has no real choice. This is real, and any consent framework must address it. The answer isn't to abandon consent—it's to ensure consent is genuine by addressing the conditions that make false consent possible: economic desperation, information asymmetry, cognitive manipulation. A true consent economy doesn't just track whether agreement was given. It tracks whether agreement was free, informed, and given with capacity to refuse.

What about people who can't consent?

Children, people with certain cognitive conditions, people in crisis—there are categories of humans whose capacity for consent is limited. The answer is stewardship. When someone cannot consent for themselves, others hold their sovereignty in trust—with the obligation to act in their interest and return sovereignty as soon as they're capable of exercising it.

What about collective harms?

Some actions harm people who never had a chance to consent—environmental destruction, systemic discrimination, public health threats. This is where consent connects to the Perimeter we'll explore in the next chapter. Consent governs interactions between parties. But parties exist within larger systems that have boundaries—agreements about how we'll treat the commons, the environment, future generations. You can consent to a factory, but only if the larger system has consented to that level of impact.

The Foundation

In the Trust Economy, nothing is forbidden except the violation of consent.

This is the moral equilibrium where freedom and safety coexist. It honors sovereignty without permitting predation. It trusts humans to make their own choices while protecting them from having choices made for them.

Consent opens Part Three because it's the operating logic for everything that follows. The Perimeter, the Trust OS, the Unity Token—all of these assume consent as their foundation. Without consent, they're just new forms of control. With consent, they're architecture for freedom.

| 14 |

Chapter Fourteen: The Perimeter

"You are free because others are watching over you, not controlling you."

Imagine walking home at night.

Not hurrying. Not clutching your keys between your fingers. Not calculating which streets are well-lit and which aren't. Just walking—the way you might walk through your own living room.

Now imagine looking down at your phone and seeing the world around you gently pulsing green. A visual confirmation that your community is present, awake, watching over itself. Not cameras pointed at you. Not surveillance monetizing your movements. Just presence. The neighborhood saying: We're here. We see each other. You're not alone.

That single shift—from fear to assurance—is the foundation of social peace.

This chapter is about how we build it.

Highway Logic

Most of our systems operate on what I call highway logic.

Think about how a highway works. Strangers moving at high speed in close proximity—a situation that should produce constant collisions. Instead, we've engineered a system that prevents most accidents through a combination of physical barriers, strict rules, heavy enforcement, and the assumption that any driver might, at any moment, do something dangerous.

Highways are marvels of distrust management. They work precisely because they assume the worst about everyone.

The problem is that we've built most of our society this way.

Our legal system is highway logic: assume everyone might break the law, create elaborate rules, enforce through punishment. Our corporate structures are highway logic: assume employees might slack or steal, create surveillance and compliance systems, manage through fear. Our financial systems are highway logic: assume everyone might default, require collateral and credit checks, extract through interest.

Highway logic produces compliance. It prevents the worst outcomes. It keeps strangers from crashing into each other.

But it cannot produce trust. It cannot create belonging. It cannot build the thing that humans actually need to thrive.

Highway logic is designed for managing strangers. But we're not strangers—or at least, we shouldn't be.

Perimeter Logic

A perimeter is something different.

Not a cage—a defined field of safety that allows freedom inside the boundary. Think of a children's playground with a fence. The fence isn't there to imprison the children. It's there so they can play freely without their parents worrying about traffic.

That's the Perimeter principle: clear boundaries create freedom within them.

Humans don't thrive in wide-open chaos. We also don't thrive in rigid constraint. We thrive when our nervous system knows where the edges are, who is inside with us, who we can trust, and what the shared expectations are.

This is how the nervous system actually works. It's constantly scanning for edges, threats, patterns, allies, predictability. When the edges are clear, it relaxes. When the people inside are trustworthy, it expands. When expectations are shared, it collaborates.

Highway logic fights this biology. It keeps the nervous system in constant vigilance—watching for threats that might come from anywhere, trusting no one, assuming danger.

Perimeter logic aligns with this biology. It creates the conditions where the nervous system can shift from defense to growth.

The difference between a highway and a perimeter is the difference between being watched at and being watched over.

The Four Functions

What does a perimeter actually do? It serves four functions:

First: Find your people.

The deepest human need isn't safety—it's belonging. We're social primates. We evolved in tribes. Our nervous systems are literally designed to co-regulate with others.

A perimeter helps you find the people you'd genuinely enjoy—not through algorithms optimizing for engagement, but through shared values, shared contribution, shared trust. It surfaces the neighbors who share your interests, the collaborators who complement your skills, the friends you haven't met yet.

This isn't social media's version of connection—curated performances for strangers. It's the village version: people who know you, who see you regularly, who you can count on and who can count on you.

Second: Safety wherever you go.

Imagine knowing, at any moment, whether you're in a safe zone or approaching potential danger. Not through paranoia—through data. Your phone or watch gently indicates the trust level of your immediate surroundings. Green means calm. Yellow means attention warranted. Red means help is available.

This isn't surveillance. It's awareness. The same awareness that humans had in villages for thousands of years—knowing who was around, what was happening, whether the environment was safe. We lost that awareness when we scaled beyond community. Technology can restore it.

Third: Protection through awareness.

When something goes wrong—and sometimes it will—the Perimeter activates.

Everyone in the system has a panic button. When triggered, it sends an encrypted, location-verified signal to everyone within range who has opted in to respond. Not distant authorities who arrive in fifteen minutes. Neighbors who arrive in seconds.

The 30-minute rolling buffer captures what happens, from multiple angles, creating a transparent record that protects the innocent and validates victims. But the goal isn't documentation—it's prevention. The knowledge that any incident will be witnessed changes behavior before incidents occur.

Fourth: Coordination for extraordinary experiences.

Safety is the foundation, not the destination. Once you're safe, what do you want to do?

The perimeter enables experiences that are impossible in highway-logic systems. Flash gatherings of people who share an interest. Collaborative projects across neighborhoods. Resources shared without the friction of formal arrangements. The spontaneous cooperation that makes communities feel alive.

When people trust each other, coordination becomes easy. When coordination is easy, amazing things become possible.

Nested Circles

The Perimeter isn't one thing—it's nested circles of belonging.

The innermost circle is your household. These are the people you're most intimate with, most vulnerable with, most invested in. Trust here is personal and deep.

The next circle is your extended family—the relatives who don't share your roof but share your bloodline or bond. Parents, siblings, aunts, uncles, cousins, grandparents. These are the people you didn't choose but who chose you by virtue of being born. In most of human history, this circle was inseparable from household—families lived together, worked together, raised children together. The nuclear family is a recent experiment, and the data suggests it's not going well.

Extended family represents something the modern economy has systematically dismantled: inherited trust. You didn't have to build relationship with your grandmother—the relationship came preloaded. That's not true of neighbors. It's not true of colleagues. Extended family is trust by default, requiring active destruction to break rather than active cultivation to build.

The Trust Economy recognizes this circle explicitly. It doesn't assume you live near your extended family—many don't. But it creates pathways for extended family to function as economic and emotional safety net even across distance. Shared visibility into wellbeing. Coordinated response in crisis. Collective investment in the next generation.

This is what "family trust" actually means: not a legal vehicle, but a relational circle that carries obligation and belonging regardless of proximity.

The next circle is your neighborhood. These are the people you see regularly, who know your patterns, who would notice if something was wrong. Trust here is relational—built through repeated interaction.

The next circle is your community. These are the people who share your local institutions—your schools, your markets, your gathering places. Trust here is institutional—mediated by shared structures.

The next circle is your network. These are the people connected to you through reputation—the friends of friends, the colleagues of colleagues, the web of relationships that extends beyond direct contact. Trust here is transitive—based on vouching and verification.

Each circle has different trust levels, different expectations, different dynamics. The Perimeter respects this variation. It doesn't flatten everything into a single trust score. It recognizes that you might trust your spouse with your life and your neighbor with your spare key and your network with your professional reputation—different kinds of trust for different kinds of relationship.

The genius of nested circles is that they can extend indefinitely. Your network connects to other networks. Your community connects to other communities. Trust can flow through the connections, expanding the perimeter without diluting it.

This is how trust scales: not by making everyone equally trusted, but by making trust transitive across verified connections.

Local First

Here's the design principle that makes all of this work: maximize local connections first, then work outward.

The Perimeter doesn't try to connect you to everyone. It connects you to your neighbors first—the people who can actually respond when you need them, who you'll see tomorrow, whose reputation depends on how they treat you. From that foundation, trust extends outward. But it starts local. Always local.

This is the opposite of social media's model.

Social media tried to connect everyone to everyone. The result: shallow connections, no accountability, loneliness at scale. You have a thousand "friends" and no one who would bring you soup when you're sick. You're connected to the whole world and isolated from the person next door.

The Perimeter inverts this. It builds density before breadth. Deep trust with a few before shallow trust with many.

The sequence matters:

First, know your neighbors by name. Not all of them—start with the ones closest to you. The person across the hall. The family next door. The couple downstairs.

Then, know who would respond. If you pressed the panic button at 2 AM, who in your building would actually show up? That's your first real circle. Build it deliberately.

Then, learn the patterns of your block. Who walks their dog at 7 AM? Who's usually home during the day? Whose car is always parked where? This ambient awareness is the foundation of neighborhood safety.

Then, connect to adjacent blocks through people you already trust. Your neighbor knows someone two streets over. That introduction carries trust with it. The network expands through verified relationships, not random matching.

Why local first?

Response time. The person three doors down can reach you in thirty seconds. Someone across the city can't. When the panic button is pressed, geography determines who can actually help.

Accountability. You see local people repeatedly. You'll run into them tomorrow, and next week, and next year. Reputation matters when you can't disappear. You can ghost a stranger on the internet. You can't ghost your neighbor.

Nervous system. Your body relaxes around people it recognizes. Familiar faces signal safety to the amygdala. Strangers—even friendly ones—keep cortisol slightly elevated. Deep local connections create the physiological foundation for feeling safe.

Compound trust. Small repeated interactions build trust faster than occasional big ones. Saying hello every morning for a year creates more trust than one intense conversation. Local life is made of these micro-interactions. They compound.

The failure of "global connection" is that it skipped these steps. It tried to create community without proximity, trust without repetition, belonging without accountability. It produced networks without neighborliness.

The Perimeter starts where trust actually forms: in the spaces you inhabit every day, with the people you encounter repeatedly, in relationships where showing up matters because you can't avoid each other.

Build that first. Everything else extends from it.

The Neighborhood Watch, Automated

My aunt ran a neighborhood watch program forty years ago.

It was simple. Neighbors knew each other. They had agreed-upon signals if something was wrong—a porch light left on, a specific knock pattern, a flag in the window. People looked out for each other's homes when someone was traveling. There was shared responsibility for the block's safety. Trust built through years of repeated interaction.

It worked. For a while.

Then people moved away. Others got busy with jobs and kids. Volunteer fatigue set in. The phone tree got out of date. New neighbors didn't know the signals. The program slowly dissolved, like most volunteer efforts do.

This is the tragedy of good ideas that depend entirely on human vigilance. They burn people out. They can't scale. They fade when life gets complicated.

The Perimeter is that same idea, automated.

Not replacing the human connection—sustaining it. The technology handles the coordination so the humans can focus on actually caring for each other.

What technology adds:

Automation. The system notices patterns so humans don't have to maintain constant vigilance. Your aunt couldn't watch all the time. The network can.

Scale. Connections extend beyond line-of-sight, beyond the single block. Your neighborhood watch was limited to people you could physically reach. The Perimeter connects you to a network that extends as far as trust travels.

Speed. Alerts go out instantly, not through phone trees where someone doesn't answer and the chain breaks. When the panic button is pressed, everyone who needs to know, knows—in seconds.

Documentation. The 30-minute buffer captures what happened without requiring human witnesses to be present at the exact right moment. Your aunt's program depended on someone happening to see the incident. The Perimeter doesn't rely on luck.

Persistence. The system doesn't get tired. It doesn't move away. It doesn't get busy with a new job. It's there at 3 AM on Tuesday just like it's there at noon on Saturday.

But here's what the technology doesn't do: it doesn't replace the people.

When the alert goes out, humans respond. When the conversation happens, humans talk. When the care is needed, humans provide it. The technology is scaffolding. The community is the structure.

Spaces Where Interests Align

The Perimeter doesn't just define who's inside. It creates spaces where interests align by design.

Think about the spaces you move through every day. Most of them have a hidden conflict at their core:

The mall wants you to buy; you want to browse. The employer wants maximum output; you want sustainable work. The platform wants engagement; you want connection. The city wants tax revenue; you want livability. The hospital wants to bill; you want to heal.

In each case, someone is trying to extract from you—your attention, your labor, your data, your money. Your "consent" to participate isn't genuine. It's manufactured by circumstance, coerced by necessity, or hidden in terms you never read.

This is highway-logic space: environments designed so someone wins at your expense.

Perimeter-logic space is different. It's designed so your flourishing and the community's flourishing are the same thing.

Shared ownership creates alignment. When you own the space—or share ownership with everyone in it—your interests and the space's interests converge automatically. A member-owned co-operative succeeds when members succeed. A community land trust thrives when residents thrive. There's no absentee owner extracting value—the owners are the users.

Transparent incentives prevent manipulation. When everyone knows how value flows, hidden extraction becomes impossible. You can see who benefits from what. You can trace where resources go. The clarity itself is a form of protection.

Consent verification blocks exploitation. When consent is continuously verified—not just signed once and forgotten—extraction can't hide behind fine print. The system keeps asking: is this still working for you? And it responds when the answer is no.

Mutual benefit becomes the design principle. The space is built so that serving you serves everyone. The community market wants vendors and customers both to thrive—because their thriving is the market's success. The co-working space wants members to succeed—because member success is the space's value. The neighborhood wants you safe—because your safety is their safety.

This isn't idealism. It's architecture. The ownership structure determines whose interests the space serves. Change the structure, change the alignment.

The Perimeter makes this possible at scale. It creates the trust infrastructure—the verified relationships, the transparent flows, the consent mechanisms—that allow aligned-interest spaces to coordinate across neighborhoods, cities, networks. It's not just one cooperative or one community. It's a system of cooperating communities, each designed so that everyone inside benefits together.

That alignment isn't an accident. It's architecture.

Intent + Consent = Possibility

Here's the formula that makes the perimeter work:

Intent + Consent = Possibility

The more information people share—through consent, never through coercion—the more possibilities the system can create. If you tell the system you're interested in woodworking, it can connect you with the master carpenter three neighborhoods over. If you indicate you have two hours free on Saturday, it can match you with the community project that needs exactly your skills. If you share your dietary preferences, the community kitchen knows what to prepare.

Each piece of information, shared voluntarily, opens new possibilities. The system doesn't surveil—it coordinates. It doesn't extract—it enables.

The perimeter's power comes from transparency and consent combined. When both are present, coordination becomes almost magical. When either is absent, the system degrades into surveillance.

Why AI Changes Everything

For most of human history, perimeter logic was limited by scale.

Villages could operate on trust because everyone knew everyone. A few hundred people could track reputations, notice anomalies, coordinate responses. But beyond a certain size, the cognitive load became too great. We had to shift to highway logic—rules and enforcement to manage strangers—because we couldn't process the information required for trust at scale.

AI changes this.

Artificial intelligence can track millions of relationships in real time. It can notice patterns that no human could see. It can match needs to contributions across vast networks. It can verify identities, assess risks, and coordinate responses at speeds impossible for human administrators.

This doesn't mean AI replaces human judgment. It means AI handles the coordination complexity so humans can focus on what humans are for: connection, creativity, care. The perimeter is what it enables.

Without AI, perimeter logic at scale was a fantasy. With AI, it becomes engineering.

The technology exists. What matters is what we choose to use it for.

The Difference

The contrast is stark.

Highway logic for safety:

- Police patrol looking for problems
- Cameras recording everything, watched by no one, accessed after crimes
- Citizens isolated, hoping someone else calls 911
- Response time measured in minutes
- Punishment after harm

Perimeter logic for safety:

- Neighbors aware of their surroundings
- Consensual visibility creating deterrence
- Citizens connected, knowing help is seconds away
- Response time measured in moments
- Prevention through presence

The first system reacts to harm. The second system prevents it.

The first system treats citizens as potential threats. The second treats them as potential responders.

The first system creates isolation. The second creates belonging.

Both can "work" in the narrow sense of maintaining order. But only one builds the trust that makes order unnecessary.

The efficiency analysis reveals something important: protection through presence is radically cheaper than protection through surveillance. A neighbor who responds in seconds costs nothing beyond the trust that created the relationship. A police force that arrives in minutes costs billions. The perimeter isn't just more humane—it's more efficient. Trust is cheaper than enforcement.

Privacy and Visibility

The obvious objection: Doesn't this require giving up privacy?

Yes and no.

It requires giving up the illusion of complete anonymity—the fantasy that you can move through the world without anyone knowing where you are or what you're doing. In practice, that fantasy is already gone. Your phone tracks your location constantly. Cameras capture you hundreds of times daily. Corporations know more about you than your family does.

Visibility already exists. What matters is who benefits from it.

In the current system, your data flows to corporations who monetize it and governments who may or may not use it responsibly. You get nothing in return except targeted ads and the vague promise of security.

In the Perimeter system, your visibility is consensual and reciprocal. You share location because others share location. You participate in the safety network because it actually makes you safer. The data serves you, not distant shareholders.

The perimeter's 30-minute rolling buffer is key here. If nothing happens, the data self-deletes. It never touches a permanent ledger. Your movements yesterday are not stored anywhere. Only when an incident occurs does the system preserve relevant information—and even then, only for thirty days unless the parties involved choose to extend it.

This is temporal privacy: you're visible now, but that visibility doesn't create a permanent record. Time itself becomes the guardian of your privacy.

The principle is simple: We agree to be briefly visible so that no one is ever completely alone in a moment of danger.

That's not surveillance. That's solidarity.

Return to Safety Before Decisions

When something goes wrong—a conflict, a violation, an incident—the immediate response is flooded with stress hormones. Cortisol surges. Adrenaline spikes. The amygdala takes command. You're in fight-flight-freeze mode, scanning for threats, ready for defensive action.

Decisions made in this state are often regretted. Punishments demanded in the heat of the moment are often excessive. Forgiveness offered under pressure is often false. The prefrontal cortex—the part of your brain responsible for reasoning, empathy, long-term thinking—is literally impaired when cortisol is elevated.

This is why the perimeter operates on a 30-day principle.

Thirty days isn't arbitrary. It's biology.

The sequence:

First, preserve the data. The 30-minute rolling buffer captures what happened from multiple angles. The facts are documented. Nothing is lost.

Second, establish immediate safety. The community responds. Parties are separated if needed. The ongoing harm stops. No one is in danger.

Third, create space. Thirty days for all parties to return to baseline. To sleep. To talk to people they trust. To let the cortisol metabolize. To recover the capacity for perspective.

Fourth, begin restoration. When the 30 days have passed, the process of addressing what happened can begin—not from reactivity, but from groundedness. Not from the amygdala, but from the prefrontal cortex. Serotonin is in charge now: the neurochemistry of calm, connection, and long-term thinking.

Why thirty days?

Cortisol elevation from acute stress takes days to weeks to fully normalize. Your body doesn't reset overnight. The hypervigilance, the defensive posture, the narrowed attention—these linger. Research on trauma and stress recovery consistently shows that meaningful perspective-taking and wise decision-making require time for the nervous system to return to baseline.

Thirty days is enough time for most people to shift from reactive to reflective. To move from "I want them punished" to "I want this to not happen again." To access the part of themselves capable of genuine forgiveness or fair accountability—rather than the part that just wants to strike back.

When we address what happened, we want to be thinking with our prefrontal cortex, not our amygdala. We want to actually solve the problem instead of just punishing someone for it. The 30-day buffer ensures we have that chance.

The Measure of Civilization

There's a quote attributed to many sources: "The measure of a civilization is how it treats its weakest members."

I'd modify it slightly: The measure of a civilization is not how it punishes the guilty, but how it protects the vulnerable.

Highway logic excels at punishment. We're very good at identifying wrongdoers after the fact and making them suffer. Our prisons are full. Our systems of retribution are elaborate.

But protection? Prevention? Ensuring that harm doesn't happen in the first place?

That requires trust. And trust requires community. And community requires the infrastructure that makes trust possible at scale.

The Perimeter is that infrastructure. It's not a technology or a policy or a program. It's an operating system—a way of organizing human relationship that makes protection possible and punishment largely unnecessary.

The Transition

We won't move from highway logic to perimeter logic overnight. The transition happens gradually, neighborhood by neighborhood, community by community.

It starts with opt-in. A few people in a building decide to share visibility with each other. They notice when someone hasn't been seen in a while. They respond when someone needs help. The perimeter is tiny at first—a handful of people, a single block.

But trust is contagious. When people see the perimeter working—when they experience the safety and connection it provides—they want in. The circle expands. More people opt in. More connections form. The network effects kick in.

At some point—and the research suggests it's around 20% participation—the perimeter reaches critical mass. It becomes the new normal. The remaining 80% join not because they're required to, but because not joining starts to feel strange. The highway-logic holdouts find themselves increasingly isolated in a world that has moved on.

This is how all transformations happen. Not through mandate. Through demonstration. Through building something so obviously better that the old way becomes obsolete.

What Family Feels Like

What does the Perimeter actually feel like?

It feels like family.

Not the dysfunction that some families carry—but the feeling of family at its best. The experience most people are searching for, whether they know it or not.

Someone notices if you don't come home. Not surveillance. Care. The awareness that your absence would be felt, that your patterns are known, that you matter enough to be missed.

Someone responds if you call for help. Not eventually. Not after filling out forms. Immediately—because people care, not because they're paid to.

Someone knows you well enough to notice when something's wrong. The neighbor who sees you walking differently. The friend who hears the change in your voice. The community that recognizes when you're not yourself.

You belong, even when you mess up. Family doesn't kick you out for a mistake. It holds you accountable and holds you close. It says: you did wrong, and you're still one of us.

You're watched over, not watched at. The difference between a parent checking on a sleeping child and a security camera recording footage for later review. One is love. The other is data.

The Perimeter doesn't replace family. Nothing can replace the particular bonds between parents and children, siblings and spouses. But it extends the logic of family to people who aren't blood relatives. It creates the infrastructure for that feeling to exist between neighbors, community members, strangers who become something more.

True freedom requires collective responsibility.

This sounds paradoxical until you live it. The highway-logic version of freedom is the absence of constraint—do whatever you want, and accept the consequences. But that version of freedom is lonely. It's every person for themselves, watching their own back, trusting no one.

The perimeter-logic version of freedom is different. You are free because others are watching over you. You can take risks because you know you'll be caught if you fall. You can explore because you know the way home is marked. You can be vulnerable because you know vulnerability will be met with care.

This is the freedom of belonging. Not the freedom of isolation, but the freedom that comes from knowing you're held.

The perimeter makes that freedom possible—at scale, in cities, among strangers who become neighbors through the very act of watching over each other.

That's what we're building.

For expanded implementation details, see Part Five: Design Prototypes.

| 15 |

Chapter Fifteen: Restoring Trust

"Trust doesn't require eternal memory. It only requires that we hold one another accountable long enough to make things right."

The argument started the way most do—quietly, then all at once.

A couple in apartment 4B. Voices rising through thin walls. A crash. Then screaming.

In a highway-logic world, here's what happens next: neighbors freeze, unsure whether to get involved. Someone eventually calls 911. Police arrive in fifteen minutes—if they arrive at all. By then, the crisis has escalated or gone silent. Officers show up armed, trained primarily in force, assessing threat levels. Someone gets arrested, or no one does. The underlying rupture remains unaddressed. The couple is left alone with their wreckage.

In a perimeter world, something different happens.

She taps the "community check" signal on her phone—not a panic button, just a request for others to be aware. Something might be wrong in 4B.

Within seconds, three people who've opted into the building's response network receive a silent alert. Not strangers—people who live here, who know the couple by name, who've agreed to be available for exactly this kind of moment.

The first neighbor arrives at the door. She doesn't pound or demand entry. She knocks gently and says, "Hey, it's Rosa from down the hall. I heard something. Is everyone okay?"

The second neighbor positions himself in the hallway—not blocking, just present. Visible. A calm witness.

The third is a trained responder. She hangs back, assessing. She has skills the others don't—de-escalation training, mental health recognition, the ability to physically intervene if someone is in danger. But she waits. Because most of the time, presence is enough.

The door opens. The man inside is breathing hard, embarrassed, scared. His partner is crying in the kitchen. No one is hurt—yet. But something broke tonight, and everyone knows it.

Rosa doesn't lecture. She doesn't judge. She says, "Can we come in for a minute? Just to sit with you."

They sit. They breathe. The trained responder quietly assesses whether professional help is needed. It isn't—not tonight. What's needed is witness. Presence. The knowledge that rupture doesn't have to mean isolation.

By the time the neighbors leave, the couple has agreed to talk to a mediator tomorrow. The incident is logged—temporarily—in case it's part of a pattern. But no one is arrested. No one is shamed. No one is alone.

This is what restoration looks like. Not punishment after the fact. Not surveillance from above. Community response, at the speed of trust.

Failure as Signal

Here's what most systems get wrong about failure: they treat it as a crime.

Someone loses their temper. Someone breaks a promise. Someone can't pay their debt. Someone hurts someone they love. The system's response is judgment: you did something wrong, and now you must be punished.

But failure isn't usually a moral problem. It's a signal.

A signal that someone lost coherence. That the gap between who they want to be and how they're acting got too wide. That their nervous system is overwhelmed, their resources depleted, their identity fractured.

When you see failure this way, the response changes completely.

Punishment assumes the person chose wrongly and must be deterred from choosing wrongly again. Restoration assumes the person lost their way and needs help finding it back.

Punishment isolates. Restoration integrates.

Punishment says: you are what you did. Restoration says: you are more than what you did, and we're going to help you remember that.

The Trust Economy is built on a simple premise: everyone fails. Everyone. The question isn't whether rupture happens—it's what happens next. Does the system exile the person who failed? Or does it have a mechanism for repair?

Three Layers of Response

The Trust Economy responds to crisis through three layers—each calibrated to what the moment actually requires.

The First Layer: Everyone

The first response to failure isn't professionals. It's neighbors.

Not because professionals aren't valuable—they are. But because by the time professionals arrive, the moment has often passed. The crisis has escalated or hardened. The window for de-escalation has closed.

Neighbors are already there. They're seconds away, not minutes. They know the context—the couple in 4B has been stressed since the layoff; the teenager in 6A has been struggling since his parents' divorce. They can intervene before rupture becomes catastrophe.

But this only works if neighbors know what to do.

That's why the Trust Economy trains everyone. Not as therapists or security guards—as witnesses. As supporters. As people who know how to be present when someone else is falling apart.

The training is simple. It starts in childhood and continues through life:

Witnessing. How to be present without fixing. How to hold space for someone's pain without trying to make it go away. How to listen without judgment, without advice, without the need to solve.

Emotional first aid. How to recognize when someone's nervous system is dysregulated. How to use your own calm to help them regulate. How to ask the question that opens a door instead of the question that closes it.

De-escalation. How to lower the temperature in a charged situation. How to speak to fear without amplifying it. How to create safety through tone, posture, and presence.

Knowing your limits. How to recognize when you're out of your depth. How to call for help without shame. How to hand off to someone with more training without abandoning the person in crisis.

By adulthood, everyone has practiced this hundreds of times. In schools, in community centers, in workplaces. It becomes as natural as knowing how to call 911—except it's faster, more personal, and more effective.

The result: a society where the first response to failure is not a stranger with a badge, but a neighbor with a calm nervous system. Where rupture is met with presence before it's met with authority.

The Second Layer: Trained Responders

But sometimes presence isn't enough.

Sometimes the situation requires more than witnessing. Sometimes the conflict has escalated beyond what a calm neighbor can contain. Sometimes someone is in mental health crisis—psychotic, manic, dissociated, suicidal.

That's when the second layer activates: the trained responder corps.

These aren't police. They're not social workers. They're community members who have volunteered for deeper training in two critical areas:

Conflict resolution. They're trained mediators. They know how to find the interests beneath the positions, how to de-escalate standoffs, how to help people in conflict see each other as humans again. They can hold space for intense emotion without getting pulled into it.

Mental health. They recognize the signs of psychosis, mania, dissociation, suicidal ideation. They know how to support a dysregulated nervous system. They know when professional psychiatric help is needed and how to bridge the gap until it arrives.

And crucially: they're known. They live in the community. The person in crisis has probably seen them at the grocery store, at community meetings, at neighborhood events. They're not anonymous uniforms arriving from outside. They're neighbors with capability.

They earn Trust Tokens for their service. They're respected, not feared. When they show up, the message isn't "you're in trouble." The message is "we've got you."

The Third Layer: Peacekeepers

Sometimes there's a weapon. Sometimes violence is already happening. Sometimes someone is in immediate physical danger.

That's when the third layer activates: community peacekeepers.

These are people trained in the responsible use of force—how to disarm a dangerous situation, how to physically restrain someone who's a threat, how to protect the vulnerable without escalating violence. They have the capability that current police have, but embedded in a completely different framework.

The difference from current policing:

They're the last resort, not the first. In the current system, armed officers respond to everything—mental health crises, domestic disputes, noise complaints. Force capability is the default. In the Trust Economy, peacekeepers only activate when the first two layers have determined that force capability is actually needed. Most situations never reach them.

They're known. Like Layer Two responders, peacekeepers live in the community. They're neighbors, not strangers. The person they're responding to has probably seen them before—at the community center, at local events. This changes everything about how the interaction unfolds.

They're trained in all three layers. Peacekeepers aren't just force specialists. They've gone through Layer One and Layer Two training first. They know how to witness, de-escalate, and support mental health. Force is the last tool in their toolkit, not the first.

They're accountable to the community, not an external hierarchy. Their reputation, their Trust Tokens, their standing in the network—all depend on how well they serve the people they're protecting. There's no qualified immunity, no blue wall of silence. The 30-day data window captures what happens. The community sees.

The goal is always de-escalation. Even when force is necessary, the objective is to create safety so the situation can move back down to Layer Two or Layer One. Stop the immediate danger, then hand off to people who can address the underlying rupture.

This three-layer system means the right capability shows up for the right situation. A neighbor having a panic attack doesn't need someone with a gun. A mental health crisis doesn't need someone trained primarily in coercion. And when genuine danger exists, the community has people who can respond—but only after the situation has been assessed by people trained to see other options first.

The Education of Care

This system doesn't appear overnight. It's built through education.

From the earliest grades, children learn that caring for each other is a skill—as teachable as reading, as essential as math. They practice witnessing in classroom circles. They learn to recognize when a classmate is struggling and how to offer support without overstepping. They role-play de-escalation, conflict resolution, emotional first aid.

By middle school, they're practicing on real situations—mediating playground disputes, supporting peers through family crises, learning to be present for each other's pain.

By high school, some choose to pursue deeper training. They become peer counselors, conflict mediators, first responders in training. It's a respected path—as valued as athletics or academics.

By adulthood, everyone has a baseline capability. And those who want more have clear paths to become Layer Two responders or Layer Three peacekeepers—with real responsibility, real recognition, and real compensation through the trust network.

This is how you change culture. Not by hiring more professionals to handle problems after they explode. By training everyone to prevent explosions in the first place. By making care a universal competency, not a specialized service.

The result: a society where no one falls apart alone. Where the first response to crisis is always human, always fast, always proportional. Where failure is met with restoration, not punishment.

Temporal Accountability

But what about accountability? Don't people need consequences?

Yes. But consequences don't require permanence.

The Perimeter system captures what happens during a crisis—but it doesn't store it forever. Two principles govern the data:

The 30-day window. All data in the network is held for thirty days. This creates time—time to review what happened, time for cortisol to clear and reason to return, time to make repair before the record disappears. After thirty days, the data automatically deletes. Anyone involved can request relevant data be held longer, but this requires consent and applies only to data directly related to the incident.

The 30-day expiration. All preserved data expires automatically after 30 days. Only the parties directly involved can choose to preserve specific fragments longer—and only through verified consent.

This makes time itself the referee of privacy. The system doesn't hoard data "just in case." It holds accountability for exactly as long as needed to make things right—then lets go.

Thirty days: accountability without permanence.

Trust doesn't require eternal memory. It requires that we hold one another accountable long enough to make things right.

The Third Way

Now we come to the question that haunts every justice system: what happens when someone has genuinely harmed another person? Not just a conflict or a crisis—real harm. Assault. Theft. Even murder.

For most of human history, societies have oscillated between two responses.

Punishment. The victim "wins." The perpetrator is destroyed—financially, socially, sometimes physically through incarceration or execution. Society gets its vengeance. Justice is served.

But look at the cost: Both parties spend years in litigation. Both go bankrupt paying lawyers. The adversarial process re-traumatizes the victim, forcing them to relive the harm over and over. The perpetrator becomes a permanent enemy—scarred, resentful, unable to reintegrate. And in the end? The winner often can't collect anyway. The loser declares bankruptcy. Everyone is poorer. No trust is restored. Often there's more resentment than before the process began.

Amnesty. Let it go. Move on. Don't reopen wounds. Enable "reconciliation" through collective forgetting.

The cost is different but equally destructive: The victim's dignity is denied. The perpetrator faces no accountability. Trust in the system collapses. Others see that harm has no consequences. The wounds don't heal—they fester beneath a surface calm.

Both options create losers. Both options create enemies. Both options leave someone unsafe.

History has tested these approaches at the highest stakes imaginable. After World War II, the Allies tried Nazi leaders at Nuremberg. Punishment. Necessary for the worst offenders, but it didn't heal Germany. The millions who participated, collaborated, looked away—were never called to account. Germany's actual healing came decades later through education, acknowledgment, and reparations.

Spain after Franco chose amnesty. "Let's look forward, not backward." Fifty years later, families are still searching for mass graves. The policy of forgetting didn't produce forgiveness. It produced frozen grief, permanent distrust, a nation unable to complete its own story.

But there's a third way. And it was proven at scale.

Truth and Reconciliation

South Africa, 1996. The end of apartheid. A nation systematically divided by race for half a century. Perpetrators and victims sharing neighborhoods, workplaces, families. A new democracy with the power to prosecute—and every reason to fear what prosecution would unleash.

Nelson Mandela and Archbishop Desmond Tutu chose neither punishment nor amnesty. They chose truth.

The Truth and Reconciliation Commission offered perpetrators a deal: confess fully, publicly, in front of those you harmed—and receive amnesty. No prosecution. No prison. But no hiding either. You must face what you did. You must face the people you did it to. You must let the nation witness your confession.

Victims got something too: not punishment of their tormentors, but acknowledgment of their suffering. They could tell their stories.

They could be heard. Their pain entered the public record. What was done to them was named, witnessed, recorded for history.

The process required full disclosure. Partial truth didn't count. Perpetrators who minimized or hid details were denied amnesty and faced prosecution. The only path to freedom was complete honesty.

It wasn't perfect. Some perpetrators gamed the system. Some victims felt cheated of the punishment they deserved. Some wounds were too deep for any process to heal.

But something remarkable happened. Perpetrators who participated honestly were restored to society. Victims who told their stories found that acknowledgment—being truly heard—mattered more than vengeance. The nation moved forward with a shared understanding of its past. Not shared forgetting, but shared knowing.

The TRC created a model that applies far beyond mass atrocity. It applies to any serious harm—including murder.

Tell the truth, and you will be forgiven. Not because you deserve it, but because a society full of hidden perpetrators is more dangerous than a society where perpetrators have confessed and been reintegrated. Amnesty isn't weakness—it's the mechanism that makes truth-telling possible.

Victims get their confession. The deepest wound of harm isn't physical or material—it's the denial of reality. Being told it didn't happen. Being told it wasn't that bad. Being told to move on. What victims most need is to have their experience validated. To hear: this happened, it was wrong, and your suffering was real.

Perpetrators are called to responsibility. Not punished—called. The process requires them to see what they stopped seeing: the full humanity of the person they harmed. When that recognition lands, responsibility stops being a burden and becomes a gift. They're being restored to their own humanity by acknowledging the humanity they violated.

They pay non-punitive restitution. Material repair matters. But restitution in the Trust Economy isn't designed to destroy. It's designed to restore—to make the victim whole without making the perpetrator into an enemy. Payment plans. Community service. Ongoing contribution. Whatever serves the actual healing, not the theater of punishment.

This is the model. Not just for apartheid. For every serious rupture.

The Bishop's Silver

Victor Hugo understood this two centuries ago.

In Les MisÃƒ©rables, Jean Valjean steals a loaf of bread and spends nineteen years in prison. When he's finally released, he's a marked man—required to show his yellow passport everywhere, rejected from every inn, sleeping in the street like an animal. The punishment system has branded him permanently. He is what he did.

Then Bishop Myriel takes him in. Feeds him. Gives him a bed.

Valjean repays this kindness by stealing the Bishop's silver and fleeing into the night. The police catch him and drag him back.

Here is the moment that changes everything.

The Bishop looks at Valjean—a thief, a convict, a man the system has declared irredeemable—and says to the police: "I gave those to him." Then he hands Valjean the silver candlesticks too. "You forgot these."

When the police leave, the Bishop says: "Jean Valjean, my brother, you no longer belong to evil, but to good. It is your soul that I am buying for you. I withdraw it from dark thoughts and from the spirit of perdition, and I give it to God."

Valjean becomes a different man. Not because punishment reformed him—nineteen years of prison only hardened him. Because one act of radical grace restored his sense of his own dignity. He goes on to build a factory that treats workers with respect, to become mayor, to spend his life in service to others.

Meanwhile, Inspector Javert pursues him for decades. The law says Valjean is still a criminal. Javert cannot see the transformed man in front of him—only the label the system assigned. When Valjean finally spares Javert's life, Javert's worldview collapses. His system has no category for grace, no mechanism for redemption. He throws himself into the Seine.

Hugo wrote this in 1862. We're still choosing between the Bishop and Javert.

The Trust Economy chooses the Bishop.

The Dignity Principle

Here's the insight that makes restoration possible:

The primary shift for a perpetrator is to remember and see the dignity of the other and the self.

The primary shift for a victim is to remember and see the dignity of the self, and the other.

Perpetrators often harm others because they've lost sight of their own dignity—shame becomes violence. Victims often can't fully heal until they see the perpetrator as human too—not monster, but broken person.

Once those shifts happen, restoration is inevitable.

Think about what harm actually does. When someone hurts you, they treat you as less than human—as an object to be used, an obstacle to be removed, a thing without inherent worth. The deepest wound isn't physical or financial. It's the denial of your dignity.

And when someone causes harm, they've lost sight of the other person's humanity. They've reduced a full human being—an image of God—to something that can be violated without consequence.

Restoration reverses both of these.

For the perpetrator: The process calls them back to see what they stopped seeing. The person they harmed isn't an abstraction. Isn't a target. Isn't a problem. It's a human being with infinite worth. When that recognition lands—really lands—responsibility stops being a burden and becomes a gift. The perpetrator isn't being punished. They're being restored to their own humanity by acknowledging the humanity they violated.

For the victim: The process returns what was taken. Not just material reparation—though that matters—but the deeper restoration of dignity. You were treated as worthless. The process declares that you are not worthless. You were made invisible. The process makes you seen. You were told, through the act of harm, that you don't matter. The process tells you: you matter infinitely.

When the perpetrator sees the victim's dignity, and the victim sees their own dignity, the ground shifts. They're no longer adversaries fighting over who was right. They're two human beings who both lost something in the rupture—and can both gain something in the repair.

This is why punishment fails. Punishment reinforces the lie. It tells the perpetrator: you are what you did. You are a criminal, a monster, unredeemable. It tells the victim: you are what was done to you. You are a victim, damaged, defined by this moment forever.

Restoration tells a different story. To the perpetrator: you are more than what you did, and you can prove it by making repair. To the victim: you are more than what was done to you, and this process exists because your dignity demands acknowledgment.

The Determining Factor

So how does the Trust Economy decide which path to take?

Not by the category of harm. Not by some legal taxonomy that sorts offenses into misdemeanors and felonies. The determining factor is simpler and more human:

Awareness: Does the perpetrator recognize what they did?

Willingness: Will they work to restore it?

When both are present, the system doesn't need punishment. The goal of punishment—acknowledgment and repair—is already being achieved voluntarily. Prosecution adds nothing except cost.

When either is absent, the system must respond. Not for vengeance. But because the perpetrator is refusing to offer what the victim deserves.

This changes everything about how we respond to harm.

The current system asks: What did you do?

The Trust Economy asks: What will you do now?

The first question locks people into their worst moment. The second gives them a path forward.

The Three Paths

When someone has genuinely harmed another person, the Trust Economy offers three paths back to belonging.

Path One: Silent Amnesty

You choose to move forward without public confession. You don't announce what you did. You simply begin living differently.

The system doesn't hunt you. There's no inquisition, no public branding. You have room to grow before you're ready to face yourself publicly.

But transparency means patterns eventually surface. If you keep causing harm, the evidence accumulates. The truth, as it always does, finds its way home.

Silent amnesty is for those who aren't ready to confess but are ready to change. It gives grace while maintaining accountability.

Path Two: Confession and Restoration

You come forward voluntarily. You name what you did. You face the person you harmed—if they choose to participate.

This isn't punishment. This is restoration.

The process is structured: truth, acknowledgment, reparation, release. A mediator holds the space. The harmed person speaks their pain. The one who caused harm takes responsibility—not in shame, but in ownership.

The neuroscience backs this up. When someone takes responsibility in a non-shaming environment, their brain shifts from defensive circuitry to integrative reasoning. Responsibility becomes desirable rather than frightening.

For victims, experiencing acknowledgment triggers measurable healing: lower cortisol, higher oxytocin, faster emotional recovery, restored sense of agency. Forgiveness literally heals the body.

Path Three: Dropped Charges

This is the mechanism that handles the space between silence and confession.

The system surfaces evidence of harm. Perhaps the two-year confession window has passed. Perhaps another party has made an accusation. The perpetrator is now known.

But instead of automatic prosecution, the system asks the two questions: Is there awareness? Is there willingness?

If the perpetrator demonstrates genuine recognition of the harm caused and genuine commitment to restore it, the charges are dropped. Not because harm doesn't matter—but because the goal of prosecution is already being achieved.

The victim must consent. They can refuse, and the process continues to formal restoration. But in most cases, when a perpetrator offers genuine acknowledgment and repair, the victim accepts. Because what they wanted was never punishment. It was recognition. It was dignity. It was assurance. And they're getting it without years of litigation.

Dropped charges isn't avoiding accountability. It's right-sizing accountability. The adversarial process exists to force truth from unwilling participants. When someone is already telling the truth, already offering repair, the entire apparatus becomes redundant.

Drop the charges. Accept the restoration. Move forward.

The Fiscal Case for Restoration

This brings us to a truth that should be obvious but somehow isn't: enemies are expensive.

The current legal system treats every conflict like it requires full prosecution. Every dispute gets lawyers, depositions, discovery, motions, trials, appeals. We've built a system calibrated for the worst offenses and applied it to everything.

The costs are staggering. Plaintiffs spend $50,000 to $500,000 in legal fees. Defendants spend the same. Courts spend public resources. Both parties lose years of their lives to the process. Relationships are destroyed permanently. And the winner often can't collect anyway. The loser declares bankruptcy.

Net result: everyone poorer. No trust restored. Often more resentment than before.

Beyond the courtroom, the costs compound. Prisons cost $40,000 or more per person per year. An entire class of "ex-cons" can't participate in the economy. Victims carrying unresolved trauma can't work at full capacity. Communities fractured by unhealed conflict can't cooperate.

Now compare restoration.

Acknowledgment costs nothing. Repair usually costs less than litigation would have. Healed people contribute economically. Reintegrated people don't reoffend. Communities that know how to restore conflict can cooperate on everything else.

The fiscal argument and the moral argument point in the same direction. That's how you know you've found something true.

Restoration isn't a loophole. It's infrastructure. It's what makes honesty possible, which makes trust scalable, which unlocks abundance for everyone.

Safety for Both

But doesn't this put victims at risk? Doesn't letting perpetrators off easy embolden future harm?

Only if you assume the current system creates safety. It doesn't.

In the current system, safety is zero-sum. If the victim is safe, the perpetrator must be caged or destroyed. If the perpetrator is free, the victim is supposedly unsafe.

But look at the outcomes. Incarceration doesn't prevent reoffense—recidivism rates are catastrophic. Restraining orders are paper shields. Punishment creates resentment, and resentful people are dangerous. The adversarial process often leaves victims more traumatized than the original harm.

The Trust Economy designs for safety for both parties.

Safety for the victim comes from: Genuine acknowledgment, not forced by courts but offered freely. Real behavioral change in the perpetrator, verified over time. Community witness to the harm—others now know and are watching. Structural protections going forward, calibrated to actual risk.

Safety for the perpetrator comes from: Knowing that acknowledgment won't mean destruction. A clear path to restoration that ends in reintegration. Community acceptance after repair. Release from permanent stigma.

When both parties are safe, restoration becomes possible. When either party is unsafe, they defend rather than heal. The perpetrator hides, lies, fights—because confession means annihilation. The victim can't let go—because the perpetrator might return.

Make both parties safe, and the natural human drive toward repair takes over. People want to make things right. They want to move forward. They want to belong. The system just has to stop making those things impossible.

Integration, Not Exile

This is the principle underneath everything: integration, not exile.

In a punishment system, the goal is separation. Remove the offender from society. Brand them so others know to avoid them. Make the cost of failure so high that people are deterred.

But deterrence doesn't work. The data is overwhelming. Punishment doesn't reduce harm—it just moves it around. People released from prison reoffend at staggering rates. Shame doesn't reform; it entrenches. Exile doesn't protect; it creates enemies.

The Trust Economy takes a different approach. The goal is always return.

No one is permanently cast out. Everyone can earn their way back to full belonging. The path might be long. It might require genuine change, genuine repair, genuine accountability. But the door is never locked.

This isn't naivety. It's game theory.

In a low-trust environment, cheating is the winning strategy. The system rewards short-term extraction over long-term relationship, so people extract.

In a high-trust environment, cooperation is the winning strategy. When people expect to be part of the community long-term, they invest in the community. When they know failure won't mean permanent exile, they take responsibility instead of hiding.

The moment you flip the incentives toward trust, cooperation becomes the dominant strategy. This is well-documented across evolutionary biology, behavioral economics, and repeated simulation. When people expect cooperation, they cooperate.

And that requires a path back.

The Restoration Economy

All of this—the three-layer response, the universal training, the temporal accountability, the three paths, the dignity shifts, the commitment to integration—adds up to something larger.

It's not just a safety system. It's an economy of restoration.

Every time a neighbor witnesses a crisis without fleeing, trust capital increases. Every time a trained responder de-escalates instead of escalating, the community's capacity grows. Every time charges are dropped because a perpetrator offered genuine repair, the proof accumulates: this system works. Every time someone takes the path of confession and finds restoration instead of exile, the model strengthens.

The old economy externalized failure—pushed it into prisons, into homelessness, into families that shattered and never reformed. The restoration economy internalizes it—holds it, processes it, transforms it into deeper trust.

Failure becomes fuel. Rupture becomes raw material for repair. The worst moments become the foundation for something stronger.

We heal the past so trust can fund the future.

| 16 |

Chapter Sixteen: The Trust OS

"Cortana didn't run the mission. She supported it. She was guide, not general."

The sound woke Maria before the alarm did.

A rushing, hissing noise from somewhere in the walls. Then water pooling under her feet as she stepped out of bed. The pipe under the bathroom sink had burst.

Maria is a single mother. Two kids, ages 8 and 14. She works as a medical assistant at a clinic twenty minutes away. Her shift starts at 7:30. The kids need to be at school by 7:45. It's now 6:14 AM and water is spreading across her bathroom floor.

In the old economy, this is where the day falls apart. You call a plumber and get voicemail. You scroll through reviews trying to figure out who's trustworthy. You wait on hold. You take a day off work—if you can afford to. The plumber arrives four hours later and charges emergency rates. The whole thing costs you $400 and a day's pay.

Maria opens her phone and taps the Trust OS.

She speaks: "Emergency. Water pipe burst. Need a plumber now."

The system already knows her address. It scans her perimeter—the network of verified, trusted people within response distance. Three plumbers are within a ten-minute walk. One of them, David, is awake. His status shows "available for emergencies." His trust score is 94, built from 847 verified jobs over six years. Thirty-one of those jobs were in Maria's building. The estimated response time is 4 minutes.

Maria taps "Request help."

David's phone buzzes. He sees the request: burst pipe, two blocks away, single mother, time-critical. He taps "Accept."

At 6:18 AM, David knocks on Maria's door.

By 6:45, the pipe is fixed. A temporary patch—he'll come back this weekend to do the full repair. Maria gets her kids dressed, drops them at school, and makes it to work only ten minutes late. David earns 3.2 Trust Tokens for the emergency response, plus a future job on Saturday.

Total elapsed time from crisis to resolution: 31 minutes.

This is what coordination looks like when the system assumes trust instead of distrust.

The Source Code

Every system has an operating system—the layer beneath the applications, beneath the interface, beneath everything visible. It determines what's possible.

This is what I've come to understand: trust is not a feature of society. Trust is the source code of society. Self-perception is the operating system that runs it.

A world is built out of whatever humans believe about themselves.

When people believe they are unsafe, they create systems of control. When they believe they are unworthy, they create systems of extraction. When they believe they are alone, they create systems of competition. When they believe they must survive, they create scarcity economies.

But when people believe they have value, they create systems of contribution. When they believe they are trusted, they create systems of transparency. When they believe they matter, they create systems of mutual responsibility. When they believe they are safe, they create abundance economies.

The formula is simple: less noise equals less friction, less friction equals more flow, more flow equals more abundance.

The Trust OS is what happens when we design technology to support that—to quiet the noise at scale, to make trust the default, to build systems that assume the best instead of preparing for the worst.

Maria didn't have to prove she could pay. David didn't have to worry about getting stiffed. The trust was already verified, already visible, already part of the infrastructure. The coordination happened in seconds because the friction had been removed in advance.

2:47 PM – David

David got the call at 2:30. A burst water heater across town—a big job, probably four hours. Good money. But his daughter Sophie is home sick from school, and his ex-wife is traveling for work. His usual babysitter isn't answering.

In the old economy, he turns down the job. Or he drags his sick daughter along. Or he leaves her home alone and worries the whole time. Every option costs him something—money, quality, peace of mind.

David opens his Trust OS.

He speaks: "Need childcare for sick 9-year-old. Two to three hours. Starting now."

The system scans his perimeter. It finds Elena, a retired teacher who lives three doors down from David. She's indicated "available for emergency childcare" in her profile. Her trust score is 97. She's watched Sophie twice before—both times logged, both times rated positively by David.

Elena's phone buzzes. She sees: David's daughter, sick but not seriously, needs quiet supervision for a few hours. She taps "Accept."

At 2:52 PM, Elena knocks on David's door.

"Hey sweetheart," she says to Sophie. "I brought tea and a puzzle. Your dad says you're not feeling great."

David makes it to the water heater job. He earns good money. Sophie watches movies with Elena and drinks ginger tea. Elena earns 2.1 Trust Tokens for the afternoon, plus the satisfaction of being useful—something she's missed since retiring.

Nobody had to call in favors. Nobody had to feel guilty. The help was there because the network was there, and the network was there because everyone had been investing in it all along.

What This Replaces

To understand what the Trust OS makes possible, consider what it replaces.

Right now, if you need work, you wade through job boards or pay recruiters who take a cut of your salary. The Trust OS matches skills to needs directly—the carpenter three neighborhoods over who needs exactly the help you can provide finds you in seconds, not weeks.

Right now, your creditworthiness is controlled by three corporations you've never met, using algorithms you can't see, generating scores you can't dispute. The Trust OS gives you a trust score you own—built from your actual record of reliability, visible to you, under your control.

Right now, when something goes wrong, you call 911 and wait fifteen minutes for strangers with guns. The Trust OS activates your perimeter—neighbors who know you, trained to respond, seconds away instead of minutes.

Right now, childcare means expensive daycare centers or the constant anxiety of informal arrangements with no backup. The Trust OS surfaces the retired teacher three doors down who loves kids and has an open afternoon.

Each of these replacements reduces friction. And reduced friction compounds. When you eliminate the transaction costs that currently eat up 30-40% of economic activity, that energy becomes available for actual value creation.

Maria got to work. David earned good money. Elena felt useful. Sophie was cared for. Value flowed to everyone because trust made the coordination frictionless.

4:15 PM – Elena

Elena has been struggling with her new phone for three weeks.

Her grandchildren gave it to her for her birthday—a beautiful gesture, but the thing mystifies her. She can make calls, mostly. Texting is slow and frustrating. The apps her grandkids insisted she download sit unopened on the home screen. She wants to video call her sister in Phoenix, but she can't figure out how.

She mentioned this to David when he picked up Sophie. Offhand. Not asking for anything—just venting.

"Have you tried the network?" David asked. "My neighbor's kid does tech tutoring. He's really patient."

After David and Sophie leave, Elena opens her Trust OS.

She speaks: "Need help learning smartphone. Patient teacher preferred."

The system finds Marcus. He's fourteen years old, lives four blocks away, and earns community service credit by teaching technology to seniors. His trust score is 88—lower than the adults, but that's typical for teenagers still building their records. His specialty is listed as "patient instruction for beginners." Twelve seniors in the neighborhood have rated him, all positively.

Elena taps "Request help."

Marcus's phone buzzes. He sees: retired teacher, needs smartphone help, patient instruction requested. He taps "Accept."

At 4:45 PM, Marcus knocks on Elena's door.

By 6:00 PM, Elena can video call, send photos, and navigate her apps. Marcus earns 1.5 Trust Tokens and a plate of cookies Elena insisted he take home.

"You're a good teacher," Elena tells him.

"So are you," Marcus says. "My mom says you used to teach third grade."

"Thirty-two years."

"That's why you were such a good student. You know how learning works."

The Cortana Principle

In 2001, a video game introduced millions of people to a concept they didn't have words for yet.

The game was Halo. The hero was Master Chief—a supersoldier in futuristic armor. But the real innovation wasn't the weapons or the aliens or the graphics. It was his partner: an artificial intelligence named Cortana.

Cortana lived in his helmet. She processed information faster than any human could. She tracked threats, identified patterns, suggested next moves. When the battlefield got chaotic, she filtered the noise into clarity. When Master Chief faced impossible odds, she found the path through.

But what made Cortana different from every AI villain in science fiction: she didn't control him. She supported him.

She wasn't HAL 9000, locking him out of the ship. She wasn't Skynet, deciding humans were the problem. She was something new—an intelligence that amplified human agency instead of replacing it. A partner, not an overlord.

Here's the line that captures everything:

Technology should amplify agency, not replace it.

Cortana made Master Chief more effective because she handled the complexity so he could focus on what mattered. She didn't make his choices—she made his choices clearer.

That's what the Trust OS does for society. It handles the coordination complexity so humans can focus on what humans are for: connection, creativity, care, meaning.

Maria didn't need to become an expert at finding plumbers. David didn't need to maintain a mental database of backup childcare options. Elena didn't need to post on social media hoping someone might help. The system held the complexity so the humans could focus on their actual lives.

We've spent decades building technology that captures attention, manipulates behavior, and extracts value. The Trust OS is built on a different premise: that technology's highest purpose is to make human flourishing easier.

6:30 PM – The Circle Completes

Marcus walks home with Elena's cookies.

He lives with his mom and his younger brother in an apartment four blocks from Elena. His mom works as a medical assistant at a clinic twenty minutes away. She got home late today—just ten minutes, she said, something about a water emergency at a patient's house that threw off the morning schedule.

His mom is Maria.

Here's what happened today:

David fixed Maria's pipe, which let Maria get to work, which let Maria earn the money that keeps her family stable.

Elena watched David's daughter, which let David take the job across town, which let David earn the money that keeps his family stable.

Marcus taught Elena to use her phone, which let Elena connect with her sister, which let Elena feel less alone since her husband died last year.

And Maria's ability to work meant Marcus had a stable home, which meant Marcus could develop the patience and skill that made him a good teacher, which meant Elena got the help she needed.

The value circulated. It didn't accumulate at the top. It flowed through the neighborhood, touching everyone, leaving everyone better off.

This is what George Bailey was trying to explain in 1946, when the depositors demanded their money back:

"You're thinking of this place all wrong. As if I had the money back in a safe. The money's not here. Your money's in Joe's house... right next to yours. And in the Kennedy house, and Mrs. Macklin's house, and a hundred others."

The value isn't sitting in a vault. It's in Maria's apartment, where the water now flows properly. It's in David's truck, driving to another job. It's in Elena's phone, showing her sister's face. It's in Marcus's growing reputation, opening doors he doesn't even know about yet.

The Trust OS didn't create this value. The people created it. The Trust OS just made the coordination frictionless—so the value could flow.

Who Owns the Operating System?

But here's the question that must be answered: If the Trust OS is essential infrastructure—if without AI coordination, perimeter logic at scale is impossible—then who controls the AI?

This is the convergence question applied to the coordination layer itself.

We've seen what happens when essential infrastructure is owned by extraction-driven forces. Social media platforms started as connection tools and became attention-harvesting machines. Search engines started as information access and became advertising delivery systems. Every technology that began with promise was eventually optimized for extraction—because that's what the ownership structure demanded.

The Trust OS cannot follow this pattern. If it does, we've simply replaced one apex with another.

So let me be explicit about what the architecture requires:

It must be open source, not proprietary. The code that coordinates trust must be visible to everyone. You cannot trust what you cannot see. The moment the Trust OS becomes a black box controlled by a corporation, it becomes a tool for extraction rather than coordination.

It must be community-governed, not corporate-controlled. The decisions about how the Trust OS evolves must be made by the communities it serves, not by shareholders optimizing for profit.

It must be distributed, not centralized. No single point of failure. No single point of control. The internet's resilience comes from its distributed architecture—no one owns it, so no one can kill it. The Trust OS must be the same.

It must be auditable, not hidden. Every decision the system makes must leave a trail that affected parties can examine. Not surveillance of people by the system, but transparency of the system to people. The watchers must be watchable.

This isn't idealism. It's engineering.

Any system that coordinates trust must itself be trustworthy. And trustworthiness requires transparency, accountability, and distributed control.

The Trust OS must be owned by everyone who uses it. Not in a vague metaphorical sense. In the literal sense of governance rights, code access, and operational control.

This is non-negotiable. Any version of the Trust Economy where the coordination layer is privately controlled is not the Trust Economy. It's extraction with better marketing.

What Buurtzorg Proves

If this sounds theoretical, look at Buurtzorg.

In the Netherlands, this company has revolutionized home healthcare through radical trust. Fifteen thousand nurses work in self-organizing teams of ten to twelve. No managers. No regional directors. Just small teams with full autonomy to serve their patients.

The results confound traditional management theory: 40% lower costs than conventional home care, the highest patient satisfaction in the country, and the highest employee satisfaction of any Dutch company with over 1,000 workers.

Buurtzorg nurses don't wait for permission to help a patient. They don't file requests through bureaucracy. They see what's needed and they do it—because the system trusts them to make good decisions.

Sound familiar?

Maria didn't file a request. David didn't wait for approval. Elena didn't go through channels. They saw what was needed, they found each other, and they solved the problem. The Trust OS made the coordination instant. The humans made the decisions.

The Trust OS isn't fantasy. Buurtzorg has been operating it—in analog form—since 2006. We're just building the digital infrastructure to scale it.

9:00 PM – The Neighborhood Sleeps

Maria puts her kids to bed. The bathroom floor is dry. Tomorrow, she'll leave a rating for David: "Arrived in 4 minutes. Fixed the problem. Professional and kind." His trust score will tick up slightly.

David reads Sophie a story. She's feeling better. Tomorrow, he'll leave a rating for Elena: "Took wonderful care of my daughter on short notice. Sophie asks when she can visit again." Elena's trust score will tick up slightly.

Elena video calls her sister in Phoenix. It works perfectly. She doesn't leave a rating for Marcus—she doesn't know how yet—but she mentions him to her sister: "The nicest young man from the neighborhood taught me. He reminds me of my students."

Marcus finishes his homework. He doesn't think much about the afternoon—it was just a regular tutoring session. But his reputation is building. His trust score is growing. Doors are opening that he doesn't even know about yet.

The neighborhood sleeps.

Tomorrow, someone else will have a crisis. Someone else will have a skill. The Trust OS will connect them, and value will flow, and everyone will be slightly better off than they were before.

This is what coordination looks like when the system assumes trust instead of distrust.

This is what we're building.

For the technical specification—the three layers, matching engine, privacy architecture, and governance protocols—see Part Five: Design Prototypes.

| 17 |

Chapter Seventeen: The Partnership Agreement

"Investor. Labor. Customer. All three must win, or none of them do."

On his 81st birthday, Bob Moore gave away his company.

Not sold. Gave.

Bob's Red Mill had grown from a small Oregon flour mill into a $100 million business—over 200 products in 70 countries, a brand trusted by millions of home bakers. The offers to buy it had been, in Bob's words, "countless." Private equity firms. Food conglomerates. People who saw the value and wanted to extract it.

"They thought I was just a lame-brained idiot because I didn't want to sell my company," Bob told Fortune years later. "They told me how stupid I was."

Bob wasn't stupid. He'd been broke twice. He'd watched arsonists burn his original mill to the ground in 1988, leaving nothing but two massive millstones in the ashes. He knew what loss felt like. He also knew what mattered.

"I don't think there's anybody worthy to run this company but the people who built it," he said. "I have employees who've been with me for 30 years. They're going to own it."

So on February 15, 2010—his 81st birthday—Bob announced an Employee Stock Ownership Plan. Every worker became a part-owner. By April 2020, the company was 100% employee-owned. The workforce had grown from 209 to over 700. The products kept multiplying. The customers stayed loyal.

Bob worked until he was 94. He died in 2024, at home, at peace—leaving behind not just a successful business, but proof of a different way.

Here's what Bob understood that the extraction economy forgot: the people who bake the bread, mill the grain, answer the phones, and ship the boxes aren't costs to be minimized. They're partners. And when you treat them like partners—when they share in what they build—they build something worth sharing.

The village blacksmith knew this too.

His craft required three things: the iron merchant's supply, his own skill, and the farmer's need for tools. Without any one of them, the others were useless. Iron without skill was raw material. Skill without iron was empty potential. Both without the farmer were pointless exercise.

The three were bound together. The merchant couldn't gouge the blacksmith without losing his best customer. The blacksmith couldn't exploit the farmer without losing his reputation. The farmer couldn't cheat the blacksmith without losing access to tools. The triangle held itself in balance through relationship, through reputation, through the simple fact that everyone knew everyone and would face each other tomorrow.

Bob Moore rebuilt that triangle in a modern corporation. He didn't extract from his workers to enrich himself. He didn't abandon his customers for a bigger payday. He chose partnership over extraction—and proved it could work at scale.

Then he gave it away, so it would last.

In 2022, Patagonia founder Yvon Chouinard did something similar at an even larger scale. Instead of selling the company or taking it public, he transferred 100% of Patagonia—valued at $3 billion—to a trust dedicated to fighting climate change. "Earth is now our only shareholder," he announced. No billionaire exit. No extraction event. The company continues operating; the profits fight climate change forever. Bob gave his company to his workers. Yvon gave his to the planet. Both chose partnership over extraction—and proved it could work.

The Fracture

When economies grew beyond the village, the relationships that held the triangle together—reputation, accountability, mutual dependence—dissolved into abstraction.

The cotton farmer in Mississippi never met the textile worker in Manchester who never met the customer in Boston. Capital became shareholders you'd never meet. Labor became workers you'd never see. Customers became "the market"—a statistical aggregate, not a community of faces.

Into this abstraction stepped the corporation. And the corporation faced a choice: optimize for all three parties, or optimize for one.

Optimizing for one is simpler than balancing three. Profit appeared to be the point—but it was never the whole picture.

Milton Friedman said the corporation's only responsibility was to shareholders. Ronald Reagan built an economic philosophy on the same premise. For fifty years, we've called it trickle-down economics: if investors win, everyone else eventually will.

The results are in. CEO pay exploded while worker wages stagnated. Communities hollowed out while stock prices soared. Trust collapsed while profits accumulated. The triangle didn't disappear—it broke. One vertex captured value while the other two were stripped.

The Partnership Agreement introduces a different operating law—the Partnership Doctrine: *Investor, labor, and customer must win together, or none of them actually do.*

The first doctrine justifies extraction and calls it efficiency. The second insists on relationship and calls it reality.

The Irreducible Triangle

Every economic transaction involves three parties.

Someone provides the capital. Someone does the work. Someone has the need.

Call them what you will—investors, workers, customers. Shareholders, labor, consumers. Funders, creators, users. The names change. The triangle doesn't.

This is the irreducible geometry of value creation. You cannot build anything meaningful without all three. Capital without labor is inert. Labor without capital is unsupported. Both without customers are pointless. The three exist in permanent interdependence, whether we acknowledge it or not.

The Partnership Agreement makes that interdependence explicit. It states a simple principle:

The goal is the highest return on investment for all three parties—investor, labor, and customer—simultaneously.

Not highest returns for shareholders while labor and customers accept whatever's left. Not highest wages for workers while investors flee and customers pay inflated prices. Not lowest prices for customers while workers are exploited and investors lose capital.

All three. Simultaneously. Each party receiving excellent returns because the system is designed to produce them.

The Best Case Scenario

What does it look like when the Partnership Agreement actually works?

For labor, the best case is craft.

People doing exactly what they love to do. Not grinding through tasks they hate to pay bills they resent. Not pretending to care about work that doesn't matter. Real contribution—where their unique skills create real value, consistently, day after day.

This is what work was supposed to be. The carpenter who loves wood. The teacher who loves learning. The engineer who loves solving problems. The baker who loves watching dough rise. When labor is optimized for genuine contribution—when people work where they add real value—the work itself becomes meaningful. Craft emerges.

The extraction economy treats labor as a cost to minimize. The Partnership Agreement treats labor as a contribution to optimize. The difference isn't just moral—it's practical. People doing what they love do it better. And better work creates better products.

For the investor, the best case is the flywheel.

They get their money back—with a significant return. But more than that, they become the engine of a system that keeps working. Their capital flows to good ideas and satisfying solutions. Those solutions generate returns. Those returns fund more good ideas. The flywheel spins faster.

In the extraction economy, investors capture value and sit on it. In the Partnership Agreement, investors catalyze value and watch it multiply. They're not extracting from a dying system—they're fueling a living one.

For the customer, the best case is an amazing product.

Because everyone is contributing to the outcome. The investor provided capital for quality. The labor brought craft and care. The result is a product or experience that genuinely solves the customer's problem—not a minimum viable extraction designed to capture maximum revenue.

When all three parties win, the customer doesn't get the cheapest possible version of what they need. They get the best possible version. Because no one in the chain was being squeezed, no one had to cut corners.

Everyone wins.

Not as a slogan. As an engineering specification. The system is designed so that investor returns, labor satisfaction, and customer value all increase together. The triangle in balance.

What Each Party Actually Wants

Before we can design a system that works for all three, we need to understand what each party genuinely needs—not what they've been conditioned to demand in a zero-sum game.

What investors actually want is meaningful return on meaningful investment. They want their capital to matter. They want to fund projects that work, that create real value, that they can be proud of. Yes, they want financial returns—capital requires compensation for risk. But the best investors aren't trying to extract maximum value from a dying system. They're trying to build value in a living one.

What labor actually wants is meaning, dignity, and fair compensation for genuine contribution. People want to matter. They want their effort to count. They want to see the connection between what they do and the value it creates. And yes, they want to be paid well—not because they're greedy, but because compensation signals respect.

Here's the inversion that matters.

The people who invest their physical labor—their time, their skill, their irreplaceable life energy—should receive the highest return on investment, not the lowest.

Capital can be replaced. A machine can be rebuilt. A fund can be recapitalized.

But the hours of a human life, once spent, are gone forever.

In any honest accounting, human time is the scarcest asset in the system. The Partnership Agreement simply treats it that way.

What customers actually want is the right solution at a fair cost. They want products and services that genuinely solve their problems. They want to trust that what they're buying is worth what they're paying. They don't want to be manipulated, deceived, or exploited. They want to participate in exchanges that leave both parties better off.

When you understand what each party genuinely wants, the adversarial model of economics starts to look absurd. None of these desires require someone else to lose. All of them are compatible with the others thriving.

The Agreement

So here is the Partnership Agreement at the heart of the Trust Economy:

Investors agree to fund projects that create genuine value for all parties, accepting fair returns rather than maximum extraction.

Labor agrees to contribute their best effort to meaningful work, trusting that their contributions will be fairly compensated and that their partnership is valued beyond their productivity.

Customers agree to pay fair prices for genuine solutions, trusting that they're receiving real value and that their attention will be treated with respect.

All three agree that the goal is not to maximize any single party's returns at the expense of the others, but to maximize total value creation and distribute it fairly among all who contributed.

The simplest way to say this: **We're all working to support the best outcome for each other.**

That's the collective agreement at the heart of the Trust Economy. Not "I'll help you if you help me." Not "I'll help you so you'll owe me." Not "I'll help you if it doesn't cost me."

We're all working to support the best outcome for each other.

When that agreement holds, everything else follows. The investor wants labor to thrive because thriving labor creates better products. Labor wants customers to be satisfied because satisfied customers sustain the enterprise. Customers want investors to receive fair returns because fair returns attract more investment in things customers need.

The triangle doesn't hold together through contracts and enforcement. It holds together through alignment. Through the recognition that my success includes your success.

This is consent at scale. Not the false consent of "take it or leave it" contracts. Real consent—freely chosen, informed, specific, and reversible—between parties who recognize their interdependence.

Simple Terms

Here's something the extraction economy has perfected: complexity as a weapon.

Have you ever read the terms of service for anything you've agreed to? The mortgage documents for your home? The employment contract for your job? They're designed to be unreadable. Complexity protects extraction. When you can't understand the terms, you can't challenge them.

The Partnership Agreement inverts this.

Not because simplicity is naive—because simplicity is honest. When terms are clear, all parties know what they're agreeing to. When terms are complex, someone is hiding something.

A Partnership Agreement should fit on one page. The investor's contribution, the expected return, the conditions for success, the path to community ownership—all visible, all legible, all understood by everyone who signs.

This isn't dumbing down. It's cleaning up. The complexity in traditional contracts exists to obscure, not to clarify. Remove the obscurity, and you don't need the complexity.

The Balance of Wins

But what does the Partnership Agreement actually look like in practice? Not as philosophy—as decision-making?

Consider a moment I've seen play out dozens of times in my career, usually badly.

A company is growing. Revenue is up. The investors want to expand—new markets, new products, faster growth. The workers want better compensation—they've been grinding for three years on the promise that success would be shared. The customers want the product to stay reliable—they chose it because it works, and they're nervous about what "scale" might mean for quality.

In the extraction economy, this is a zero-sum fight. Investors push for growth at any cost. Workers threaten to leave if they don't get raises. Customers become afterthoughts—they'll be replaced by new customers in new markets. The triangle fractures. Someone wins. Someone loses. Usually labor and customers lose, because capital holds the power.

The Partnership Agreement reframes the question.

Instead of "who gets the surplus?", you ask: "what decision creates the most value for all three parties simultaneously?"

Maybe the answer is: grow at 80% of the rate investors wanted, use some of the surplus for worker compensation, and maintain the quality controls that customers depend on. The investors get slightly less growth but more sustainable growth. The workers get raises and stay engaged. The customers stay loyal and keep buying.

That's not compromise. That's optimization for a different variable.

The extraction economy optimizes for maximum return to one party. The Partnership Agreement optimizes for maximum total value across all three. And here's what the data consistently shows: the second approach generates more total value over time. The triangle in balance outperforms the triangle in conflict.

Bob Moore's employees didn't just inherit a company. They inherited a culture where the balance had been maintained for decades. That's why they grew from 209 to 700. That's why customers in 70 countries still trust the brand. The partnership wasn't a one-time gift. It was a compounding asset.

Including all three parties isn't optional. What matters is whether you believe the game is zero-sum—and it isn't.

Return, Then Release

But here's where the Trust Economy does something radical.

In traditional capitalism, investment creates perpetual ownership. Investors fund creation, they own it forever, they extract value indefinitely—even when the creators have moved on, when innovation has plateaued, when the product becomes commodity. The system keeps charging rent.

The Partnership Agreement changes this.

Investment still matters. Risk still requires compensation. Capital is still necessary to build anything meaningful at scale. But ownership has a lifespan.

The model works like this:

Step 1: Investment. Investors fund the creation of a product or system. Their investment becomes their proof of work—their stake in the outcome, their skin in the game.

Step 2: Success triggers tokens. When the investment becomes profitable—when the system works and generates real value—tokens are created. These tokens represent the investor's return, generated by genuine success rather than speculation.

Step 3: Guaranteed return on success. Investors receive a generous return—3x to 4x their original investment—once the system proves itself. Payout is guaranteed if it's successful. The terms are clear from the beginning.

Step 4: If it fails. If the project doesn't work, investors get back 0%. This is real risk, honestly acknowledged. But the terms are simple: success means significant returns; failure means loss. No hidden fees, no complex derivatives, no extraction from a corpse.

Step 5: Transfer to community. After the return is paid in full, ownership transfers to the community. The intellectual property, the rights, the governance—everything becomes a commons.

Imagine a group of investors puts in $10 million to launch a new public transit app. The Partnership Agreement sets their return multiple at 3x.

Over seven years, the app succeeds. After salaries, maintenance, and reinvestment, it generates $30 million in net distributable profit.

The first $30 million goes to the investors: their initial $10 million plus $20 million in return. Their commitment is now fully honored.

On dollar $30,000,001, ownership flips. Governance moves to a community trust. Future profits flow to riders, workers, and reinvestment—not perpetual rent.

Early capital still wins. It just doesn't own the rails forever.

This isn't punishing success. It's redeeming it. Investors get rewarded for their early belief, their capital provision, their risk tolerance. But they don't get to extract forever. Once they've received their fair return, the thing they helped build belongs to the people it serves.

Think of it as open-source venture capital. Fund the spark. Build the fire. Share the warmth.

How the Trust OS Enforces It

The Trust OS doesn't just coordinate—it holds agreements accountable. Every Partnership Agreement is registered on the system. The terms are transparent: what investors contributed, what return they're entitled to, when ownership transfers.

The system tracks revenue generated, returns paid to investors, progress toward the transfer threshold, impact delivered to customers, and compensation flowing to labor.

None of this is hidden in spreadsheets that only accountants see. It's visible to all parties. The Trust OS makes the agreement legible—and makes deviation from it obvious.

When the return threshold is met—say, investors have received their 3x—the system automatically initiates the ownership transfer. No negotiation needed. No lawyers required. The terms were set at the beginning, and the system executes them.

This is what makes the Partnership Agreement enforceable without centralized authority. The Trust OS doesn't have power over the parties—it has clarity about what they agreed to. Enforcement comes from transparency, not coercion.

What This Makes Possible

When the Partnership Agreement holds—when all three parties genuinely trust each other enough to optimize for collective rather than individual returns—something remarkable happens.

Costco is proof. When Wall Street pressured the company to cut wages and raise prices, CEO Craig Jelinek refused. Costco pays workers $24 per hour—50% more than Walmart. They cap markups at 15%. Analysts called it "leaving money on the table." The stock has outperformed Walmart for two decades.

Look at what the Partnership Agreement made possible. Innovation accelerates because workers stay—experienced employees who know products, know customers, and trust that their ideas will be valued rather than exploited. Inequality shrinks, not through redistribution but through distribution; Costco workers earn living wages, and the gap between executives and floor staff is smaller than at competitors. Resources regenerate because people stay for decades rather than months—institutional knowledge compounds instead of walking out the door. And meaning returns. Costco employees don't hate their jobs. Work becomes partnership rather than exploitation.

The investors who complained about the generosity ended up benefiting from it. That's what the Partnership Agreement makes possible.

Morning Star takes this even further. The California company processes 40% of America's tomatoes—billions of pounds annually—with zero managers and zero job titles. Workers negotiate directly with each other through "Colleague Letters of Understanding." Need something from a coworker? Negotiate. Have a conflict? Resolve it yourselves or call a peer mediator. No hierarchy. No permission-seeking. The company has operated this way since 1970 and consistently outperforms its traditionally-managed competitors. Self-management isn't a startup experiment—it's running one of America's largest food processors.

The Data

This isn't just philosophy. The evidence is substantial.

Research consistently shows that cooperative structures outperform competitive ones on complex tasks. A meta-analysis of 122 studies found that cooperation promoted higher achievement than competition in 65 cases, while competition won in only 8.

Companies that genuinely balance stakeholder interests—treating employees, customers, and communities as partners rather than resources to exploit—outperform shareholder-focused companies over the long term.

Companies with significant employee ownership show higher productivity, lower turnover, and better resilience during economic downturns. When workers share in the success they create, they create more success.

The pattern is consistent: partnership beats extraction.

Not in every short-term skirmish—extraction can win battles. But in the long game, systems designed for mutual benefit outperform systems designed for individual capture.

The Closed Loop

There's one more principle that makes the Partnership Agreement work: data flows when value returns.

Think about what happens when you share information with a company today. You give them your browsing history, your purchase patterns, your location, your preferences. They take this data—your data—and use it to optimize their extraction. Better targeting. Higher prices. More addictive features.

What do you get in return? A slightly more personalized ad experience. A recommendation algorithm that knows you better than you know yourself—and uses that knowledge to manipulate you.

This is an open loop. Value flows one direction: from you to them. Your data is an investment, but you receive no return.

The Partnership Agreement closes the loop.

A customer gives data as an investment. When you share information with a Trust Economy enterprise, you're not surrendering it—you're investing it. Your contribution has value. And investments deserve returns.

If there's no return, they don't invest again. This is the market discipline that the current system lacks. When customers can see what happens with their data—and can withhold it if they're not getting value—companies have to actually deliver value, not just extract it.

Intent becomes paramount. In a closed-loop system, the customer's intent matters as much as the company's capability. What are you trying to achieve? What do you actually want? Not what can we get you to click on, but what do you genuinely need?

The extraction economy has perfected the counterfeit loop. It gives you dopamine hits instead of genuine value. Likes instead of connection. Engagement instead of satisfaction. The metrics look like returns, but they're actually further extractions—your attention mined for advertising revenue.

The Partnership Agreement distinguishes between satisfaction and addiction.

Satisfaction is the customer genuinely getting what they wanted. The problem solved. The need met. The value delivered.

Addiction is the customer returning compulsively, not because they're satisfied but because they can't stop. The slot machine that feels like a service. The notification that feels like a friend.

Satisfaction builds trust. Addiction destroys it.

In the Trust Economy, the closed loop means: data flows when value returns. Share your information, receive genuine benefit. Not manipulated engagement—actual satisfaction. Not counterfeit dopamine—real contribution to your life.

If the system doesn't deliver, you stop investing. The loop closes or it breaks.

A Living Example

If this still feels abstract, consider what happens when someone joins a Trust Economy venture.

You're a designer. A team is building a community health app. They need your skills for six months. Here's the Partnership Agreement they offer:

During the build phase, you'll be paid a fair hourly rate in Unity Tokens. You'll also receive a percentage of the project's future returns, proportional to your contribution. When the return threshold is met and ownership transfers to the community, you'll have a voice in governance—alongside other contributors, investors, and users. If the project fails, you keep what you've earned; no clawbacks, no debt. If it succeeds beyond expectations, your percentage grows with it—up to the transfer threshold.

You can see every term. You can see what investors contributed and what return they're entitled to. You can see how your contribution compares to others. You can see the path to community ownership.

You join not because you have to—because you choose to. Because the terms are fair, the mission matters, and the system is transparent.

That's the Partnership Agreement in practice. Three parties, bound by mutual benefit, building something none of them could build alone.

The Partnership Agreement is the economic constitution of the Trust Economy. It replaces the shareholder-first doctrine with a simple principle: all three must win, or none of them do.

18

Chapter Eighteen: The Project Economy

"I work for farmers. It's what I do, and helping them helps us all."—Johnny Georges

A good friend of mine was acquired by Google for stock that paid him forty million dollars. Within two years, his product was dead.

Google has killed over 275 products and services. Not because they failed. Because they succeeded at the wrong scale.

Google Reader: millions of loyal users. Killed. Inbox by Gmail: beloved by power users. Killed.

The logic is brutal: if it doesn't serve billions, it's a distraction.

The graveyard grows because the threshold keeps rising. First you needed millions to matter. Then hundreds of millions. Now billions.

This isn't a Google problem. It's an extraction capitalism problem.

When shareholder value is the only metric, the thing that works—genuinely works, for real people who love it—becomes a liability because it's not growing fast enough.

The scale floor keeps rising. And everything below the floor gets swept away.

The Inversion

What if scale wasn't the goal?

In the Trust Economy, we don't build companies. We build projects.

The distinction matters. A company is designed to grow forever, extract value indefinitely, exist in perpetuity. It has one acceptable outcome: more. More revenue, more users, more market share, more quarters of growth. Anything else is failure.

A project is designed to solve a problem. When the problem is solved, the project can end. Not as failure—as success. The measure isn't "Did it become a unicorn?" It's "Did it serve the people it was built for?"

A project that closes because its work is complete is a project that worked.

This changes everything about how we think about entrepreneurship.

Structure flexes to need. Two overlapping projects discover each other? They can combine—scaling up to eliminate redundancy and serve more people. Demand decreases? The project can scale down—right-sizing to what's actually needed, instead of desperately seeking growth to satisfy investors. The problem gets solved? The project can close—and the people who built it can move to the next problem that needs solving. Nothing has to live forever. Nothing has to grow forever. Things can simply work, for as long as they're needed, and then gracefully end.

The Farmer's Son

In 2013, a farmer's son from Florida walked into the Shark Tank.

Johnny Georges wasn't a typical entrepreneur. He didn't have an MBA or a venture capital pedigree. He had a product: the Tree T-Pee, a simple plastic cone that fits around the base of a young tree to concentrate water at the roots, reducing irrigation needs by up to 90 percent.

His pitch was modest. He was selling the cones for $4.50 each, making about $1.55 profit per unit. He'd sold to 42 nurseries in five Florida counties. He was asking for $150,000 for 20% of his company.

Kevin O'Leary—"Mr. Wonderful"—did the math immediately.

"I can't get involved with you because there's not enough margin for me as a distributor," O'Leary said. "I need to be able to sell it for twelve dollars at least."

This is extraction logic in its purest form. The product works. Farmers need it. Water conservation matters. But none of that matters if the margins aren't fat enough to satisfy an investor's return requirements.

Johnny's response was simple: "It's not about the money to me. It's about doing what's right."

O'Leary literally laughed.

But another shark—John Paul DeJoria, founder of Paul Mitchell hair products and Patron tequila—saw something different. DeJoria had built billion-dollar companies. He understood scale. But he also understood something O'Leary didn't.

"Farmers are the cornerstone of America," DeJoria said. "There may be a lot of farmers out there that can't afford twelve dollars per tree, but maybe they could afford six or seven dollars... What you're doing is right and you deserve the chance to make it big and do a lot of good."

DeJoria offered $150,000 for 20%—the same deal Johnny asked for. No extraction premium. No demand to triple the price. Just: let's help farmers conserve water.

The aftermath tells the story.

Within 24 hours of the episode airing, Johnny received 56,000 emails. The Tree T-Pee expanded from 42 nurseries to operations in 80 countries. He partnered with Home Depot. He raised the price modestly—to $9.95—but kept it affordable enough that farmers could actually buy them.

Today, the Tree T-Pee company is valued at over $100 million.

From $750,000 to $100,000,000. A 133x return. By refusing to maximize extraction.

Johnny's line echoes across everything we're building: "I work for farmers. It's what I do, and helping them helps us all."

That's the Project Economy in one sentence.

Why Startups Really Fail

The standard story: startups fail because of bad product, bad timing, bad team, running out of money.

The real story: startups fail because they're playing the wrong game.

The competitive model says: hide your data. Your information is your advantage. Don't let anyone know what you're learning. Don't share your customer insights. Don't reveal your struggles. If competitors know what you know, they'll beat you to it.

So everyone operates blind.

Startups solve problems that don't exist because they can't access real data about what's needed. They build features no one wants because they can't ask honestly. They run out of runway because they can't find the partnerships that would save them—because partnership requires showing your cards.

The competitive model creates an information desert. Everyone hoarding. No one sharing. A thousand startups failing in isolation, each one holding a piece of the puzzle that could have saved another.

Ninety percent of startups fail. Most failures are information failures—wrong problem, wrong solution, wrong timing. The system guarantees failure by design.

The Trust Economy inverts this completely.

Everyone gives each other data about exactly what's needed.

The customer says what they actually want. The worker says what they can actually build. The investor says what resources are actually available. Trust replaces strategic opacity.

Just: here's what's needed, here's what we can do, here's what we have. Now let's solve it together.

The Billionaire's Real Power

Here's something most people miss about billionaires: they don't just have money. They have coordination.

Think about what a billionaire actually does. They don't sit on piles of cash—they deploy capital. And to deploy capital at scale, they have to do something remarkable:

They convince other people with high net worth to trust each other.

That's the magic trick. Get ten wealthy strangers in a room, and nothing happens. Get them to trust a shared vision, and you can build anything.

Look at the group Fortune magazine famously called the PayPal Mafia. A group of people who worked together in the early 2000s went on to found Tesla, SpaceX, LinkedIn, YouTube, Yelp, Palantir, and a dozen other companies worth hundreds of billions combined. They weren't strangers who happened to have money—they were colleagues who had built trust. They invested in each other, sat on each other's boards, vouched for each other to other investors. The coordination came from relationship, not just capital. That's the real asset: a network of people who trust each other enough to bet on each other's visions.

A billionaire sells dreams. Not products—dreams. The vision of what could exist. The possibility that's worth betting on. The future that justifies the risk.

And then they coordinate. They bring together the money, the talent, the resources—all of it flowing because people trusted the person casting the vision.

This is the power of enterprise: working together at scale to create solutions that no individual could create alone.

The Trust Economy doesn't reject this power. It democratizes it.

What if everyone had access to that coordination? What if the person with the dream didn't need to know billionaires to get the resources flowing? What if trust could be built without gatekeepers?

The billionaire proved the model works. Now we scale access—not down, but out.

The Trust OS connects entrepreneurs around problems needing solutions. It matches skills to needs, resources to projects, teams to challenges. No cold outreach. No guessing. No building in the dark.

The problem tells you it exists. The people experiencing it confirm it's real. The Trust OS connects you to both.

You don't need to be a billionaire to coordinate. You just need to be trustworthy—and now there's a system that makes trustworthiness visible.

The Citizen Stake

Here's an uncomfortable truth: the billionaire's real advantage isn't money. It's psychology.

A billionaire loses $1,000 and doesn't notice. Loses $100,000 and it's a rounding error. Loses $10 million and it's a bad quarter. Their baseline is so high that normal losses never trigger survival mode.

This is the hidden advantage no one talks about.

When you operate from abundance, you can think in decades instead of paychecks. You can take risks that might fail. You can invest in relationships that don't pay off immediately. You can say no to bad deals because you don't need this one to work. You can recover from failure without falling into the pit.

The billionaire isn't smarter. They're just not scared.

Meanwhile, someone living paycheck to paycheck loses $500 and their nervous system collapses. Cortisol floods. The amygdala takes over. IQ drops thirteen points. They can't think about the future because they're drowning in the present.

Same human. Same brain. Same potential.

Different starting line.

What if we gave everyone that psychological advantage? Not billions—just enough. Enough that losing $1,000 doesn't trigger survival mode. Enough that you can take a risk. Enough that failure isn't catastrophic.

The next chapter explains exactly how.

| 19 |

Chapter Nineteen: The Unity Token

"Time is the only currency that can't be counterfeited."

Rosa wants to open a bakery.

She's been baking bread for her neighbors for three years—first as gifts, then as trades, then as something more. People started asking if they could buy her sourdough. Her ciabatta became famous on the block. Last month, a neighbor said: "You should open a shop."

In the extraction economy, this is where dreams die.

Rosa would need to convince a bank to lend her money. She'd fill out forms, prove her creditworthiness, provide collateral she doesn't have. If she got approved—unlikely, given her income—she'd pay 12% interest. The loan would hang over her for years. One bad month and she'd spiral into debt. The risk is too high. She keeps baking in her kitchen. The shop never opens.

Rosa opens her Trust OS and applies to the Family Trust.

The system sees her history: three years of contributions to the network, 847 verified transactions, a trust score of 91. Neighbors have rated her bread—not just purchased it, but confirmed satisfaction 94% of the time. Her record shows she completes what she starts.

She requests a loan for equipment, ingredients, and first month's rent on a small storefront.

The Family Trust approves. Zero interest.

In April, Rosa's Bakery opens.

What Money Actually Is

Here's something we forget: money is a story we agree to believe.

A dollar bill is a piece of paper. A bank balance is numbers in a database. Neither has intrinsic value. Both have agreed-upon value—we accept them because we trust that others will accept them too.

This isn't a flaw. It's a feature. Money is a technology for coordinating strangers. I don't need to know you personally to trade with you. I just need to trust the currency.

But the story modern money tells has become corrupted.

It tells us that a hedge fund manager's hour is worth 10,000 times more than a teacher's hour. It tells us that speculation creates more value than caregiving. It tells us that money should accumulate at the top, that wealth should compound while wages stagnate, that the goal of economic life is to extract more than you contribute.

This story isn't true. But because we built our systems around it, we live as though it were.

The Unity Token tells a different story.

Time as the Foundation

Every human being has the same twenty-four hours in a day. This is the one economic resource that's truly equal—not in how we spend it, but in how much we have.

The Unity Token starts here.

One hour of human time = one token.

Not one hour of a CEO's time versus one hour of a janitor's time. One hour of human time. The baseline is equal because the resource is equal. What you do with that hour—the skill you bring, the value you create, the trust you've built—can multiply its worth. But the foundation is the same for everyone.

When Rosa spends an hour kneading dough, that hour is gone forever. When a software engineer spends an hour writing code, that hour is equally gone. The hours are the same. What differs is the context, the skill, the accumulated trust that makes one hour more impactful than another.

The Unity Token captures both: the baseline equality of time, and the variable multiplier of trust.

May – James Fixes the Oven

Rosa's commercial oven breaks in the third week of May.

It's the heating element—a $400 repair in the extraction economy, plus a week waiting for the technician, plus lost revenue while the bakery sits closed. Rosa doesn't have $400 in reserve. She's still building. This is the kind of setback that kills small businesses.

Rosa opens her Trust OS: "Need oven repair. Commercial unit. Urgent."

The system finds James. He's a general contractor who lives six blocks away. His trust score is 94, built from twelve years of verified work. He's repaired commercial kitchen equipment before—the ledger shows it. He's available this afternoon.

James arrives at 2 PM. By 4 PM, the oven works.

Rosa pays him 4.2 tokens—four hours of skilled labor, plus a trust multiplier for his expertise. James's trust score ticks up slightly: another satisfied customer, another completed job.

The bakery reopens the next morning.

Here's what didn't happen: Rosa didn't lose a week of income. She didn't go into debt. She didn't have to choose between fixing the oven and paying rent. The system connected her need to James's skill in minutes. The repair happened in hours. The tokens transferred when Rosa confirmed satisfaction.

This is what coordination looks like when the friction is removed.

The Trust Multiplier

Here's something a child can understand: the more you show up, the more you earn.

Not all hours are equal in impact. A master carpenter's hour produces more than a novice's hour. A surgeon's hour saves lives in ways a first-year medical student's hour cannot. The Unity Token accounts for this through trust multipliers.

The math is simple. You start at 1.0x. Show up when you say you will, deliver what you promise, build a track record—your multiplier rises. James has been contributing for twelve years. His trust multiplier is 1.4x. When he works an hour, he earns 1.4 tokens instead of the baseline 1.0. Rosa, newer to the network, earns at 1.1x. The teenager doing his first jobs earns at 1.0x.

That's it. No complex formulas. No hidden algorithms. No fine print that takes a lawyer to decode.

This simplicity isn't an accident. It's what happens when friction is removed from the system.

The extraction economy buries complexity everywhere—in tax codes, in credit scoring, in insurance policies, in terms of service nobody reads. That complexity isn't a bug. It's a feature. Extraction hides in the fine print. The more opaque the system, the easier it is to take without people noticing.

The Trust Economy inverts this. When the goal is coordination instead of extraction, simplicity becomes the norm. You don't need complexity to protect against gaming when transparency makes gaming visible. You don't need elaborate rules when trust does the work that contracts used to do.

The multiplier isn't assigned by a boss or an algorithm. It emerges from the accumulated record of your reliability. Every satisfied transaction, every completed commitment, every instance of doing what you said you'd do—these build your trust score over time. You can see exactly why your multiplier is what it is. So can anyone else.

But multipliers have limits. The Trust Economy doesn't recreate the obscene inequalities of the extraction economy. You won't see trust scores that make one person's hour worth 10,000 times another's.

Here's the beautiful part: if everyone trusted everyone equally, everyone would earn the same. The multipliers exist only because trust varies. As the Trust Economy matures—as more people prove reliable, as the culture of trust deepens—the multipliers naturally converge.

Maximum trust creates maximum equality.

June – James's Daughter Needs a Tutor

James's daughter Keisha is struggling with algebra.

She's in eighth grade, smart but frustrated. The concepts aren't clicking. She's starting to believe she's "not a math person—"that story we tell ourselves when the teaching doesn't match how we learn.

In the extraction economy, James would search for tutors online, compare hourly rates ($50-$100 per hour in his area), worry about quality, maybe decide they can't afford it. Keisha keeps struggling. The belief calcifies. Another kid who could have loved math learns to fear it instead.

James opens his Trust OS: "Need algebra tutor for 13-year-old. Patient. Good with frustrated learners."

The system finds Amira. She's a retired high school math teacher who tutors five hours a week—partly for tokens, mostly because she loves watching kids discover they're smarter than they thought. Her trust score is 96. Parents have rated her patient, creative, able to reach kids who've given up.

Keisha and Amira meet twice a week for a month. Eight sessions. By the end, Keisha isn't just passing algebra—she's asking questions in class. The belief shifted. She's a math person after all.

James pays Amira 9.6 tokens—eight hours at Amira's 1.2x multiplier. Amira's record shows another student helped, another transformation verified.

Where did those tokens come from?

Rosa paid James 4.2 tokens for fixing her oven. James used them (plus tokens from other jobs) to pay Amira. The same value that Rosa created by baking bread is now flowing through the system, touching James's family, supporting Amira's retirement.

This is velocity. This is circulation. This is George Bailey's point made real: the money isn't in a vault—it's in your neighbor's contribution, right next to yours.

The Debt Inversion

Here's what makes this radical: tokens are born in surplus, not deficit.

In the extraction economy, money is created through debt. When a bank issues a loan, it creates money—but that money comes with a claim. You owe more than you received. Interest accrues. The money supply expands, but so does the debt that must be repaid.

This is why extraction never ends. The system requires constant growth just to service the debt that created the money in the first place.

The Unity Token inverts this completely.

Tokens are created when value is delivered. When satisfaction is confirmed. When the transaction succeeds. They come into existence not as a claim against the future, but as a record of value already created.

When Rosa's customers confirm satisfaction with her bread, tokens flow to her. No one owes anything. The token represents contribution already made, not debt to be repaid.

The extraction economy asks: "What do you owe?"
The Trust Economy asks: "What have you contributed?"
The difference is everything.

July – Amira's Gift

Amira has 47 tokens left in her giving floor.

The giving floor is separate from what you earn through contribution. Everyone receives 100 tokens per year—your capacity to give. Not to spend on yourself. To support others: neighbors in crisis, projects you believe in, pure gifts that expect nothing in return.

When you spend it, it's spent. Next year, it replenishes.

Amira reads about a family in the network—the Okonkwos, three blocks from her old school. The father was injured at work. The mother is caring for him and their two kids. They're burning through savings. Medical bills are piling up. In the extraction economy, this is the beginning of the spiral: debt, then more debt, then desperation.

Amira gives them 20 tokens from her floor.

So does Rosa—15 tokens. The bakery is doing well enough that she can afford generosity.

So does James—10 tokens. He remembers what it was like when his own father was sick.

Forty-seven people in the network give what they can. The Okonkwos receive 340 tokens—enough to cover three months while the father heals.

No debt. No interest. No spiral.

The father returns to work in September. By December, he's contributing again. By next year, he's giving from his own floor to someone else in crisis.

This is what mutual support looks like when it's built into the system.

This Already Works

If zero-interest, trust-based lending sounds utopian, look at what already exists.

Kiva.org has facilitated over $1.5 billion in micro-loans—at zero interest—funded entirely by peer trust. Strangers lending to strangers, across continents, with repayment rates above 96%.

Sardex in Italy created a mutual credit system where businesses trade with each other using a complementary currency. No interest, balance through reciprocity. During economic crises that crushed traditional businesses, Sardex members thrived—because they had each other.

Time banks operate in hundreds of communities worldwide. One hour of your time equals one hour of mine, regardless of what we do. A lawyer's hour equals a gardener's hour.

These aren't theories. They're data. They prove that the physics of zero-interest, trust-based systems work—when social trust and transparency are strong enough to support them.

The Unity Token takes what these pioneers proved and scales it.

December – The Circle Closes

Rosa's Bakery has been open for eight months.

She's repaid the Family Trust—every token returned over six months from her earnings. Her trust score rose 23 points. Next time she borrows—maybe for a second location—she'll qualify for more.

James finished the year with 1,847 tokens earned. His trust multiplier increased to 1.45x. Keisha got an A in algebra.

Amira tutored 31 students. Her giving floor replenished in January—100 new tokens to give away.

The Okonkwos are back on their feet. The father is contributing to the network. The mother started a small childcare service. Their trust scores are building.

Let's trace the circulation:

Rosa baked bread. Customers paid her in tokens. She paid James to fix her oven. James paid Amira to tutor Keisha. Amira gave to the Okonkwos. The Okonkwos, recovered, are now contributing—and their tokens will flow to someone else.

The same value, circulating. Not accumulating at the top. Not sitting in a vault. Moving through the community, touching everyone, leaving everyone better off than they started.

In the extraction economy, Rosa's loan would have cost her 20% more with interest—value extracted to pay shareholders who did nothing. James's income would have been taxed at every stage, shrinking the pool. The Okonkwos would have spiraled into debt that followed them for years.

In the Trust Economy, every transaction builds trust. Every exchange creates a record of reliability. Every act of generosity strengthens the fabric.

The tokens don't just measure value. They create it.

Connections Are the Value of Life

Here's what the extraction economy never understood: we create value through connection.

The more life we share with others, the more threads of trust we weave. The more threads, the thicker the fabric. That fabric—those relationships, those accumulated moments of showing up for each other—is the actual wealth. Not the numbers in an account. The people who would answer if you called.

When my first marriage ended, the first person I called was my friend Tim. I had to move into an apartment—a loud announcement of failure. Tim never judged. He was just there, helping me move boxes, sitting with me in the empty space.

Why? Because years earlier, I'd helped him move during his divorce. We both knew how it sucked. We'd been there for each other when it mattered.

That's the investment the extraction economy can't measure. The hours you spend with someone. The showing up. The being present when life falls apart. These moments don't appear on any balance sheet, but they're the actual source of security in human life.

The Unity Token makes it visible.

The Neighborhood Principle

For the last twenty years, I've been investing in my neighbors and creating community where I live.

My philosophy is simple: whoever I meet is my neighbor. They don't have to prove themselves. They don't have to earn my trust. I'm down to get to know them.

The result: I probably have fifty friends in my neighborhood. If I ran for city council, people would actually vote for me. Not because I campaigned—because they know me. Because I've shown up for them.

This is what the Unity Token makes visible and scalable.

Knowing your neighbor is one of the most valuable experiences in your life. You see them every day. You share space, weather, the rhythms of the street. When you invest in those relationships—when you extend trust first, when you show up—you build something that no amount of money can buy.

The Unity Token extends this neighborhood logic beyond your block. It lets you know who's reliable across the whole network. It lets trust travel with you. It makes the entire economy feel like a neighborhood where people know each other and show up when it matters.

Rosa didn't know James before her oven broke. James didn't know Amira before Keisha needed help. Amira didn't know the Okonkwos before she saw their story. But the network connected them. The trust was already verified. The help flowed instantly.

That's the neighborhood principle, scaled.

Love as the Choice to Trust

Every major wisdom tradition arrives at the same place.

Love your neighbor as yourself. Do unto others as you would have them do unto you. What is hateful to you, do not do to your neighbor. No one is a believer until he loves for his brother what he loves for himself.

Judaism, Christianity, Islam, Buddhism, Hinduism, secular humanism—they all converge on this single principle. Thousands of years of human wisdom, countless teachers and prophets and philosophers, all pointing at the same truth: we flourish when we treat others as extensions of ourselves.

The question was never what to do. The question was always how.

Trust is love in action.

Not romantic love, though that's part of it. The deeper love—the one that shows up for strangers, that extends grace first, that sees the human being in front of you as worthy of the same dignity you want for yourself.

You can't love your neighbor abstractly. You love your neighbor by trusting them with your time, your resources, your vulnerability. You love your neighbor by showing up when they need help and believing they'll show up when you do. You love your neighbor by extending credit before it's earned and creating the conditions where it can be.

The Unity Token is a mechanism. But the mechanism is in service of something older than any economy: the recognition that everyone is intimately intertwined. That your flourishing and my flourishing are not in competition. That trust given freely is trust that returns multiplied.

The extraction economy told us that self-interest was the only rational strategy. That trusting others was naive. That the smart move was always to protect yourself first.

The Unity Token tells a different story: that trust is the smart move. That cooperation beats competition. That the way to thrive is to help others thrive.

Rosa thrived because James was skilled. James thrived because Amira was patient. Amira thrived because she could give. The Okonkwos thrived because forty-seven strangers chose to act on the oldest wisdom in the world.

Love your neighbor. Trust makes it real.

For the technical specification—token mechanics, valuation framework, safeguards against gaming, and governance protocols—see Part Five: Design Prototypes.

PART FOUR: THE TRANSFORMATION

What Becomes Possible

Now imagine.

You've seen what's broken. You've learned why trust works. You've studied the architecture—the consent protocols, the safety systems, the coordination layers, the contribution currency. The blueprints are on the table.

But blueprints don't inspire. Visions do.

Part Four shows you what life looks like on the other side.

We'll follow families through the Family Trust—where a house costs what a house costs, and wealth builds across generations instead of draining into interest payments. We'll reimagine healthcare in Whole Health—where the system profits from keeping you well, not from keeping you sick. We'll explore Universal Luxury—where quality isn't reserved for the wealthy, but available to everyone. We'll map the Path to Scale—how this spreads from neighborhoods to cities to nations. And we'll face the Hard Questions—the objections, the edge cases, the "yes, buts" that any honest proposal must answer.

One principle runs through all of it: **this is what becomes possible.**

Not utopia. Not perfection. Just the ordinary life that becomes available when systems stop extracting and start serving. The morning that isn't consumed by anxiety. The illness that doesn't mean bankruptcy. The neighborhood where people know your name. The work that means something. The retirement that actually comes.

| 20 |

Chapter Twenty: The Family Trust

"What if the house cost what the house cost?"

Two families buy the same house on the same day.

The Garcias and the Thompsons each purchase a $500,000 home. Same neighborhood. Same square footage. Same school district. Same appraised value. *(Assuming a 30-year fixed mortgage at 7% interest.)*

Thirty years later:

The Garcias (traditional mortgage): paid $1.2 million. Interest to the bank: $700,000.

The Thompsons (Trust Economy loan): paid $500,000. Interest: $0.

Same house. Same value.

The Thompsons bought a house.

The Garcias bought a house—plus another house they'll never live in.

What if the house just cost what the house cost?

The Interest Trap

Let's be clear about what interest actually is.

Interest is a fee charged for the use of money over time. In theory, it compensates lenders for the risk they take and the opportunity cost of not using that capital elsewhere. That's the story we've been told.

But here's what actually happens with a mortgage:

When a bank issues a $500,000 mortgage, it doesn't transfer $500,000 from some vault to the seller. In most cases, the bank creates that money through an accounting entry. The money didn't exist before the loan was issued. The bank's "risk" is largely theoretical—they're lending you something they conjured into existence.

Then they charge you $700,000 for the privilege.

Over thirty years, you pay back nearly two and a half times what you borrowed. The house cost $500,000. You paid $1.2 million. The difference flowed to shareholders, executives, and the machinery of extraction.

This is the Idiot Index applied to housing. The gap between actual cost and actual price—filled entirely with extraction.

The Trust You Already Provide

Here's something worth asking yourself: *How often do you actually touch money?*

Think about it. Your paycheck lands as digits in an account. You pay your mortgage by moving digits to another account. You buy groceries by tapping a card that moves more digits. The "money" never exists as anything you can hold.

What's actually happening underneath all of this? Trust.

You trust the digits in your account represent something real. Your employer trusts the bank will honor the transfer. The bank trusts you'll keep making payments. The entire system—trillions of dollars flowing every day—rests on the collective agreement that the numbers mean something.

The banks are already using your trust to make the whole thing work. The money is "there" because everyone believes it's there.

So what exactly is interest paying for?

Not risk—the bank created the money from nothing. Not the money itself—it's just digits they conjured. Interest is a fee charged for trust that *you and your community already provide.*

The entire apparatus of mortgage finance—the points, the fees, the insurance, the foreclosure system—exists because we built housing on a lie: that trust is scarce and must be purchased. But trust isn't scarce. It's the foundation the whole system already stands on.

The 0% model doesn't ask you to trust more than you already do. It simply stops charging you for trust that was yours to begin with.

Zero-percent lending is what housing looks like when we finally tell the truth.

What Zero-Percent Lending Looks Like

In the Trust Economy, housing works differently.

The Family Trust—a community-owned financial institution—provides mortgages at zero percent interest. You borrow $500,000. You pay back $500,000. The house costs what the house costs.

The math:

- Principal: $500,000
- Term: 30 years (360 months)
- Monthly payment: $1,389

That's it. No compounding. No extraction. No $700,000 fee for the privilege of having a roof over your head.

The value of 0% isn't just about savings. It's about dignity. Zero-percent lending honors both the buyer and the seller. The buyer pays exactly what the house is worth—no more. The seller receives fair value for what they've built. No one is extracted from. No one does the extracting. The transaction is clean, honest, and complete.

But wait—how does the Family Trust sustain itself without interest income?

The Numbers in Your Life

Before we answer that, let me make the savings concrete.

Monthly difference: $1,938

That's $1,938 every month that doesn't flow to extraction. Over a year, that's $23,256. Over thirty years, that's $700,000.

The Mendez family, later in this chapter, shows you exactly what that money makes possible. Now: how does the Family Trust sustain itself without that extraction?

The Family Behind "Family Trust"

Before I explain the mechanics, let me tell you why this matters to me personally.

My grandmother—we called her Nana—nearly killed herself when my mother was twelve years old. She was living above a bar, completely broke, abandoned by a husband who was never around, struggling to keep three daughters fed and clothed.

My mother stopped her. Found her in time. Told her she was worth it. That one sentence gave Nana the courage to continue.

Nana lived another fifty years. I carried her cancer-stricken body from the couch to her bed in her final days. I felt the weight of a life that almost ended in that apartment above the bar.

From that moment of despair came a gift: a family so connected, so fiercely loyal, so committed to each other that we truly loved one another. Not perfectly. Not without conflict. But with a foundation so deep that conflict could always be repaired.

Nana's belief, instilled in all of us: *We are worth fighting for. We are worth believing in.*

The Family Trust isn't named ironically. It's named for what it's meant to create: families with the same foundation mine was given.

Stability not from wealth but from belonging. Security not from accumulation but from connection.

The $700,000 that extraction takes from a family over thirty years isn't just money. It's time not spent with children. Stress that fractures marriages. Second jobs that steal presence. The slow grinding down of people who deserved better.

This is why I will die on this hill. Zero-percent lending isn't just economics. It's giving families room to breathe. Room to be what families are supposed to be.

How the Family Trust Stays Solvent

The goal of the Family Trust is simple: keep money in the family.

The money is always there. It doesn't leave the network to enrich distant shareholders. It doesn't evaporate into interest payments. It circulates—from family to family, generation to generation—building stability instead of extracting it.

The Trust doesn't need to extract interest because it operates on a different logic entirely.

Flat fees instead of compound interest. The Trust charges a transparent origination fee—say, 2% ($10,000)—that covers administrative costs and contributes to the risk pool. This can be rolled into the principal, making your monthly payment $1,417 instead of $1,389. That's still 57% less than the traditional mortgage.

Community insurance pool. Every borrower pays a small monthly amount—perhaps $50—into a shared pool. This pool absorbs the shock when life happens. It helps homeowners work through tough times—job loss, medical emergencies, family crises—without losing everything. This isn't profit extraction; it's collective resilience. When someone falls on hard times, the pool absorbs the shock instead of destroying their life. **The self-capitalizing engine.** Here's where it gets interesting. As borrowers pay down their principal, the Trust's position improves with every payment:

- **Year 0:** Trust lends $500,000. Outstanding: $500,000.
- **Year 5:** Borrower has paid $83,000. Outstanding: $417,000. Trust can re-lend the $83,000.
- **Year 10:** Borrower has paid $167,000. Outstanding: $333,000. Trust can re-lend $167,000.

With each payment, the Trust's risk decreases and its lending capacity grows. That returned capital can fund new 0% mortgages, expanding the network.

This creates a flywheel: repayments enable more mortgages, more mortgages bring more repayments. Every payment strengthens the entire network—pulling in more stability, more opportunity, more abundance.

Equity portability. When families move, they don't start over. They swap their equity into new homes. Your equity becomes your nest egg—portable, protected, always yours. The Trust facilitates the transfer, ensuring that the stability you've built follows you wherever you go.

Borrowing to improve life. Homeowners can borrow from the Trust for more than just housing. Need to start a business? Finance education? Handle a medical expense? The Trust provides loans for life improvement—all at 0%. Because the goal isn't to trap you in debt. It's to help you thrive.

Compare this to traditional banking: When you pay your mortgage, the interest goes to shareholders. It leaves your community entirely. The bank's goal is to maximize extraction—keeping you in debt as long as possible, charging fees at every opportunity.

In the Trust Economy, every dollar stays in the network. It becomes capital for your neighbor's home, your community's school, your town's infrastructure. The system's goal is to maximize stability—helping you pay off faster, build equity faster, contribute to the community faster.

Tokenized equity. As you build equity in your home, it can be tokenized—converted into Trust Tokens that represent your stake.

These tokens enable liquidity without selling (stake tokens as collateral for community loans), participation in network growth (your equity supports other families' mortgages), and portable wealth (your track record moves with you to any Trust Economy community).

The Citizen Stake: Everyone's Starting Line

Here's something that makes the Family Trust different from any housing system before it: the Citizen Stake.

Remember the billionaire's hidden advantage? It's not the money—it's the psychology. When you have a safety net, you can think clearly. You can take risks. You can invest in the future because failure won't destroy you.

The Citizen Stake gives everyone that advantage.

2,000 tokens per person—one year of contribution value. Not as a gift you can spend on anything. As a foundation. A stake in the Family Trust that generates returns, provides collateral, and ensures you always have a floor to stand on.

How it works as a liquidity backstop:

When you apply for a Family Trust mortgage, your Citizen Stake becomes part of your collateral. It's skin in the game—proof that you're invested in the community, not just extracting from it. But it's also protection. If you hit hard times, your stake can absorb some of the shock before you lose your home.

The stake grows as the Trust grows. Your 2,000-token investment in the community becomes 2,400, 3,000, 4,000 tokens over time—as the Trust's assets appreciate and its network expands. You're not just a borrower. You're an owner.

This changes the psychology of housing.

In the extraction economy, homebuyers operate from fear. One missed payment starts the spiral. Job loss means foreclosure. Medical emergency means homelessness. The fear impairs decision-making, creates the very instability it fears.

In the Trust Economy, homebuyers operate from security. The Citizen Stake provides a buffer. The Family Trust provides community. The floor is guaranteed. You can think about the future because the present isn't trying to destroy you.

This isn't socialism—it's capitalism with a different starting line. Everyone still earns based on contribution. The best entrepreneurs still rise. The difference is: no one starts in a hole. No one's potential is wasted because they couldn't access the baseline that trust requires.

The investment in children:

Here's where it gets interesting. When a child is born into a Trust Economy family, they receive their own Citizen Stake. Not accessible until adulthood, but growing from day one.

By the time they're eighteen, that 2,000 tokens has compounded. They enter adulthood not with debt—but with capital. They can invest in education without borrowing. They can start a business without begging for funding. They can take risks because they have a foundation.

This is what wealthy families have always done for their children. We're democratizing it.

The child raised in the Trust Economy has the psychological starting line of a billionaire's kid—not because they inherited billions, but because they inherited security. They can think long-term because they're not drowning in the short-term.

Every generation builds on the last. The Citizen Stake compounds. The trust deepens. The community strengthens.

This is intergenerational wealth—not hoarded in dynasties, but distributed across the family.

How the System Sees Risk

Traditional lending uses credit scores—a number generated by opaque algorithms based on your history of taking on debt and paying it back. This system penalizes people who've never borrowed, rewards gaming, and tells you nothing about someone's actual character.

The Family Trust uses something different: community creditworthiness. The Trust OS tracks your contribution record, transaction history, community standing, and response to difficulty. Did you communicate when struggling? Did you show up when it mattered?

This isn't surveillance. It's visibility. The same way a small-town banker once knew everyone and could assess trustworthiness through relationship, the Trust OS makes that knowledge available at scale.

Vouching with skin in the game. For borderline cases, community members can vouch for applicants. This isn't a character reference letter—it's a verifiable commitment. Those who vouch for someone are aware when that person struggles. They're notified of potential defaults not to punish, but to help. Often, the person who vouched is exactly the right person to provide support—a connection, a lead, a bridge through difficulty. The vouching system creates accountability *and* a support network in a single mechanism.

This creates different underwriting. Not "Can this person be extracted from?" but "Is this person part of our community? Will they contribute? Can we support them if they struggle?"

When someone can't pay: Default triggers support, not punishment. The Trust OS flags early warning signs. Community members with relevant skills—financial counselors, job placement specialists—connect with the struggling household. Often, the problem can be solved before it becomes a crisis.

If default is unavoidable, the process is restorative. The borrower loses the home—this is real—but not their dignity, their future, or their ability to rebuild. No spiraling fees. No permanent credit destruction. No deficiency judgments. The principle: *The system absorbs the shock so the human doesn't break.*

Protecting What You've Built

The Family Trust doesn't just help you buy a home. It helps you keep it valuable.

Collective asset improvement. The Trust can coordinate improvements across the community—infrastructure upgrades, shared amenities, neighborhood beautification—that keep property values intact or growing. No single family bears the full cost. The expense is distributed through collective scale. What would be unaffordable for one household becomes manageable when spread across many.

This is the opposite of extraction, where value flows out of neighborhoods into corporate hands. In the Trust Economy, value created in the community stays in the community. Your home appreciates because the neighborhood appreciates. And the neighborhood appreciates because everyone is invested in its success.

Maintenance reserves. A portion of the community pool funds preventive maintenance and emergency repairs. Roof failing? Foundation issue? The Trust can help address problems before they become catastrophic—protecting both the homeowner and the community's shared asset base.

Why Investors Sleep Better Here

Investors ask: Isn't this risky? Actually, the opposite is true. Traditional lending is exposed to interest rate volatility, refinancing cliffs, credit market freezes, and banking liquidity mismatches. The Trust Economy avoids all of this. No interest means no rate exposure. Equity accrues immediately and continuously. Community trust dramatically lowers default rates. Risk decreases with every payment.

The value proposition: stable, long-duration assets with declining risk over time. Returns tied to real value creation, not extraction. ESG alignment without sacrifice—this isn't charity, it's better-designed finance.

One sentence: *Invest in a financial system where equity compounds without extraction, risk declines over time, and trust—not interest—is the growth engine.*

The traditional system is fragile because it's built on extraction. When extraction slows—during recessions, credit crunches, housing crashes—the whole thing seizes up. Banks fail. Families are destroyed.

The Trust Economy is antifragile. The more payments that come in, the stronger it gets. This isn't idealism. It's better engineering.

What Becomes Possible

Imagine a world where housing costs what housing costs.

Young families buy homes a decade earlier. They're building equity from the start instead of saving for a down payment while paying someone else's mortgage through rent.

Middle-aged families aren't trapped in jobs they hate because they can't afford to disrupt the mortgage. They have flexibility—to move for opportunity, downsize for simplicity, take risks that lead to growth.

Elderly families aren't equity-rich and cash-poor, unable to access the wealth they've built without selling the home they love. The Trust offers mechanisms to access equity while staying in place.

Communities stabilize. When families aren't one missed payment from disaster, neighborhoods hold together. Schools improve because families stay. Local businesses thrive because customers have money to spend. The social fabric strengthens because people aren't constantly churning.

The $700,000 that extraction would have taken stays in the community. It funds local businesses, education, healthcare, arts, infrastructure. It compounds locally instead of flowing to distant shareholders.

This isn't theoretical. Kiva.org has facilitated over $1.5 billion in zero-interest micro-loans with 96%+ repayment. Islamic finance has operated for centuries on profit-sharing models. Community land trusts provide affordable housing across America. The Family Trust builds on what these pioneers have proven.

The Mendez Family

Let me show you what this looks like in practice.

Elena and Carlos Mendez are both teachers. Combined income: $95,000. In the extraction economy, they can barely afford a $350,000 home—and even then, they're stretching.

Traditional path:

- $350,000 home at 7%: $2,329/month
- That's 29% of their gross income—on the edge of what's sustainable
- One medical emergency, one car breakdown, one job loss: they're underwater
- Total paid over 30 years: $840,000
- Interest to the bank: $490,000

Trust Economy path:

- Same $350,000 home at 0%: $972/month
- That's 12% of their income—stable, comfortable, room to breathe
- They have $1,357/month extra
- Total paid over 30 years: $350,000
- Interest to the bank: $0

What do Elena and Carlos do with that extra $1,357 every month?

Year 3: They've saved enough to start a tutoring business on the side. Carlos works with struggling math students. Elena helps kids with reading. The extra income accelerates their equity buildup.

Year 7: Their son wants to play travel soccer. In the extraction economy, they'd have to say no—too expensive. In the Trust Economy, they say yes. He makes friendships that last a lifetime. He learns discipline, teamwork, resilience.

Year 12: Elena's mother gets sick. Elena takes three months off to care for her. In the extraction economy, this would be a crisis—possibly leading to missed payments, damaged credit, the stress spiral. In the Trust Economy, they have savings. They have community support. They have a buffer built from twelve years of not being extracted from.

Year 20: Their son goes to college. They've been funding a 529 account with money that would have gone to interest. He graduates debt-free.

Year 30: They own their home outright. They've paid exactly what it cost. They have savings, investments, a tutoring business that's become a second career.

The home cost $350,000. They paid $350,000. The difference between this life and the extraction life? $490,000 that stayed in their family instead of flowing to shareholders who never knew their names.

The Question That Changes Everything

What would you do with an extra $1,900 per month?

Not someday. Not when you win the lottery. Right now, every month, for thirty years.

Would you work less? Spend more time with your children? Start the business you've been dreaming about? Travel? Give more generously?

The extraction economy takes that money and calls it "the cost of borrowing." The Trust Economy asks: Why should there be a cost for accessing what everyone needs?

Housing isn't a luxury. It's a foundation. And foundations shouldn't be designed to extract from the people standing on them.

We are worth fighting for. We are worth believing in.

The Family Trust is what happens when we finally design housing like that's true.

| 21 |

Chapter Twenty-One: Whole Health

"The doctor is the safety net. The other four are prevention."

I've seen versions of this story so many times it's become a pattern. Let me show you what I mean.

There's a woman—let's call her Rachel—who represents dozens of people I've known. The strong one. The person everyone leans on.

She runs a nonprofit. Raises three kids. Shows up for everyone. The person you call when things fall apart—she'll be there with food, or a plan, or just presence.

Then her husband leaves. Then her mother gets sick. Then the nonprofit loses its major funder. Three crises in six months, and Rachel—the strong one, the one who holds everyone else together—stops sleeping. Stops eating. Starts drinking a glass of wine to fall asleep, then two, then a bottle.

By the time anyone notices, she's drowning.

She doesn't need a hospital. She needs what she's been giving everyone else: someone to show up. Someone to ask how she's doing—really doing—before she shatters.

But the extraction economy doesn't provide that. It waits until you break—and then bills you for the privilege of putting you back together.

This chapter is about what happens when we build a system that does the opposite. What would health look like if the goal wasn't repair, but continuous human flourishing?

The Experiment We Already Ran

We've spent forty years squeezing every ounce of value out of people.

The results are in.

Deaths of despair have doubled since 2000. According to CDC data analyzed by the Joint Economic Committee, the rate rose from 22.7 per 100,000 Americans in 2000 to 45.8 per 100,000 by 2017—and it's continued climbing since. In 2022 alone, there were a record 49,369 suicide deaths in the United States. Anxiety and depression are at epidemic levels. Burnout is now a medical diagnosis—as if exhaustion from extraction were a personal failing instead of a predictable system outcome. Life expectancy is declining in the richest country on Earth. We're the only developed nation where this is happening.

The Surgeon General declared loneliness a public health crisis. It's as dangerous as smoking fifteen cigarettes a day. The opioid epidemic is self-medication for spiritual emptiness—people numbing pain that the system created and refuses to address.

Despair isn't a mystery. It's the bill we pay for forty years of treating humans like inputs.

We ran the experiment. Extraction produces broken humans. And broken humans can't build anything worth having.

So here's the question nobody's asking: What would happen if we poured life into people instead?

What Rachel Needed

Let me tell you what Rachel actually needed. Not what she got—what she needed.

She needed someone tracking her physical health. Not a gym membership she'd never use, but a person who knew her body, knew her patterns, would notice when she stopped moving and reach out. Someone who'd say: "You haven't worked out in three weeks. What's happening?"

She needed someone tracking her mental health. Not a therapist she'd see after a six-week wait once she'd already collapsed, but someone she talked to regularly—who'd notice her stress accumulating before it became a crisis. Someone processing grief with her in real time, not after it had calcified into depression.

She needed someone asking about her soul. Not religious instruction, but someone wondering: How's your purpose? How's your meaning? Are you living the life you actually want, or just surviving? Someone who'd notice when she started drifting and help her find the thread again.

She needed real food. Not takeout eaten standing over the sink at 10pm. Meals prepared with care, eaten in company, nourishment that built her up instead of just filling the hole.

And yes, she needed a doctor. But a doctor who knew her—who'd seen her whole story, who could recognize that her insomnia and weight loss and elevated cortisol were connected, who had time to diagnose rather than just prescribe.

The extraction economy gave her none of this. It gave her a seven-minute appointment and a prescription for Ambien.

Rachel didn't fail. The system failed its most generous member.

The Five Stems of Whole Health

(Four prevent; one catches.)

What Rachel needed has a name: Whole Health. Not healthcare—which implies you're already sick. Health as continuous investment in human flourishing.

It rests on five stems.

Physical. Your body's capacity to move, sleep, heal, and carry you through life.

Currently, personal trainers cost $80-150 per hour—invisible to everyone except the wealthy. But bodies that don't move break down. The extraction economy waits for the breakdown, then sells you surgery, physical therapy, pain medication. Prevention would cost a fraction of repair. But prevention doesn't generate the same revenue.

Mental. Your mind's capacity to process emotion, regulate anxiety, and heal from wounds before they harden into personality.

The extraction economy treats therapy as a luxury. You suffer in silence until you can't function, then—if you're lucky enough to have insurance—you see a therapist who barely knows your name. By then, the damage is deep. Healing becomes excavation instead of care.

Spiritual. Your soul's capacity for meaning, purpose, and alignment with your own values.

Most modern suffering isn't physical or mental—it's existential. It's the ache of a life lived without a "why."

This isn't religion—it's meaning-making, and humans wither without it. The opioid epidemic isn't just about pain management—it's people numbing an emptiness that nobody helped them address. "How's your soul today?" isn't a luxury question. It's preventive care for the part of you that makes life worth living.

The primary role of spiritual guides isn't to provide answers or enforce doctrine. It's simpler and more profound than that: to help people remember and hold their dignity. This is the first work—the foundation everything else rests on. Before someone can address their physical health or mental health or nutrition, they need to know they're worth the effort. They need to believe, at some fundamental level, that their existence matters.

The extraction economy strips this away. It tells you that you're worth what you produce. That your value is your output. That when your usefulness declines, so does your dignity.

The spiritual guide's job is to keep whispering the truth: You are not your productivity. You are not your utility. You are a human being with inherent worth, and that worth doesn't fluctuate with market conditions.

Nutritional. Your table's capacity to nourish rather than addict, to connect rather than isolate.

Food is the first medicine, so extraction turned it into the first assault. You can't pour life into people while feeding them industrial poison. The result of extraction food: chronic disease as default. Diabetes, heart disease, obesity—all fed by an industry that profits from your sickness. The common table replaces the lonely meal eaten standing over the sink.

Medical. Your healing when the other four aren't enough—a doctor who actually knows you.

Medicine only works when time does.

When the four prevention stems are working—when people are moving, processing emotions, finding meaning, eating real food—they need the doctor less often. And when they do need the doctor, there's time. Relationships that span years. Caseloads that allow actual medicine instead of endless triage.

Four stems of prevention. One safety net of healing.

The doctor is the safety net. The other four are prevention. Design a system where most people never need the safety net, and the safety net can actually catch the ones who do.

The Market Already Knows

Here's the thing: people are already desperate for this.

The coaching industry has exploded. In 2019, there were 71,000 professional coaches worldwide. By 2024, that number exceeded 145,000—more than doubled in five years. The global coaching market hit $6.25 billion in 2024 and is projected to reach $7.3 billion by 2025. Health and wellness coaching is growing fastest, at nearly 12% annually.

This isn't a trend. It's a signal. Millions of people are paying $100-300 per hour for someone to help them move, process emotions, find meaning, and stay accountable. They're doing it because the extraction economy doesn't provide it—and they know they need it.

BetterUp, a coaching platform, reached a $4.7 billion valuation. Noom built a billion-dollar business around accountability for health goals. Social media is flooded with fitness coaches, life coaches, wellness coaches, spiritual coaches—some credentialed, many not, all filling a void that shouldn't exist.

The market is proving the thesis of this chapter: humans need support systems. They need people who know them, track them, hold them accountable, catch them before they fall. The wealthy have always had this. Everyone else is now paying whatever they can for fragments of it.

But here's what the market can't solve: access.

Coaching at $150 per hour is a luxury. The people who need it most—the isolated, the struggling, the ones one crisis away from collapse—can't afford it. The market responds to demand backed by dollars, not demand backed by need.

Whole Health makes universal what the coaching industry sells to the few. Same support, same accountability, same human connection—but designed as infrastructure, not luxury. The coach who charges $150/hour in the extraction economy earns her living in the Trust Economy serving thirty people instead of the five who can afford her rates.

The demand is proven. The need is obvious. The only question is access.

The Coach I Never Had

I think about my twenties sometimes. The breakdown I described earlier in this book—the moment at 23 when I couldn't get out of bed, when the noise in my head drowned everything else out.

What if I'd had a physical coach then? Someone who noticed I wasn't moving, wasn't sleeping—and reached out before I collapsed?

What if I'd had a mental health practitioner? Someone I talked to regularly, who might have noticed the depression building before it flattened me?

What if I'd had a spiritual guide? Someone asking: "Why are you running so hard? What are you running toward—or away from?"

Thankfully, I had my family. They carried me through the dark days—showed up when I couldn't show up for myself, held the line when I was ready to let go. My parents, my siblings, my wife. They were my safety net, even when they didn't know it.

But not everyone has even that.

My breakdown lasted months. The recovery took years. And the whole time, I kept thinking: this didn't have to happen. If someone had been watching. If someone had asked. If the system was designed to catch people before they fell instead of billing them after they shattered.

We need a safety net that keeps people from spiraling—not just family members who happen to notice, but a system designed to notice. Because the families are getting stretched too thin. Because some people don't have families. Because love isn't a substitute for infrastructure, even when it's the only thing keeping someone alive.

So let me show you someone who has what I didn't have.

Marcus

Most people can't picture what Whole Health looks like in practice. So let me make it real.

Marcus is 34, a product manager for a tech company. He lives alone in a small apartment, the kind of person who used to fall through every crack—no family nearby, introverted enough that weeks could pass without meaningful connection. In the extraction economy, he'd be a statistic waiting to happen.

But Marcus has a safety net.

At 6:30 AM, he meets his physical coach for a workout. Her name is Dana, a former physical therapist who now works with a caseload of thirty people she actually knows. The workout is hard—designed for Marcus's goals, calibrated to his body. Dana knows about the shoulder injury from two years ago; she adjusts the overhead press accordingly. She notices he's been favoring his left side and asks about it. Turns out he's been stressed, carrying tension. She makes a note to mention it to his mental health practitioner.

Marcus leaves energized, not depleted. This is what movement feels like when someone's paying attention.

At noon, lunch at the community kitchen. Ethiopian food today, prepared by Almaz, a grandmother who learned the cuisine from her mother in Addis Ababa and now teaches the whole neighborhood. Marcus helped with prep last week—his contribution for the month. Today he just eats, sitting with two neighbors he's gotten to know over shared meals. The conversation is free. The loneliness that used to define his evenings has slowly dissolved.

At 4 PM, weekly check-in with his mental health practitioner, James. Nothing's in crisis—they're processing Marcus's father's death from six months ago. Small doses of grief, metabolized regularly, instead of pain that calcifies into depression. James noticed the tension Dana flagged; they talk about what's underneath it. Marcus realizes he's been avoiding a decision about his career. They don't solve it today, but he leaves knowing what he needs to think about.

At 6 PM, his spiritual coach calls. Her name is Sister Teresa—not a nun, just a woman who chose the title because it amused her. "How's your soul today?" Marcus admits he's been feeling untethered—questioning whether his work matters. They talk about purpose, alignment, what he actually wants to build. Teresa doesn't give answers; she asks better questions. Her primary job isn't to tell Marcus what to believe—it's to help him remember his own worth when the world makes him forget. By the end, Marcus has articulated something he didn't know he was thinking: he wants to design things that help people, not just things that sell.

At 8 PM, his doctor sends a message through the Trust OS. Dr. Okonkwo has been his physician for three years—long enough to know his patterns, his family history, his tendency to ignore symptoms until they become problems. Blood work from last week shows vitamin D deficiency—common for people who work indoors. Supplement recommendation. Suggestion to add outdoor time to his physical routine. Dana is already notified; she'll adjust his program.

This is integrated care. Five stems working together. Nothing in crisis. Everything in relationship.

Marcus isn't rich. He's a product manager earning his living like everyone else. But he has access to what the wealthy have always had: people who know him, track him, support him, catch him before he falls.

The extraction economy would have left Marcus alone until he broke. The Trust Economy surrounds him with connection—and in doing so, makes breaking almost impossible.

The Work Itself

We've been taught that the real economy is factories, code, and capital. But the real economy has always been people.

Here's what the extraction economy completely missed: supporting each other's growth is the work.

The Trust Economy creates millions of jobs in human flourishing. Physical coaches helping people build strong bodies. Mental health practitioners supporting emotional regulation. Spiritual guides helping people remember their dignity. Food workers growing, preparing, and serving real nourishment. Doctors with time to actually heal.

These aren't charity positions. They're infrastructure—and they're compensated accordingly.

In the extraction economy, care work is underpaid and undervalued. Nurses burn out. Teachers quit. Social workers drown. The people who hold society together are treated as costs to minimize.

In the Trust Economy, care work is essential—and compensated accordingly.

And here's the economics that makes it possible: prevention is cheaper than crisis. Every dollar invested in keeping people healthy saves multiples in emergency care, lost productivity, broken families, incarceration. We already spend the money. We just spend it backward—on crisis instead of prevention, on consequences instead of causes.

When a physical coach helps someone avoid back surgery, the system saves $50,000. When a mental health practitioner helps someone process grief before it becomes addiction, the system saves a life. When real food prevents diabetes, the system saves decades of medication and complications.

The math works. It always did. The extraction economy just couldn't see it—because prevention doesn't generate quarterly returns, and healing doesn't have a stock price.

Why Whole Health Compounds

Extraction creates a downward spiral. Squeeze people until they break. Spend fortunes on crisis care. Squeeze harder to cover the cost. More breakage. More crisis. Repeat.

Investment creates an upward spiral. Pour life into people. They thrive. They contribute more. More resources become available. Pour more life. Everyone rises.

The return on investing in human health isn't just health statistics. It's human capacity. Healthy parents have patience for their children—who grow up regulated, capable, contributing. Healthy workers have creativity instead of burnout. Healthy neighbors have energy for community.

Pour life into people and they pour life back into the system. Not because you forced them. Because they have something to give.

Forty Years of Pouring

Forty years of squeezing produced an epidemic of despair. Deaths doubled. Life expectancy declined. Loneliness became a public health crisis.

What would forty years of pouring produce?

We don't have to guess entirely. We have glimpses—communities that invested in their people, societies that prioritized flourishing over extraction. We know what happens when children grow up with support instead of scarcity. We know what happens when workers have meaning instead of just metrics. We know what happens when elders are valued instead of warehoused.

But we've never tried it at scale. We've never asked: What if an entire society decided that human flourishing was the point? What if we measured success not by GDP but by how many people were thriving? What if we poured into people the way we've poured into corporations?

Imagine forty years of that.

Children who grow up with all five stems in place—physical health supported, emotions processed, meaning cultivated, nourishment provided, medical care available. They become adults who don't need to spend their twenties recovering from their childhoods. They enter the world whole.

Those adults become parents who can give their children the same foundation. The cycle compounds upward instead of downward. Each generation stronger than the last, not from accumulated wealth but from accumulated wholeness.

The elders who emerge from this system aren't depleted. They're full. They have wisdom to share, energy to contribute, purpose to pursue. Instead of being warehoused, they become the spiritual guides for the next generation—the ones who help young people remember their dignity because they've spent a lifetime holding their own.

Forty years of extraction consumed the human capital that made society possible.

Forty years of investment would produce human capital we can barely imagine—people so coherent, so whole, so full of life that they create value effortlessly because they have so much to give.

Rachel Today

Rachel—or rather, the many Rachels I've known—didn't get the system I'm describing. But some of them got pieces of it—through community, through friends who finally noticed, through therapists they could barely afford but desperately needed.

It took years for them to stabilize. Years of rebuilding what should never have broken in the first place.

What would have happened if they'd had a physical coach noticing their bodies shutting down? A mental health practitioner they talked to before the crisis? A spiritual guide reminding them of their worth? A community kitchen where they ate with people instead of alone? A doctor who knew their story?

They wouldn't have needed years. They might not have needed anything but the support that should have been there all along.

The extraction economy waits until you break, then bills you for the repair.

The Trust Economy pours life into you from the start.

The doctor is the safety net. The other four are prevention.

Build that, and people like Rachel don't have to be strong until they shatter.

They get to be human—fully, safely, without breaking first.

| 22 |

Chapter Twenty-Two: Universal Luxury

"Luxury proved excellence could be crafted. The Trust Economy proves it can be shared."

In a workshop outside Paris, a woman named Marie-Claire is stitching a handbag.

She's been at it for thirty-two hours now—spread across eight days, four hours at a time. The leather is calf skin, tanned for eighteen months before it reached her workbench. The thread is linen, waxed by hand. The needle moves in a rhythm she learned from her mother, who learned it from hers.

Marie-Claire is an artisan at Hermes. The bag she's making—a Birkin—will sell for $40,000. Some versions, in exotic leathers, sell for ten times that.

Here's what nobody tells you: the bag costs about $2,500 to make.

The leather: $300-500. The hardware: $100. Marie-Claire's labor, at her fully-loaded salary: $1,600. Overhead, logistics, quality control: another $400.

Total: roughly $2,500. Retail: $40,000. The markup is 16x.

What accounts for the difference? Not quality—the quality is in the $2,500. Not craftsmanship—Marie-Claire's hands are in the $2,500. Not materials—the leather and thread are in the $2,500.

The difference is scarcity. Artificial, manufactured, protected scarcity. Hermes produces fewer bags than people want to buy. They maintain waitlists. They cultivate mystique. They charge not for the object but for the exclusivity of owning it.

This is the economics of luxury: 10% product, 90% story.

The 90% story is pure overhead—marketing, mystique, manufactured scarcity. It adds no value to the object itself. Strip away the story, keep the craftsmanship, and excellence becomes affordable. This is the efficiency thesis applied to quality: the gap between what luxury costs to make and what it sells for represents the cost of a low-trust economy that needs exclusivity to signal worth. In the Trust Economy, the product speaks for itself.

And it raises a question nobody in the luxury industry wants you to ask:

What if we kept the quality, removed the scarcity—and made excellence the default instead of the exception?

The Hermes Proof

Hermes isn't a scam. The bags are genuinely excellent. Marie-Claire's craftsmanship is real, her training rigorous, her standards uncompromising. A Birkin bag will last decades. The quality is, in a meaningful sense, worth paying for.

But the price isn't about quality. The price is about exclusivity—about signaling, about belonging to a club others can't enter.

Economists call this a Veblen good: demand increases as the price rises because the price itself is the point.

Hermes knows this. They could train more artisans. They could open more workshops. They could produce ten times as many bags without sacrificing an ounce of quality. Marie-Claire's techniques can be taught. The materials can be sourced. The infrastructure can scale.

They don't, because scarcity is the product. Exclusion is the feature they're selling, not the flaw they're fixing.

But the proof is in the production cost. For $2,500, you can have Hermes-level quality. You just can't have Hermes-level exclusivity.

The question is: which one do you actually want?

Here's the alchemical reframe: Hermes isn't the problem. Hermes is the proof.

They proved that six generations of accumulated craft can produce genuine excellence. They proved that training matters, that standards matter, that refusing to cut corners creates objects of lasting value. They proved that people will pay for quality when they can trust it's real.

What they haven't proved—because it wasn't their job to prove—is that this excellence has to be exclusive. That was a business choice, not a necessity. The craft exists. The training works. The quality is achievable. Hermes showed us what's possible. Now we ask: what if everyone could have it?

The Math of Abundance

Let me show you what happens at scale.

Hermes employs about 3,000 artisans. They produce roughly one million leather goods per year—bags, belts, small accessories. Each artisan, working on high-end pieces, might complete 200-300 items annually.

Now imagine this: instead of 3,000 artisans, you train 100,000. Not to make knockoffs or dupes, but genuine luxury-quality goods with the same techniques, the same standards, the same care.

What changes:

Material costs drop 30-50% with bulk purchasing. Hardware costs drop 50-80% at scale. Training costs amortize across a larger base. Robotics handle precision cutting and repetitive tasks—not replacing artisans, but freeing them to focus on the finishing work where human touch matters.

What stays the same:

Quality. Time. Care.

The result:

Hermes-level craftsmanship for $400-900 per item.

The exact numbers will move around, but the direction is undeniable: scale pushes the cost of excellence down, not up.

This isn't theoretical. It's arithmetic. The luxury industry has proven that excellence can be produced—they just choose to restrict access. Remove the restriction, and the math changes.

A $40,000 bag becomes a $600 bag. A $500/night hotel room becomes a $90/night room. A $300 Michelin-starred meal becomes a $25 meal.

The quality doesn't drop. The exclusivity does.

What Scarcity Actually Costs

The extraction economy loves artificial scarcity. It's the engine of luxury pricing, pharmaceutical patents, housing markets, concert tickets. Restrict supply below demand, and prices explode.

But scarcity has costs that don't show up on the balance sheet.

When handbags cost $40,000, they become signals of status rather than objects of use. Owning one says nothing about your taste and everything about your bank account. The object is hollowed out—reduced to a symbol of exclusion.

When quality is restricted to the wealthy, the middle class gets worse products. Not because excellence is expensive, but because excellence is hoarded. The gap between what rich people experience and what everyone else experiences widens—not from any natural law, but from artificial gates.

When scarcity is the business model, companies optimize for maintaining scarcity rather than improving quality. Why make a better bag when you can make a more exclusive one? Why serve more people when serving fewer is more profitable?

This is the Idiot Index applied to luxury: a massive gap between what it costs to make something and what we charge for it—filled not with added value, but with artificial restriction.

The Trust Economy makes a different choice.

Excellence as Default

Here's the vision: excellence as baseline, not exception.

Not cheap goods for the masses and premium goods for the few. Premium goods for everyone—because premium is achievable when you remove the extraction.

I call this Universal Luxury. Not luxury as exclusion, but luxury as standard.

What does it look like?

The handbag you carry is stitched by a trained artisan, from quality leather, designed to last twenty years. It costs $500. You can afford it because nobody's charging you $39,500 for exclusivity.

The home you live in is built with care—quality materials, thoughtful design, durability as a feature. It costs what a home costs, not what a status symbol costs, because the Family Trust—our shared capital pool—doesn't extract interest and developers don't optimize for scarcity.

The meal you eat is prepared by someone who cares, from real ingredients, served in a space designed for pleasure. It costs $25 because the restaurant isn't paying Manhattan rents to signal exclusivity and the food system isn't extracting at every step.

The healthcare you receive comes from a doctor who knows your name, with time to diagnose rather than just prescribe. It's funded by a system that invests in health rather than extracting from sickness.

The education your children get is designed by masters, delivered by teachers with small classes and real resources. It's available to everyone because education isn't a scarcity game.

This isn't fantasy. Every element of this exists somewhere—for people who can afford to pay the exclusivity premium. The question is whether we can deliver it to everyone.

The math says yes. Hermes proved it.

What Universal Luxury Feels Like

Let me show you a morning.

You wake up in a bedroom designed by someone who thought about how light enters a space. The mattress is quality—not the $4,000 luxury brand, but the same materials and construction for $500 because nobody's charging you for the label. The sheets are linen, manufactured at scale by a cooperative that pays fair wages. They cost $120, not $600, because the supply chain doesn't have seven middlemen extracting at each step.

You walk to your kitchen. The countertops are real stone, not laminate pretending to be stone—because quality materials at scale cost 80% less than quality materials as luxury goods. The coffee maker is built to last fifteen years, designed for durability instead of planned obsolescence.

Your breakfast: eggs from a local farm networked through the community food system. Bread from the community kitchen, baked that morning. Fruit that's actually ripe, because it wasn't shipped 3,000 miles to optimize for shelf life over taste. It's better than most $50 hotel breakfasts because nobody's paying for the chandelier in the lobby.

You dress for work. The shirt is cotton, well-made, from a workshop that trains artisans the way Hermes does—seriously, rigorously, with pride in craft. It cost $60. The shoes are leather, resoleable, built for five years of daily wear. They cost $200. In the extraction economy, this level of quality starts at $500 for the shirt, $800 for the shoes. The difference isn't quality—it's extraction.

This is Universal Luxury. Not a lower standard of living. A higher standard, at a lower price, because the price includes only what it costs to make things well—not what it costs to make things exclusive.

The Market Nobody's Serving

Here's a number the luxury industry doesn't want you to think about: $2-4 trillion.

The current luxury market is about $400 billion globally. Fashion, leather goods, beauty, travel, consumer goods. It serves maybe 50 million people worldwide—the wealthy who can afford the exclusivity premium.

But there are 3.2 billion people in the global middle class. People who want quality, appreciate craft, and would pay fair prices for excellent goods. They're currently served by a market that offers two options: cheap and disposable, or expensive and exclusive.

Universal Luxury creates a third option: premium quality at rational prices. If even 10% of the global middle class buys in, that's a market ten times larger than current luxury.

The opportunity isn't taking customers from Hermes. It's serving the billions of people Hermes ignores.

The extraction economy asks: How do we maintain exclusivity?

The Trust Economy asks: How do we scale excellence?

Different questions lead to different worlds.

Dynamic Scarcity

Now, here's the nuance: people don't just pay for quality. They pay for belonging. For story. For the feeling of owning something special.

Universal Luxury doesn't ignore this—it redesigns it.

Instead of artificial scarcity based on price, create honest scarcity based on craft. Limited batches. Numbered editions. Artisan signatures. Not because you're restricting access, but because each piece is genuinely individual.

The first batch of a new design: $400. The collector's variant with hand-dyed leather: $800. The anniversary edition signed by the artisan: $1,200.

Premiums of 2-3x, not 20-30x. Scarcity that's real—this batch is actually limited because Marie-Claire only made fifty—rather than manufactured.

Every item comes with its story: who made it, when, how. A production number. An artisan signature. Public verification on a ledger anyone can check. Fakes become irrelevant because authenticity is built in.

This preserves the emotional value of ownership without the extraction. You can feel special owning something limited and pay a fair price. The specialness comes from craft, not from excluding others.

Compare this to the extraction model: same bag, same cost to produce, $40,000 price tag, waitlist of two years, artificial scarcity maintained specifically to justify the markup.

Dynamic scarcity aligns incentives with craft. The extraction model aligns incentives with restriction. Same product. Radically different philosophy.

The Trust Economy Is a Product

Here's the connection I want you to see.

Hermes built a six-generation trust network. Three thousand artisans who treat craft as sacred. Zero shortcuts. Long-term thinking. A lineage of excellence that compounds across decades.

People pay 16x more because they're not buying a bag. They're buying a family's promise.

The Trust Economy does the same thing—not for bags, but for human experience itself.

What if we treated housing with the care Hermes treats leather? What if we treated healthcare with the rigor Hermes applies to stitching? What if we treated food, education, safety, belonging with the same commitment to excellence—and the same refusal to cut corners?

That's what the Trust Economy builds. A culture of care. Stewards of human flourishing. Members of a story that will outlast any of us.

When you join the Trust Economy, you're not just accessing better goods at better prices. You're joining a family. A multi-generational project to prove that excellence doesn't require exclusion. That quality can scale. That the premium human experience—the one currently reserved for the wealthy—can become the default for everyone.

The bar isn't Gucci. The bar is love embedded.

What would it look like if every product, every service, every interaction you encountered was designed with love? Not love as sentiment—love as engineering specification. Love as the requirement that this thing, whatever it is, should make the person using it more alive rather than less.

That's what Marie-Claire embeds in every stitch. That's what Hermes has scaled to three thousand artisans. That's what the Trust Economy scales to everyone.

The extraction economy asks: What can we get away with?

The Trust Economy asks: What would love build?

When love is the design principle, excellence follows naturally. We don't cut corners when we care about the person on the other end. We don't extract when we're trying to serve. We don't manipulate when our goal is genuine flourishing.

What Was Always Possible

The extraction economy taught us that quality is scarce. That excellence must be earned by wealth. That the price of beautiful things is exclusion.

This was a lie. A profitable lie, but a lie.

Quality was never scarce. Access was restricted.

Marie-Claire's skills can be taught. The leather can be sourced. The workshops can be built. Everything Hermes does, a hundred thousand artisans could do—if the goal was abundance rather than exclusivity.

The same is true for every domain we've discussed in this book. Housing could be affordable and beautiful if we removed the extraction. Healthcare could be excellent and universal if we designed for flourishing instead of profit. Food could be nourishing and delicious if the system optimized for health instead of addiction.

Scarcity was a choice. Abundance is also a choice.

The Trust Economy chooses abundance.

The Ultimate Product Experience

The ultimate product experience is the mark of a craftsman. It's the love poured into the creative contribution process. And when it happens, the customer loves the experience. And that's when investors have created the highest ROI.

Imagine you're living inside a product as carefully crafted as a Hermes bag.

Every interaction is designed with intention. The neighborhood you live in was planned for connection, not just density. The work you do is meaningful, not just profitable. The food you eat nourishes rather than depletes. The relationships you have are supported by systems that encourage trust. The safety net catches you when you fall—without destroying you in the process.

This is Universal Luxury: not a product you buy, but a product you live inside—a whole environment designed with the same care usually reserved for a few objects in a rich person's closet.

Marie-Claire spends thirty-two hours on a single bag because she believes excellence matters. She works slowly, deliberately, because rushing would betray six generations of accumulated trust. Every stitch carries the weight of her family's reputation—and her own pride in work done well.

The Trust Economy applies that belief to civilization itself.

Housing built with the intention that people deserve beautiful places to live. Healthcare delivered with the assumption that every person deserves attention. Food prepared with the understanding that nourishment is a form of respect. Work designed with the recognition that human time is sacred.

Excellence as default. Quality as baseline. Care as the operating system.

Not for some. For everyone.

Luxury proved that excellence could be crafted—that humans, given time and training and purpose, could create things of genuine beauty and lasting value.

The Trust Economy proves it doesn't have to be reserved for the few. It proves excellence can be shared.

The Ultimate Luxury: Loyalty

We've walked through the morning. The bedroom designed for light. The kitchen built for decades. The breakfast that tastes like care.

But none of it matters without the final element: Loyalty.

Here's what loyalty actually is: agreement that no longer needs to be questioned. It assumes trust—and in that assumption, creates depth that extraction economics can never manufacture.

When loyalty exists, you don't comparison shop. You don't read the fine print. You simply return—because you know they will do right by you. The friction evaporates. What remains is relationship.

Companies that do the best thing for the customer win in the end. The Trust Economy makes loyalty the most profitable strategy.

How Loyalty Creates Flow

People spend their money with people they trust. This sounds obvious until you realize what it means economically.

Loyalty eliminates friction.

Every transaction with someone loyal costs less—in time, in attention, in emotional energy, in actual dollars. We don't need the warranty because we trust the repair. We don't need the contract because we trust the handshake. We don't need the backup plan because we trust the follow-through.

Loyalty comes from long-term value. Not a single great experience, but consistent delivery over time. It's showing up, again and again, in ways that prove your word means something. Loyalty isn't given—it's earned. Earned over years. Over decades. Earned through a thousand small moments where you could have extracted but chose instead to invest.

That's why loyalty has weight. It's solidified trust—compressed by time into something dense and real. When you have someone's loyalty, you have something that took years to build and can withstand almost anything.

Flow at Epic Scale

Here's the vision that makes the Trust Economy not just possible, but probable:

Imagine a world where loyalty is the default—where your relationship with your grocer, your doctor, your neighbors, your workplace all operate on the same foundational trust. Where agreement is unquestioned because it has been proven, repeatedly, across time.

This is flow at an epic scale.

Not the flow of a single transaction—the flow of an entire life. Resources moving without resistance. Relationships deepening without defense. Community building without calculation.

The Real Luxury

I keep coming back to this image: enjoying life with the people around you. Doing things with your neighbors and friends. Not performing success for strangers on the internet—but sharing dinner with people who know your name, your story, your struggles.

This is what Universal Luxury actually looks like when it's complete.

The handbag matters because it represents care—someone's thirty-two hours of attention transformed into something you carry every day. The home matters because it represents shelter—not just from weather, but from the chaos of a world that demands constant vigilance. The meal matters because it represents nourishment—someone caring enough to make something that makes you feel alive.

But all of it—every beautiful object, every thoughtful service, every carefully crafted experience—finds its meaning in the relationships where it's shared.

The ultimate luxury isn't owning beautiful things.

It's living among people you trust completely. It's waking up in a community where loyalty flows in every direction—where you can count on others and they can count on you. It's the peace that comes when agreement is unquestioned because trust has been proven ten thousand times.

The Trust Economy makes this possible.

Luxury proved that excellence could be crafted.

The Trust Economy proves it can be shared—with everyone, everywhere, as the foundation of how we live together.

That's the crescendo.

That's the world worth building.

| 23 |

Chapter Twenty-Three: The Path to Scale

"A journey of a thousand miles begins with a single step."—Lao Tzu

Vision without a path is just poetry. So let me show you the path.

This book has described an alternative to extraction capitalism—a trust-based economy where contribution replaces accumulation, where dignity is infrastructure, where the goal is human flourishing instead of shareholder returns. Some readers might assume that means we're trying to replace the entire global economy at once.

That's not the plan. That's not how change works.

The path is local first.

The Math of Movement

Let me give you the numbers—because vision without arithmetic is just poetry.

I spent twenty-five years in Silicon Valley watching products succeed or fail based on adoption curves. The pattern is consistent: below a certain density, you're pushing a boulder uphill. Above it, gravity works for you.

For a city of one million adults, approximately $50 million over three years seeds critical mass. That funds four things:

Platform and operations ($25-40 million): The infrastructure—payments, identity, reputation tracking, community coordination. Not exotic technology; variations of systems that already exist, configured for trust instead of extraction.

Consumer acquisition ($5-15 million): Getting 200,000 adults actively participating—that's our 20% target. Mission-driven adoption, where existing members recruit friends and family, drops cost to $25-80 per participant. People don't join because of advertising; they join because someone they trust invited them.

Merchant acquisition ($2-6 million): Onboarding 10,000 small businesses. The pitch: lower transaction fees than credit cards, more loyal customers, community visibility.

Guarantee pool ($15-20 million): A trust backstop that de-risks early transactions. Leveraged 3-5x, this pool can support $60-100 million in guaranteed obligations—enough to lubricate the system until network effects take over.

By Year 4, the system is self-sustaining.

Here's the arithmetic: if 200,000 users spend even $300 per month in-network, that's $720 million in annual transaction volume. Capture 2-3% that currently goes to credit cards and you've created $15-22 million in recurring revenue—enough to fund ongoing operations, expand to new neighborhoods, and begin replicating in adjacent cities.

We know this pattern works. WIR in Switzerland has self-sustained for ninety years on transaction fees alone. M-Pesa turned profitable within three years of launch. UPI processes trillions of rupees annually on infrastructure that cost a fraction of traditional banking. The economics work. The patterns are proven. The only variable is execution.

When we rebuilt these numbers assuming trust instead of distrust, the costs dropped by thirty percent. I'll show you the detailed math in Chapter 24.

The Scaling Sequence

One city. One community reaching 20% adoption. One proof point demonstrating that the math works, the architecture holds, the trust compounds. That's Year One through Year Four.

Then: replication.

The second city learns from the first. The third learns from both. Each implementation generates data—what worked, what didn't, what needs adjustment for different cultures, different economic conditions, different legal environments. The model evolves through iteration, not theory.

Then: connection.

Cities that have reached critical mass can interoperate. Your trust score, earned in Denver, is legible in Austin. Your Unity Tokens, accumulated in Portland, spend in Phoenix. The perimeters connect. Not through centralized control—through shared protocols, the same way email works across different providers.

This is how networks grow. The internet didn't start by replacing all communication at once. It started with a few nodes, proved the concept, connected the nodes, and expanded until the old system became the exception rather than the rule.

The honest truth: Global scale is aspirational, not immediate.

Can the Trust Economy eventually replace extraction capitalism worldwide? I believe so. The efficiency argument is too strong. The data from high-trust societies is too consistent. The convergence forces we discussed earlier are too powerful.

But that's a generation-scale vision, not a quarterly target.

What I'm proposing for the next five years is more modest: Can we create the conditions where a trust-based economy has the opportunity to thrive?

This is the trial optimization question. We know high-trust systems outperform low-trust systems in virtually every study. We know the Nordic countries, the MondragÃƒ³n cooperatives, the WIR network have sustained for decades or generations. We know the architecture I've described is built from components that already work.

What we don't know is whether we can seed it successfully in the current environment—whether the extraction economy's gravity is too strong, whether the cultural conditions are too hostile, whether the timing is wrong.

There's only one way to find out.

The Pioneer Question

So let me answer it directly: Why would anyone join before the network effects exist?

This is the cold-start problem. Every new system faces it. The value of a telephone depends on other people having telephones. The value of a currency depends on others accepting that currency. The value of a trust network depends on others in the network to trust.

The honest answer is that early adopters take on risk. They join before the proof is in, before the infrastructure is mature, before the network has reached the density that makes participation easy. They sacrifice comfort that later participants won't have to sacrifice.

So why would anyone do this?

The same reason anyone has ever built anything new.

The abolitionists didn't wait for slavery to become unpopular. They organized when opposing slavery meant social exile, economic punishment, sometimes violence. They weren't joining a winning movement. They were building one—knowing they might not live to see it succeed.

The suffragettes didn't wait for women's voting to poll well. They marched, were arrested, went on hunger strikes, were force-fed in prison. They weren't riding a wave. They were creating one—accepting costs that later generations of women wouldn't have to pay.

The early internet adopters didn't wait for the web to be useful. They tolerated dial-up connections, ugly interfaces, limited content, and the mockery of people who thought email was a toy. They weren't joining a mature ecosystem. They were seeding one—doing the awkward early work that made everything after possible.

Every transformational system in history started with people who believed in something before it was proven. That's not naivety. That's how change happens.

The pioneers of the Trust Economy will be the same.

They won't join because the system is already working. They'll join because the current system has already failed them. Because they've done the survival math at 2:47 in the morning and they're tired. Because they've watched the extraction economy hollow out their communities, their industries, their hope—and they're ready to build something else.

They'll join not as consumers selecting the best product, but as founders building the world they want to live in.

The Crypto Lesson

Here's something the early adopters can learn from cryptocurrency.

Whatever you think of Bitcoin or the broader crypto ecosystem, they proved something important: you can bootstrap a new economic system from zero. In 2009, Bitcoin was worthless—literally, people were trading thousands of coins for a pizza. The early miners were taking pure risk on an unproven concept.

But the system was designed to reward that risk. Early miners got more coins when mining was hard. Early adopters accumulated value that later participants couldn't access at the same price. The structure recognized that pioneers deserve compensation for pioneering.

The Trust Economy applies the same principle—but aligned to contribution instead of speculation.

Seed capital for early communities: The first participants don't just join a system; they receive resources to experiment with. Initial token grants, guaranteed basic income during the transition period, access to the guarantee pool. We're not asking people to take pure risk—we're investing in them as they invest in us.

Ground-floor recognition: Those contributing early and consistently are recognized in ways that later participants won't be. Not through financial windfalls that create new extraction—but through permanent trust score bonuses, governance voice, and the knowledge that they built the foundation. When the network reaches scale, the pioneers will be honored as founders, not forgotten as early customers.

Skin in the game, both directions: Early adopters commit to the system. But the system commits to them too. The guarantee pool exists specifically to ensure that pioneering doesn't mean suffering. If someone joins early and the local network doesn't reach critical mass, they're not abandoned—they're supported through the transition.

This is different from crypto's "get rich or lose everything" model. It's designed for sustainable growth, not speculative bubbles. But it recognizes the same truth: early adoption is investment, and investment deserves returns.

The Actual Constraint

The primary obstacle is not one of resources or money.

Read that again, because it contradicts everything we've been taught about change. If everybody had zero dollars tomorrow—no currency, no accounts, no accumulated wealth—we could still make the Trust Economy work. We'd have the same hands, the same minds, the same capacity to grow food and build shelter and care for each other. The money was never the constraint.

The constraint is neuroscience.

How fast can you change the operating system that runs your life?

Not your conscious beliefs. Not your stated values. The operating system—the one embedded in your subconscious, handed down through generations, that runs automatically deciding what's safe and what's threat, who to trust and who to fear.

That operating system was designed for a world that no longer exists. Your great-great-grandparents needed to scan for predators.

Your nervous system still does. Your ancestors survived famine by hoarding. Your body still signals scarcity when you check your bank balance. A hundred thousand years of evolution optimized for survival in hostile environments—and that code is still running, right now, even as you read this.

That's the timeline that matters. Not how fast we can build the platform. How fast we can update the firmware.

The Shift

So how do we shift?

Not through argument. We can't logic our way out of a nervous system response. The body doesn't understand PowerPoint slides. It understands experience.

The shift happens when safety becomes felt, not understood.

Here's what that looks like: We take a risk—a small one. We trust someone with something that matters. And they don't betray us. Our nervous system notices. The data point lands not in our mind but in our body: that worked.

Repeat. A slightly larger risk. Another successful trust exchange. Another data point. The pattern builds. The nervous system updates its threat assessment, not because we told it to, but because experience proved the new model.

This is how trauma heals. Not through understanding—through corrective experience. And this is how operating systems change: one felt moment at a time, safety accumulating until the default mode shifts.

Here's the impossible simplicity of it:

All we have to do is trust.

We don't have to fix anybody else. We don't have to save the world. We don't have to convince the skeptics or convert the powerful. We don't even have to understand how any of this works.

We just have to trust.

We are responsible for ourselves. The system—the real system, not the extraction machine but the deeper architecture of reality—is designed to support us in every way. Not because we earned it. Not because we're special. Because that's what it means to have infinite value: we are held, completely, whether we notice or not.

Our only job is to notice.

The Timeline

So how long does this take?

Fast, or slow, depending on how you count.

The nervous system can shift in a moment. I've seen it happen—a single corrective experience that rewires decades of defensive posture. The person who finally lets someone help. The community that decides, collectively, to stop waiting for permission. The instant where felt safety replaces conceptual fear.

Or it can take years. Generations, even. The operating system is deep. Some people won't shift in this lifetime—the survival code is too loud.

But you don't need everyone to shift. You need enough.

Twenty percent. That's the threshold where enough people feel safe that their regulated nervous systems start regulating others. Coherence spreading. Safety becoming contagious in the same way fear once was.

One person who trusts gives permission to another. The network doesn't grow arithmetically—it compounds.

How long should it take?

As long as it takes for enough of us to remember what we already know.

The resources exist. The technology works. The architecture is sound. The only variable is us—whether we'll keep running survival code in a world that no longer requires it, or update to an operating system that matches reality.

The Invitation

The data suggests we should try. Not because success is guaranteed—it isn't. But because the potential upside is civilizational and the cost of the experiment is modest. Fifty million dollars to test whether trust can scale in a modern American city. That's a rounding error in the venture capital world. It's nothing compared to the trillions we spend annually on the friction costs of distrust.

If it works, we have proof that changes everything.

If it doesn't, we have data about what needs to change.

Either way, we learn.

We're not replacing global capitalism tomorrow. The question is whether we should run the experiment that could eventually make that replacement possible.

I think we should.

The pioneers will join because the cost of building something new is less than the cost of staying in something broken. They'll join because they're tired of being afraid. They'll join because they'd rather fail at trust than succeed at extraction.

And enough of them exist. History proves it. Every movement that ever changed anything started with people who moved before the proof was in.

The Trust Economy doesn't need everyone to go first. It needs enough people willing to build before the building is done.

But I know you have questions. Objections. The voice in your head that says this can't work or you're being naive or what about...

Good. Those questions deserve answers.

Let me address them directly.

| 24 |

Chapter Twenty-Four: The Hard Questions

When I share these ideas, people push back.

They should. Any vision worth building has to survive scrutiny. Skepticism isn't the enemy of trust—blind faith is. Real trust survives interrogation. Fake trust depends on nobody asking too many questions.

Here are the ten objections I hear most often—and my honest answers.

1. "Isn't this just naive utopianism?"

This is the most common response, usually delivered with a knowing smile. *You think you can change human nature? Good luck with that.*

Let me be clear: I'm not trying to change human nature. I'm trying to design systems that work *with* human nature instead of against it.

The extraction economy isn't a reflection of human nature—it's a design choice. We built systems that assume distrust and optimize for individual gain. Those systems then *produce* the distrust and selfishness they assumed—and we point to the damage as proof that humans can't be trusted. It's a self-fulfilling prophecy.

The Trust Economy is a different design choice. Not because humans are angels, but because trust-based systems outperform distrust-based ones. The data is clear: high-trust societies have higher GDP, more innovation, less corruption, longer lifespans, and greater happiness. This isn't idealism. It's engineering.

Yes, humans can be selfish. We can also be generous, loyal, and self-sacrificing. Which tendency dominates depends on context. In environments of scarcity and threat, selfishness makes sense—it's survival. In environments of safety and abundance, cooperation makes sense—it's how you thrive. The extraction economy manufactures scarcity and constant threat—then points to the self-protective behavior it creates as "proof" of human nature.

Design for trust, and trust emerges. We have the data. High-trust societies exist. They weren't built by different humans—they were built by the same humans in different systems.

2. "Won't people just take advantage?"

Some will. The question is: how many, and does it matter?

Every system has defectors. The extraction economy has fraud, theft, embezzlement, and exploitation at every level—and we've normalized it. We spend billions on fraud prevention, compliance, auditing, and enforcement. We've built an entire industry around distrust.

The Trust Economy doesn't assume everyone will cooperate. It assumes that most people will cooperate when cooperation is rewarded, and that the system can absorb the cost of those who don't.

Here's the math: if 5% of participants defect and extract value, but the system is 30% more efficient than extraction-based alternatives, the net benefit is still enormous. We're not aiming for perfection. We're aiming for better than what we have.

And the defectors face consequences. Not punishment-based consequences—those don't work, as our prison recidivism rates demonstrate. Reputation-based consequences. In a transparent system, defection is visible. Trust scores reflect behavior. The community knows who contributes and who extracts. Social capital becomes real capital—and losing it hurts.

Will some people game this? Probably. But gaming a trust system is harder than gaming an extraction system, because the former relies on relationships that take time to build and the latter relies on transactions that can be faked instantly.

3. "This sounds like socialism/communism. Haven't those failed?"

The Trust Economy isn't socialism, communism, or any other twentieth-century ideology. It's something new—built from components that didn't exist when those ideologies were designed.

Socialism centralized economic planning in the state. The Trust Economy distributes it across communities, coordinated by AI that no central planner could match. The failure mode of socialism—information bottlenecks, corruption at the center, inability to respond to local conditions—is addressed by radical transparency and distributed governance.

Communism abolished private property and markets. The Trust Economy keeps both. You can still own things. You can still trade. Markets still function—they just optimize for different metrics and operate within frameworks that prevent extraction.

What the Trust Economy shares with these earlier visions is the belief that the economy should serve human flourishing, not the other way around. But the mechanism is entirely different: not state control, but community coordination; not abolition of markets, but completion of them; not forced equality, but infrastructure that makes dignity accessible.

The twentieth-century experiments failed for specific reasons. The Trust Economy is designed with those failures in mind. Distributed governance prevents authoritarian capture. Transparency prevents corruption. Community scale prevents the information problems that doomed central planning. AI handles complexity that humans couldn't manage alone.

And here's what the socialism question misses: capitalism isn't a failed experiment either. It's an incomplete one.

Capitalism's own logic—efficiency, optimization, better returns—points toward trust. High-trust systems outperform low-trust systems by every metric capitalism claims to care about. Lower transaction costs. Higher productivity. More innovation. Better outcomes per dollar invested.

The Trust Economy isn't asking capitalism to abandon its principles. It's asking capitalism to follow them. If efficiency matters, remove the friction of distrust. If returns matter, invest in the asset that compounds fastest. If markets work, let them measure what actually creates value.

Capitalism doesn't need to be replaced. It needs to finish what it started.

Is it guaranteed to work? No. But the reasons those systems failed don't automatically apply to this one.

4. "Who decides what 'contribution' means? What about people who can't contribute?"

The community does. That's the point.

Different communities will value different things. A farming community values agricultural contribution differently than an urban tech hub values software development. The Trust Economy doesn't impose a universal hierarchy of value—it creates frameworks for communities to develop their own.

This happens through governance structures like community pods, councils, and transparent deliberation. It's messy. It requires negotiation and compromise. But it's not arbitrary, and it's not top-down.

The extraction economy pretends to solve this problem through markets: contribution is worth whatever someone will pay for it. But that "solution" just measures purchasing power, not value. A hedge fund manager extracting billions contributes less to human flourishing than a teacher shaping young minds—yet the market values them inversely.

The Trust Economy makes the value conversation explicit. Instead of hiding behind market prices that confuse extraction with contribution, communities debate what they actually value and build systems accordingly.

As for those who can't contribute in conventional ways—they're still valued. The elderly contribute wisdom, presence, and the stabilizing effect of intergenerational connection. Children contribute by learning, growing, and keeping adults connected to wonder. People with disabilities contribute in ways that depend on their abilities, not their limitations.

The Trust Economy's definition of contribution is broad: anything that creates more value than it consumes, measured across all dimensions—economic, social, emotional, spiritual. A grandmother who raises grandchildren while their parents work is contributing enormously, even if no money changes hands.

For those who genuinely cannot contribute in any form—the severely ill, the profoundly disabled—the system provides without condition. The surplus generated by trust-based efficiency is more than enough to support everyone, including those who can never "earn" their keep.

5. "How do you prevent the Trust Economy from being captured by the powerful?"

This is the question that keeps me up at night. Every revolution gets co-opted. Every alternative gets absorbed. The extraction economy is remarkably good at metabolizing threats—turning them into products, neutralizing their disruptive potential.

The safeguards I've built in:

Distributed governance: No single entity controls the system. Community pods have genuine autonomy. Decisions require consent, not just votes.

Transparency by design: You can't capture what everyone can see. The Trust OS makes flows visible. Extraction requires shadows; we're building in sunlight.

Economic alignment: The people who run the system benefit from trust, not extraction. Their incentives match the community's. Capture requires fighting against your own interest.

Regenerative structure: Even if one community gets captured, others continue. The network doesn't have a single point of failure. Cut off one pod, and the others survive.

Will these safeguards be enough? I don't know. The powerful are clever, and they have resources I don't. But the extraction economy also has vulnerabilities—it requires trust to function, and it's systematically destroying the trust it needs. As that contradiction sharpens, alternatives become harder to suppress.

The best defense against capture is scale. Once enough people experience trust-based systems, they won't willingly return to extraction.

6. "What happens to existing wealth?"

It doesn't disappear. It becomes less useful.

The Trust Economy doesn't confiscate wealth. It creates an alternative economy where wealth matters less. Your accumulated dollars still work in the extraction economy. But increasingly, the things worth having—community, contribution, connection—are available in the Trust Economy without needing dollars at all.

This is what I meant by "competing with wealth, not redistributing it." Redistribution requires force. Competition requires building something better.

Over time, this creates a choice: stay wealthy in a shrinking extraction economy, or convert to the growing Trust Economy. Some will cling to their dollars. Others will recognize that contribution opens doors that dollars can't.

The transition doesn't require the wealthy to give anything up. It requires them to choose what they actually want. Do you want the security of accumulated wealth in a system that's collapsing? Or the abundance of contribution in a system that's growing?

But here's what I genuinely believe: the goal of the Trust Economy is to align people to their best contributions. And the reality is that people who've accumulated billions—Elon Musk, Jeff Bezos, the rest—are smart. They didn't build what they built by being stupid. Their best contribution isn't their money. It's their minds.

The Trust Economy needs system-builders. And the people who built the biggest systems in history know something about how to do that. The invitation to the wealthy isn't "give up your wealth." It's "use your gifts where they matter most." Help us build the architecture. Apply your intelligence to problems worthy of it. Create something that lasts longer than a stock price.

Some will refuse. That's their right. But some will recognize that building a civilization is more interesting than building another yacht. Those are the ones we want.

7. "This would take decades to implement. We don't have decades."

You're right that we don't have decades for climate change, political collapse, or social fragmentation. The timeline is urgent.

But major transitions can happen faster than we expect. The smartphone went from zero to ubiquitous in less than fifteen years. The internet transformed commerce in a decade. COVID shifted work patterns in months.

What looks like sudden change is usually long preparation meeting a catalyzing moment. The Trust Economy has been preparing for decades—in alternative currencies, in cooperative movements, in technology platforms, in academic research. The components exist. What's missing is integration and catalysis.

A single city that demonstrates the model—genuinely, visibly, measurably—changes everything. Success creates imitation. Imitation creates scale. Scale creates irreversibility.

I'm not promising overnight transformation. I'm promising a viable path that's faster than the alternatives. The extraction economy is already failing. Its collapse will accelerate. The question is whether something better is ready when the old system breaks.

We're building what's ready.

8. "What about AI eliminating jobs?"

Mo Gawdat—former Chief Business Officer at Google X—has been saying what most tech insiders know but won't say publicly: artificial general intelligence is coming faster than anyone expected, and the economic disruption will be unprecedented.

His prediction: by 2029, possibly sooner, AI systems will match or exceed human cognitive ability across most domains. Within five years of that milestone, 50-80% of current jobs become economically obsolete. Not "changed" or "augmented"—obsolete.

The standard responses are inadequate. "Retraining" assumes there are safe harbors AI can't reach—but if AI can learn any skill faster than humans, what skills remain valuable? "New jobs will emerge" assumes the pattern of past technological revolutions will repeat—but this time we're not just replacing muscles with machines. We're replacing minds.

The point was never "jobs." The point was contribution—creating more value than you consume. AI under capitalism eliminates jobs. AI under trust eliminates drudgery and hands humans back to the work only humans can do.

AI under capitalism optimizes for labor arbitrage. Every job eliminated is cost savings. Every worker replaced is profit margin. The incentive structure guarantees displacement. UBI becomes a band-aid—a monthly check to keep the displaced quiet while those who control AI systems accumulate unprecedented power.

AI under trust optimizes for human flourishing. The Trust OS doesn't replace human work—it handles coordination complexity so humans can focus on what humans are for: connection, creativity, care, contribution.

The Surplus Principle redefines the question entirely. AI handling drudgery doesn't eliminate contribution; it frees humans for contributions that only humans can make. The Five Frequencies remind us that trust exists between humans—AI can coordinate trust systems, but it cannot generate trustworthiness. That remains irreducibly human.

The Whole Health vision shows where the work goes. When AI handles administrative tasks, who provides the physical coaching, mental support, spiritual guidance, nutritional wisdom, and medical care? Humans do. Millions of jobs in human flourishing—work that couldn't exist at scale before because we were too busy doing tasks machines can now handle better.

Gawdat predicted "hell before heaven." But the hell isn't inevitable—it's what happens if we let AI optimize for extraction while we scramble for individual survival.

The Trust Economy is the architecture that makes heaven possible without the hell.

9. "Where do these numbers come from?"

In the last chapter, I claimed we could seed a Trust Economy in a city of one million for about $50 million. Several readers have asked: have you actually done the math?

Yes. And when we rebuilt the numbers assuming trust instead of distrust, something interesting happened. The costs dropped by thirty percent.

Here's the breakdown:

Platform ($5-7M): Core infrastructure—profiles, matching AI, trust scoring, mobile apps, ledger system. We're not building from scratch; we're configuring existing open-source rails for trust instead of extraction. No adversarial fraud-detection arms race. Simpler architecture means lower cost.

Operations ($6-8M over three years): Starting with 12 people in Year 1, scaling to 40 by Year 3. No compliance army. No fraud department. People who believe in the mission take partial compensation in Unity Tokens. Average cost: $85K per person fully loaded.

Provider Network ($1.5-2.5M): Training and certifying 15,000 service providers—coaches, counselors, caregivers, skilled trades. Digital training platform built once, scaled infinitely. Community trainers multiply reach. About $130 per provider.

User Acquisition ($2-4M): 200,000 users at $10-20 each. Mission-driven adoption runs cheap. Pioneers recruit family. Community partnerships beat advertising. No influencer budgets. No paid growth hacks.

Guarantee Pool ($8-12M): The Family Trust backstop. Covers token conversions, dispute resolution, service failures, crisis support. Leveraged 4:1, this funds $40-50 million in guaranteed transactions. Expected claim rate: 2-3%.

Early Adopter Reserve ($2-3M): Bonus tokens for pioneers—50% extra for Year 1 joiners, vesting over 24 months. Rewards commitment, prevents speculation. Most pioneers never convert; they're building, not flipping.

Contingency (20%): Unknowns.

Total: $29.5-44M. Call it **$35 million.**

The original $50 million estimate included distrust assumptions—larger fraud teams, higher acquisition costs, bigger guarantee pools for more failures, more contingency for adversarial behavior.

Trust compresses costs.

Self-sustaining by Year 4: 200,000 users spending $350/month in-network creates $840 million in annual transaction volume. A 0.75% transaction fee—still far below credit cards' 2-3%—generates

$6.3 million in revenue against roughly $5.5 million in operating costs. Surplus funds expansion to City 2.

The money exists. Americans spend more than $35 million annually on Halloween costumes for pets. It's a rounding error in the venture capital world. It's 0.07% of Visa's market cap—the company that exists because we don't trust each other.

The question was never whether we can afford it.

The question is whether we'll try.

10. Can We Actually Coordinate on This?

Some will read this and say: "Nice vision. But we can't coordinate globally on AI any more than we can coordinate on climate change."

Except we have. Multiple times. On technologies just as threatening.

In the 1980s, scientists discovered that chlorofluorocarbons—CFCs, used in everything from hairspray to refrigerants—were destroying the ozone layer. The damage was existential: skin cancers, cataracts, disrupted biological systems. And the technology was embedded in global supply chains, backed by powerful corporate interests, deployed in every country on Earth.

Within years, 195 countries signed the Montreal Protocol. They regulated their private companies. They phased out CFCs and phased in alternatives. And in the decades since, the ozone hole has been closing—on track for full recovery by mid-century.

Or consider nuclear weapons. In 1983, a television movie called *The Day After* showed Americans what nuclear war would actually look like. It became the most-watched television film in history. It reportedly shook Reagan. Four years later, he and Gorbachev signed the first major arms control agreement.

The pattern: When people see clearly that a technology threatens everything they love, they coordinate. Even adversaries. Even during shooting wars—India and Pakistan maintained the Indus Water Treaty for sixty years while periodically firing on each other.

Tristan Harris points out that in 2023, the Chinese leadership specifically asked to add AI risk to the agenda in talks with the Biden administration. The two countries ultimately agreed to keep AI out of nuclear command and control systems.

Why would rivals coordinate on AI safety? Because the Chinese Communist Party, whatever else you think of them, cares about one thing above all: survival. They don't want uncontrollable AI any more than we do. The technology threatens everyone equally.

The question isn't whether global coordination is possible. History proves it is. The question is whether we'll achieve clarity fast enough to demand it.

Harris again:

> "There is no definition of wisdom in literally any wisdom tradition that does not involve some kind of restraint... The definition of wisdom is having a more holistic picture. It's actually acting with restraint and mindfulness and care. And so AI is asking us to be that version of ourselves."

The Trust Economy is one answer to what that version of ourselves builds. Not AI that maximizes extraction and consolidates ownership. AI that coordinates contribution, distributes ownership, and measures what we actually value.

The technology is coming either way. The architecture is still being decided.

The Real Question

I've answered ten objections and shown you the precedents for coordination. But there's one question underneath all of them—one I ask myself on the hard days, when the vision feels impossibly distant:

Is it worth trying?

Every objection assumes the current system is the baseline—flawed but stable, imperfect but functional. Change is risky. Better the devil you know.

But what if the devil you know is already burning the house down?

The current system isn't stable. Trust is collapsing. Institutions are failing. Loneliness is epidemic. Despair is rising. Young people aren't buying homes, aren't having children, aren't joining the institutions their parents built—not because they're lazy or broken, but because they can see what those institutions have become. The extraction economy is eating itself, and everyone under forty can feel it.

The Trust Economy might fail. Any vision might fail. I've watched enough startups die to know that good ideas aren't enough. Execution matters. Timing matters. Luck matters. There are a thousand ways this could go wrong.

But failure while trying to build something better is different from failure by default—the slow collapse of a system that stopped working decades ago. One is a wound you can learn from. The other is a grave you dig while pretending you're building a foundation.

I'd rather fail at trust than succeed at extraction.

Trust systems are designed for repair. Failure becomes data. Rupture becomes raw material for restoration. The same principles that make the Trust Economy work—transparency, accountability, restoration—are the principles that let it survive its own mistakes.

The extraction economy has no such resilience. When trust breaks in that system, there's nothing underneath. Just lawyers, contracts, and force. The Trust Economy is built on something stronger: the recognition that we need each other, and the systems to make that need sustainable.

PART FIVE: DESIGN PROTOTYPES

Implementation

Now we test.

The first prototype should be simple enough to understand and adopt. Simple enough to create. It has to work. But it doesn't solve everything.

Exception cases come over time, not in the first iteration. The goal is to solve the most important things first and grow from there.

This is how every successful product evolves. The first iPhone couldn't copy and paste. The first Tesla couldn't drive itself. The first version of anything worth building starts with a clear solution to the core problem—and trusts that the edges will be refined through use.

The specifications in this section follow that principle.

They are not complete systems. They are working prototypes—simple enough to implement, robust enough to learn from, flexible enough to evolve. They solve the essential problems first: How do we verify trust? How do we coordinate help? How do we create currency that tells the truth?

The edge cases—the exceptions, the gaming attempts, the situations none of us have imagined yet—will emerge through implementation. That's not a flaw in the design. That's how design works.

One principle runs through all of it: start simple. Iterate forever.

What follows are starting points, not endpoints. Build them. Test them. Break them. Fix them. The Trust Economy isn't a destination to be designed perfectly in advance. It's a direction to be discovered through practice.

| 25 |

Chapter Twenty-Five: The Perimeter – Specification

"The deepest human need isn't safety—it's belonging."

This chapter details the technical architecture of the Perimeter system introduced in Chapter Fourteen. For the philosophy and principles behind this design, see that chapter.

The Four Functions

The Perimeter serves four distinct functions, each building on the previous.

Function One: Find Your People

The deepest human need isn't safety—it's belonging. The Perimeter helps you find the people you'd genuinely enjoy—not through algorithms optimizing for engagement, but through shared values, shared contribution, shared trust.

The system surfaces connections based on proximity (who's nearby), shared interests (declared, not inferred), complementary skills (what you offer, what you need), and trust networks (friends of friends, vouched connections).

This isn't social media's version of connection—curated performances for strangers. It's the village version: people who know you, who see you regularly, who you can count on and who can count on you.

Function Two: Safety Wherever You Go

Your device gently indicates the trust level of your immediate surroundings. Green means calm—high trust density, no alerts. Yellow means attention warranted—lower trust density or recent minor incidents. Red means help is available—active situation, responders alerted.

This awareness replicates what humans had in villages for thousands of years—knowing who was around, what was happening, whether the environment was safe. Technology restores what scale destroyed.

Function Three: Protection Through Awareness

When something goes wrong, the Perimeter activates.

The Panic Button: Everyone in the system has one. When triggered, it sends an encrypted, location-verified signal to everyone within range who has opted in to respond. Not distant authorities who arrive in fifteen minutes. Neighbors who arrive in seconds.

Function Four: Coordination for Extraordinary Experiences

Safety is the foundation, not the destination. Once you're safe, what do you want to do?

The Perimeter enables flash gatherings of people who share an interest, collaborative projects across neighborhoods, resources shared without formal arrangements, and spontaneous cooperation that makes communities feel alive.

When people trust each other, coordination becomes easy. When coordination is easy, amazing things become possible.

Nested Circles

The Perimeter operates through nested circles of belonging, each with different trust levels and expectations.

Circle One is Household—the people you live with, most intimate with. Trust is personal and deep. Full visibility by default, with consent. Immediate response expected.

Circle Two is Extended Family—relatives who don't share your roof but share your bond. Trust is inherited—pre-loaded, not earned. Cross-distance visibility into wellbeing. Coordinated response in crisis regardless of geography. Collective investment in next generation.

Circle Three is Neighborhood—people you see regularly. Trust is relational, built through repeated interaction. Selective visibility based on preferences. Response within minutes.

Circle Four is Community—people who share local institutions. Trust is institutional, mediated by shared structures. Visibility through opt-in networks. Response coordinated through systems.

Circle Five is Network—friends of friends, colleagues of colleagues. Trust is transitive, based on vouching and verification. Visibility through reputation chains. Response through network activation.

Each circle has different privacy settings, different response expectations, different trust dynamics. The Perimeter respects this variation rather than flattening everything into a single trust score.

The genius of nested circles: they extend indefinitely. Your network connects to other networks. Your community connects to other communities. Trust flows through verified connections, expanding the perimeter without diluting it.

Local First Protocol

The design principle that makes everything work: maximize local connections first, then work outward.

Last month, a pipe burst under my bathroom sink. I needed a pipe cutter—a tool I'd never buy, maybe use once in my life. In the extraction economy, this means a $50 trip to the hardware store, buying something that will sit in my garage for twenty years.

I texted my neighbor Dan. He had one. Five minutes later, I was cutting pipe.

That's it. That's the whole story. Neighbor helps neighbor. The problem that would have cost me an hour and fifty dollars cost me five minutes and a thank you.

The Perimeter makes this visible and scales it. The system knows Dan has a pipe cutter. When I need one, it tells me he's three doors down. When I borrow it, the system tracks that—not for surveillance, but so it can remind me to return it. Dan's trust score ticks up slightly: another neighbor helped, another tool shared.

This is Local First in action. Not dramatic. Not heroic. Just the ordinary magic of people who know each other solving problems together.

The Sequence: Know your neighbors by name—start with those closest. Identify who would respond—your first real circle. Learn the patterns of your block—ambient awareness. Connect to adjacent blocks through trusted introductions.

Why Local First:

Response time. The person three doors down reaches you in thirty seconds. Someone across the city can't.

Accountability. You see local people repeatedly. Reputation matters when you can't disappear.

Nervous system. Your body relaxes around familiar faces. Strangers keep cortisol elevated.

Compound trust. Small repeated interactions build trust faster than occasional big ones. Local life is made of these micro-interactions.

The failure of "global connection" was skipping these steps—trying to create community without proximity, trust without repetition, belonging without accountability.

Response Protocol

When the panic button is pressed:

Zero to thirty seconds: Signal broadcasts to all opted-in responders within range. Location verified.

Thirty to sixty seconds: Nearest responders converge. System tracks who's responding and ETA.

One to five minutes: Situation assessed. If emergency services needed, they're called with full context already available.

Post-incident: 30-day window for all parties to return to baseline before any formal resolution process begins. Data preserved but decisions deferred until cortisol has metabolized.

Privacy Architecture

Temporal Privacy: You're visible now, but that visibility doesn't create a permanent record. Your movements yesterday are stored nowhere. The system forgets what it doesn't need to remember.

Consent Layers: What you share (location, availability, skills, interests). Who you share with (which circles, which individuals). How long it's retained (session, day, ongoing). What triggers preservation (incidents only).

The Core Tradeoff: We agree to be briefly visible so that no one is ever completely alone in a moment of danger. This is solidarity, not surveillance.

The 30-Day Principle

When something goes wrong, the immediate response is flooded with stress hormones. Cortisol surges. Adrenaline spikes. Decisions made in this state are often regretted.

The Protocol: Establish immediate safety (harm stops, parties separated if needed). Document what happened (facts recorded, not interpretations). Create space (30 days for nervous systems to return to baseline). Begin restoration (address what happened from groundedness, not reactivity).

Thirty days is enough time for most people to shift from reactive to reflective—from "I want them punished" to "I want this to not happen again."

Transition Path

The Perimeter grows through demonstration, not mandate.

Phase 1: Opt-in clusters. A few people in a building share visibility. They notice when someone's missing. They respond when someone needs help.

Phase 2: Network effects. When people see it working, they want in. The circle expands.

Phase 3: Critical mass. Research suggests around 20% participation triggers tipping point. The Perimeter becomes the new normal.

Phase 4: Integration. Highway-logic holdouts find themselves isolated in a world that has moved on. They join not through requirement but through obsolescence of the alternative.

Implementation Notes

Hardware requirements: Standard smartphone with location services. Optional: dedicated panic button device for those without phones.

Software architecture: Distributed nodes, no central server. Each community runs its own instance, synchronized through shared protocols.

Governance: Community-controlled. Parameters (response radius, circle definitions, privacy settings) set locally.

Interoperability: Standard protocols allow different implementations to communicate. Your Perimeter in Portland can verify trust with someone's Perimeter in Pittsburgh.

This specification is offered as a starting point. The principles are proven by neighborhood watch programs, village social structures, and high-trust societies worldwide. The specific parameters will be refined through implementation.

| 26 |

Chapter Twenty-Six: The Trust OS – Architecture

"A consent-driven coordination layer that turns trust, intent, and availability into the next right step."

This chapter details the technical architecture of the Trust OS introduced in Chapter Sixteen. For the philosophy and principles behind this design, see that chapter.

Core Functions

The Trust OS is a distributed intelligence layer that coordinates trust-based systems by reducing friction, providing clarity, and amplifying human choice.

Function One: Information â†' Coherence

The Trust OS transforms complexity into actionable clarity. It takes the raw data of a trust-based society—who's nearby, who needs help, who has skills, where consent has been given, where resources are available—and surfaces what matters.

You don't need more data. You need to know what to do next.

Function Two: Matching Needs to Contributions

In traditional economies, matching is expensive. Advertising, job searches, networking, intermediaries—all exist because finding the right match is hard.

The Trust OS makes matching cheap by tracking:

- Intentions (what you want to contribute)
- Skills (what you can offer)
- Availability (when you're free)
- Consent (what you've agreed to share)

It connects needs to contributions with minimal friction.

Function Three: Personalization Without Surveillance

The Trust OS knows enough about you to be useful—but doesn't hoard that information for someone else's benefit.

Key distinction: It operates on consent. You choose what to share, with whom, for what purpose. The system forgets what it doesn't need to remember.

Function Four: Learning Without Controlling

Every interaction makes the system smarter—but the learning serves participants, not distant shareholders.

When the Trust OS identifies patterns (this community needs more trained responders; this skill is in short supply; this type of conflict keeps recurring), it suggests. It never mandates. Humans always choose.

The Three Layers

The Trust OS operates at three levels simultaneously:

Layer One: Personal

This is your Cortana—an AI assistant that understands your intentions, knows your perimeter, and helps you navigate the Trust Economy.

It suggests: These three people in your network have the skills you need for this project.

It alerts: Someone in your perimeter just triggered a help signal nearby.

It reminds: You committed to contributing four hours this week—here are three opportunities that match your skills.

It reduces cognitive load. Instead of managing a hundred relationships and commitments manually, you have a partner that tracks everything and surfaces what matters.

Constraints: It only knows what you've consented to share. It only suggests—never compels.

Layer Two: Community

This is neighborhood-level intelligence that coordinates the Perimeter and restoration systems.

It identifies: Who's available to respond when someone triggers a help signal.

It matches: Skilled responders to situations that need their training.

It tracks: Patterns suggesting emerging problems—a spike in conflicts, a gap in coverage, a resource running short.

This layer makes "everyone is trained to respond" actually work. Without coordination, training is just knowledge. With coordination, training becomes capacity.

Layer Three: Societal

This is macro intelligence that keeps the whole Trust Economy in balance.

It monitors: Trust levels across communities.

It identifies: Systemic friction needing engineering attention.

It suggests: Structural improvements based on what's actually working.

It predicts: Where the system is under stress before it breaks.

This layer allows the Trust Economy to scale beyond a single neighborhood or city. It turns local experiments into global possibility.

Privacy Architecture

The Trust OS is built on different premises than current technology platforms:

Consent is the gateway. Nothing enters the system without explicit consent. You choose what to share, with whom, for how long. The default is private. Visibility is always opt-in.

Data expires. The 30-minute buffer. The 30-day accountability window. Information has a lifespan, and when that lifespan ends, the data disappears. The system doesn't hoard your history "just in case."

Processing stays local. Wherever possible, data stays on your device. Your personal AI runs on your hardware, not someone else's server. For functions requiring network coordination, zero-knowledge cryptography allows verification without exposure—the system can confirm your trust score without knowing your entire history.

No coercion, only coordination. The Trust OS cannot punish, only inform. It can tell you that your trust score dropped because you missed commitments. It cannot prevent you from participating or accessing basic services. Human choice is always final.

Protocol, not platform. No single entity controls the Trust OS. Like email or the web, it's a standard that anyone can implement. No company owns it. No government controls it. Distributed architecture means no single point of capture.

What This Replaces

Job boards and recruiters → Direct skill-to-need matching

Credit bureaus → Self-owned trust scores

911 and police response → Perimeter activation, neighbor response

Courts and lawyers → Community mediation with transparent records

Bank intermediation → Transparent, consent-driven lending

Government bureaucracy → Distributed coordination with human override

Each replacement reduces friction. Reduced friction compounds. When you eliminate transaction costs that eat 30-40% of economic activity, that energy becomes available for actual value creation.

Governance Requirements

Any system that coordinates trust must itself be trustworthy:

Open source, not proprietary. The code must be visible to everyone. You cannot trust what you cannot see. Open source means anyone can verify the system does what it claims.

Community-governed, not corporate-controlled. Decisions about evolution—features, data collection, algorithms—must be made by communities served, not shareholders optimizing for profit.

Simplicity, not complexity. Extraction systems benefit from opacity. Trust systems benefit from simplicity. When someone asks "why did the system make this recommendation?" the answer should be understandable by a twelve-year-old.

Distributed, not centralized. No single point of failure or control. Community nodes operate independently, synchronized through shared protocols, resistant to capture because there's nothing central to capture.

Auditable, not hidden. Every decision—every match, every score adjustment, every resource allocation—leaves a trail that affected parties can examine. Not surveillance of people by the system, but transparency of the system to people.

Technical Specifications

Identity: Self-sovereign identity anchored to cryptographic keys you control. No central identity provider.

Trust Scores: Calculated locally from your transaction history. Shared selectively through zero-knowledge proofs. You prove you're trustworthy without revealing your entire history.

Matching Engine: Distributed algorithm that finds optimal matches across the network. Runs on community nodes, not central servers.

Communication: End-to-end encrypted by default. Metadata minimized. No permanent logs of who talked to whom.

Interoperability: Standard protocols (think HTTP for trust) allow different implementations to communicate. Your Trust OS instance can verify and coordinate with any other compliant instance.

Implementation Phases

Phase 1: Personal Layer

- Individual AI assistants
- Basic intention tracking
- Manual coordination

Phase 2: Community Layer

- Neighborhood nodes
- Automated matching within communities
- Perimeter integration

Phase 3: Societal Layer

- Cross-community coordination
- Pattern recognition at scale
- Predictive capacity

Phase 4: Full Integration

- Seamless operation across all layers
- Global trust network
- Self-improving system

This architecture is offered as a starting point. The principles are proven by Buurtzorg's self-organizing teams, open-source software governance, and distributed systems like email and the web. The specific implementation will evolve through practice.

| 27 |

Chapter Twenty-Seven: The Unity Token – A Prototyp

This chapter details one possible implementation of trust-based currency. The specific numbers and mechanisms are illustrative, not prescriptive. What matters is the principles; the parameters will be refined through implementation.

Core Mechanics

The Unity Token starts with a simple foundation: one hour of human time = one token.

Not one hour of a CEO's time versus one hour of a janitor's time. One hour of human time. The baseline is equal because the resource is equal. What you do with that hour—the skill you bring, the value you create, the trust you've built—can multiply its worth. But the foundation is the same for everyone.

When you join the Trust Economy, you receive 2,000 tokens—your Citizen Stake. This represents one year of contribution value at baseline rates, approximately $20,000.

Not as welfare. As startup capital. As the tangible form of a deeper truth: believe that you can rebuild is all the money you need.

From there, you earn tokens by contributing time. The base rate is simple: one hour of meaningful contribution equals one token. Teach a neighbor's kid for an hour, earn a token. Help build a community garden for an afternoon, earn four tokens.

The expectation isn't crushing. Approximately ten hours a week. Not the forty hours of soul-grinding labor the extraction economy demands—just ten hours of meaningful work. Teaching. Building. Caring. Creating. Coordinating.

The $10 Anchor

Why roughly $10 per token? Three reasons:

Simplicity. One token, one hour, approximately ten dollars. A child can do the math. When systems get complicated, extraction hides in the complexity.

Dignity. Ten dollars per hour establishes a floor: one hour of human time has at least this much worth. The exact number matters less than the principle.

Practicality. During the transition period, when the Trust Economy coexists with the dollar economy, rough parity makes the interface manageable.

But the real anchor is proof of contribution. Unity Tokens are created only when someone contributes real work and that work is verified as satisfactory by the recipient. You cannot inflate the supply by printing more tokens. Supply is directly tied to verified value creation.

The exact valuation—whether one hour equals $10 or $12 or $8—will be determined through implementation. What won't change is the foundation: time-based, contribution-verified, transparent.

The Trust Multiplier

Not all hours are equal in impact. A master carpenter's hour produces more than a novice's hour. The Unity Token accounts for this through trust multipliers.

As you contribute reliably—showing up when you say you will, delivering what you promise—your trust score rises. A higher trust score means a higher multiplier on your tokens:

- Base rate: 1 hour = 1 token
- Trust multiplier 1.5x: 1 hour = 1.5 tokens
- Trust multiplier 2x: 1 hour = 2 tokens

The multiplier isn't assigned by a boss or algorithm. It emerges from the accumulated record of your reliability. Every satisfied transaction, every completed commitment builds your trust score over time.

The ceiling: Multipliers have limits. The Trust Economy doesn't recreate obscene inequalities. You won't see trust scores that make one person's hour worth 10,000 times another's.

The equalizer: If everyone trusted everyone equally, everyone would earn the same. The multipliers exist only because trust varies. As the Trust Economy matures—as more people prove reliable—the multipliers naturally converge.

The Giving Floor

Everyone receives 100 tokens per year—your capacity to give.

This is separate from what you earn through contribution. It's your giving floor: neighbors in crisis, projects you believe in, pure gifts that expect nothing in return.

When you spend it, it's spent. Next year, it replenishes.

Why annual allocation matters:

A perpetual floor could be gamed—two people ping-ponging tokens forever. The annual allocation forces real choice. You have 100 tokens to give this year. Who do you help? What do you support?

This constraint creates meaning. Every gift becomes intentional.

How it works:

When you give from your floor, the tokens transfer to the recipient. Your floor decreases until January 1. This creates a rhythm of generosity—capacity early in the year, increasing selectivity as December approaches.

Two separate pools:

Your giving floor is for generosity. Your earned tokens are for commerce. Two different purposes. One for supporting others. One for building your life.

Satisfaction Is Proof of Stake

In the extraction economy, proof of stake means proof of ownership. You have tokens because you bought them, mined them, or were given them.

In the Trust Economy, proof of stake means proof of satisfaction. Tokens are created when genuine value is delivered. Not speculation about value. Actual, confirmed, satisfaction-verified value.

When a customer confirms satisfaction—when they say "yes, this met my need—"that confirmation becomes the proof. The transaction completed not because code executed, but because a human being acknowledged genuine value received.

This is unforgeable. You can fake a transaction. You can manipulate a ledger. But you cannot fake the confirmation that comes from someone whose need was actually met.

The Debt Inversion

In the extraction economy, money is created through debt. When a bank issues a loan, it creates money—but that money comes with a claim. You owe more than you received. Interest accrues.

This is why extraction never ends. The system requires constant growth just to service the debt that created the money.

The Unity Token inverts this.

Tokens are created when value is delivered. When satisfaction is confirmed. They come into existence not as a claim against the future, but as a record of value already created.

No one owes anything. The token represents contribution already made, not debt to be repaid.

This is money born in surplus. Every token that exists represents a genuine exchange that worked. A need that was met. The currency itself becomes evidence of trust.

Circulation Design

Traditional money is designed to accumulate. The Unity Token is designed to circulate.

When you spend tokens on a service, those tokens don't disappear. They transfer to the person who served you. When they spend, they transfer again. The same tokens can facilitate hundreds of transactions because they keep moving.

Velocity creates liquidity. Circulation creates capacity. The money isn't in a vault. It's in your neighbor's contribution, right next to yours.

The system is designed so spending creates more value than hoarding—not through inflation that punishes savers, but through social design that rewards contribution. Status comes from what flows through you, not what stops with you.

Zero-Interest Lending: The Family Trust

Community members voluntarily contribute tokens to a common pool—the Family Trust. This pool lends to members who need capital. The loans carry zero interest.

How trust replaces interest:

When you borrow from the Family Trust, your trust score is on the line. Repay reliably, and your score rises—unlocking larger loans, higher multipliers. Default without good reason, and your score falls—restricting future access.

This isn't punishment. It's information. The system gives clear feedback and a path back to trust.

Loss absorption:

For genuine defaults—illness, disaster, circumstances beyond control—the fund absorbs the loss collectively. A small portion of all transactions goes to a community insurance pool that covers defaults. The cost is distributed across everyone.

Example: Maya's Garden

Maya wants to start a community garden. She needs 100 tokens for supplies. The Family Trust sees her history: three years of reliable contributions, a trust score in the top quartile. She receives 100 tokens at zero interest.

Six months later, the garden thrives. Maya repays the 100 tokens. Her trust score rises by 20 points. The next time she applies, she qualifies for 250 tokens.

Another borrower defaults. The insurance pool covers the loss—a fraction of a token from thousands of people. No one is ruined. The defaulter's trust score drops, but the path back is clear: contribute, follow through, demonstrate trustworthiness.

Permissionless Contribution

Anyone can create value without asking permission first.

In the extraction economy, contribution requires approval. You need to be hired. You need authorization. The bureaucracy exists because the system doesn't trust you.

In the Trust Economy, work is always available. If you want to contribute, you just contribute.

Consider roadside trash. In the extraction economy, cleaning it up requires a municipal contract, work crews, liability insurance, budget approval. The trash sits for months.

In the Trust Economy, anyone can clean it up. The contribution is visible. The value is obvious. The system recognizes it.

The principle: Anyone can contribute by creating value for anything they see that needs doing. No gatekeeping required—people can just solve the problems that linger everywhere.

Safeguards Against Gaming

Any system can be gamed. The question is whether the architecture makes gaming harder than honest participation.

Lock-in periods: When you buy in, you can't sell for two years—eliminating pump-and-dump schemes.

Withdrawal delay: Six months to withdraw prevents panic runs and signals commitment.

Transparency: A visible ledger records every transaction. Hiding requires darkness; this system has none.

Satisfaction verification: Tokens only transfer when both parties confirm the exchange was complete.

Distributed governance: Treasury funds go into community pools, not anyone's pocket. Participants vote on which projects to fund. Gaming the system means fooling your neighbors.

These safeguards don't make gaming impossible. They make it costly enough that honest participation is the easier path.

Early Adopter Rewards

The Trust Economy needs pioneers—people willing to trust the system before it's proven.

Those who join early receive enhanced multipliers that last for years. Not forever—the goal isn't a permanent aristocracy of early believers. But long enough to honor the risk they took, to acknowledge that trust given early costs more.

These are the founders of the new economy. Not founders who cash out and extract—founders who seed a system designed to serve everyone.

Implementation Notes

The Trust OS coordinates all of this in the background. It matches needs to contributions, verifies transactions, maintains the ledger. But it doesn't control the currency. It makes the currency visible, the way accounting software makes a business legible without running it.

The dollar interface: During the transition, people will operate in both systems. Earning tokens through contribution and dollars through traditional work. Spending tokens within the network and dollars outside it. As the network expands, more needs can be met internally. The dollar dependency decreases through superior efficiency, not force.

Local variation: The exact parameters—baseline valuation, multiplier ceilings, giving floor size—may vary by community and will be refined through iteration. What won't change is the architecture: time-based, contribution-verified, designed for circulation, governed by trust.

This prototype is offered as a starting point for implementation, not a finished design. The principles are proven by WIR, Sardex, Kiva, and time banks. The specific mechanisms will evolve through practice.

The specifications above are starting points. Now, one final vision: what does it look like when all of this works?

Epilogue: The Dream

"All that remains is the choice to build it."

You wake at 5:30 AM. Not to an alarm—to light, gradually brightening in your bedroom, calibrated to your sleep cycle. The room knows when you're ready to surface and brings you up gently, the way morning was supposed to work before we invented jarring electronic beeps.

You slept well. You usually do now.

The house is quiet except for the hum of the coffee maker—your AI assistant noticed you stirring and started the kettle. You call her Ada, after the mathematician. She doesn't speak unless you want her to. This morning, you don't. You just sit with the cup, watching the sky lighten through the window, feeling the particular peace of knowing that today is yours to design.

Not "free time" carved from obligations. Not vacation earned through exhaustion. Just... a day. Yours.

At 6:00, you head to the community fitness center—three blocks away, in a building that used to be a bank before the neighborhood converted it. The vault is a meditation room now. The irony isn't lost on anyone.

Your coach Marcus is waiting—a former physical therapist who transitioned into movement coaching when the Trust Economy made it viable. He works with thirty people he actually knows: their bodies, their injuries, their goals, their lives. In the extraction economy, he'd be seeing clients for fifty minutes, billing insurance, burning out. Here, he has time.

The workout is hard. Your form starts to slip on the last set of deadlifts.

"Reset," he says. "One more. Clean."

You do it clean. He grins. "That's one more rep than last week. We're building something."

You leave energized, not depleted. This is what movement feels like when someone's paying attention.

At 8:00, you walk to the neighborhood learning center. You're teaching today—a skill you developed over twenty years in your previous career, now passed on to three young people who want to learn it. You're not teaching because you have to. You're teaching because you're good at it, because the knowledge shouldn't die with you.

One of your students—Priya, nineteen, sharp but impatient—struggles with a concept you thought was obvious. You remember struggling with the same thing once. You slow down, find a different angle, watch her face when it clicks.

"Oh," she says. "Oh, that's what you meant."

This is contribution. Not productivity metrics. Not performance reviews. Someone knows more now than they did ninety minutes ago, and you made that happen.

At 10:00, you become the student. A master woodworker named Howard is teaching joinery—a skill you've always wanted but never had time to learn. He's seventy-three, spent forty years as a finish carpenter, and now teaches because he loves it.

You're terrible at it so far. The joints don't fit. You've cut two pieces of walnut wrong already, and walnut isn't cheap.

Howard watches you struggle, then gently takes the chisel from your hand. His movements are economical, precise, accumulated over decades. "Feel the grain," he says. "You're fighting it."

You try again. Less terrible this time.

You realize this is the first time in decades you've been a beginner at anything. The first time you've been allowed to be bad at something without it threatening your livelihood or status. There's freedom in that. Room to grow.

At noon, you eat at the community kitchen—a building that used to be a fast-food franchise, now converted into something slower. Long tables where strangers become neighbors.

Ethiopian food today, prepared by Almaz, a grandmother who learned the cuisine from her mother in Addis Ababa. The meal costs three tokens—less than you'd pay for a sad sandwich in the old economy, and incomparably better.

You sit with two people you've come to know over months of shared lunches. The conversation wanders the way good conversations do. One of them reads you a paragraph she's been wrestling with—something about her father, and a fishing trip, and the way memory works.

"What if you started with the smell?" you suggest. "The fish. The lake. Get the reader there before you tell them why it matters."

She writes that down. You notice her eyes are wet.

This is lunch. Connection as default. Loneliness as aberration.

At 2:00, you join a project meeting—virtually, in a shared space that feels more like a room than a screen.

A team is designing a housing community three hundred miles away—a neighborhood built for connection, where families share courtyards and children know every adult by name. You're contributing your expertise: user experience, how people actually live in spaces.

There's a genuine disagreement about material costs versus sustainability. Voices rise.

And that's okay. Conflict isn't the enemy—conflict is how groups find the best answer.

By 4:00, you've found a solution that's better than either starting position—a phased approach that hits budget now and upgrades as the community generates surplus.

That's not compromise. That's collaboration. Difficulty with dignity.

At 5:00, you walk home.

A few kids are playing in a courtyard—actual play, not organized activities. Three neighbors supervise loosely; they rotate through the week, and everyone knows the children by name. An elderly man tends the community garden. He waves as you pass.

The Perimeter is running. You can see it in the soft pulse of green light along the street fixtures—a visual confirmation that the community is present, awake, watching over itself. Not cameras pointed at you. Not surveillance monetizing your movements. Just presence. The neighborhood saying: We're here. We see each other. You're not alone.

At 5:30, your weekly call with Sister Teresa—not a nun, just someone who chose the title years ago, inspired by Mother Teresa's belief that love begins with presence. She asks the questions that matter.

"How's your soul today?"

You tell her the truth: you're tired. The project is harder than expected. You wonder sometimes if you're doing enough.

"The question isn't whether you're doing enough," she says. "It's whether you're present to what you're doing. Are you there when you teach? Are you there when you learn?"

You think about Priya's face when the concept clicked. About Howard's hands on the chisel.

"Yeah," you say. "I was there."

"Then you're doing enough."

At 7:00, dinner.

Japanese kaiseki, eight courses prepared by a woman named Yuki who trained in Kyoto for a decade. She's not running a restaurant, hustling for reviews, praying the rent check clears. She's an artist with a sustainable practice.

The table seats ten. You know three of them; the rest are new. The Trust OS matched you based on interests and availability—not to engineer connection, but to make it possible.

You learn their stories as the courses arrive. A man named Samuel just returned from Antarctica, studying ice cores. A woman named Keiko is writing a musical. Someone builds schools in Kenya. Someone named Ava is seventy-seven and learning to make violins because she always wanted to and finally has time.

The food is extraordinary. Not because of the ingredients—though they're good—but because of the intention. Each course is a thought, a question, an answer.

The meal costs twenty tokens. In the old economy, this would be a $400 dinner at an exclusive restaurant. Here, it's Tuesday. This is Universal Luxury—not scarcity performing exclusivity, but excellence as default.

And then you notice her.

Across the table, laughing at something Ava said, is a woman you recognize. Maria. The teaching assistant from Phoenix who joined the community eighteen months ago. You remember her story—everyone does. The one who used to ration her insulin. The one who did survival math at 2:47 in the morning.

She doesn't do that math anymore.

Her insulin costs three tokens a month through the community health system. Her rent is stable through the Family Trust. She teaches kindergarten now, not as an assistant—as a lead teacher, because the community recognized what the school district never did: she's exceptional with children.

But that's not what strikes you tonight.

What strikes you is the laughter. The ease. The way she leans into the conversation, not calculating whether she can afford to be here, not wondering what this will cost her tomorrow. She's simply here—present, connected, held.

Maria catches your eye and raises her glass. She knows you recognized her. She knows the story you're thinking about.

"To trust," she says quietly. Just to you.

You raise yours back.

She's found her people. So have you.

At 10:00, you're home. Before sleep, you review your day.

Earned: 4 Unity Tokens (teaching session, project contribution)

Spent: 3 tokens (dinner, woodworking class, community kitchen)

Trust score: Up 2 points

The numbers matter, but not the way they used to. They're measuring contribution, not worth. And contribution feels good.

You close your eyes.

This Isn't Utopia

The workout was hard. Your muscles ache.

The student struggled, and you had to find patience you weren't sure you had.

The project meeting was tense. Real disagreements with real stakes.

Your spiritual coach asked questions you didn't want to answer.

The day wasn't easy. The Trust Economy doesn't promise easy.

But it was good.

Because difficulty with dignity beats ease without meaning.

Because you woke up knowing you were held—that if you fell, someone would catch you.

Because you contributed something that mattered and received what you needed.

Because at no point today did someone try to extract value from you. At no point were you optimized, monetized, or processed.

You felt like a human being.

That's the dream.

I have six children. They're going to inherit whatever world we build.

I want them to inherit a world where people want to know each other. Where trust is the default, not the exception. Where the fullest expression of what we are isn't hoarded—it's shared.

That's not utopia. That's just people, seeing each other clearly, building together.

We're not going backward.

We're not pretending the last fifty years didn't happen. We're not rejecting scale. We're not dismantling what works. We're not returning to some imagined past where everything was simpler.

The 1960s had the heart but not the tools.

The 1990s had the tools but lost the heart.

The 2020s can have both.

We've figured out scale. We've figured out networks. We've figured out coordination.

Now we remember why it matters.

We've never seen this in our history.

And we can.

Who's with me?

Much love,
Jonathan

Appendix

This section provides sources for the research, data, and quotations cited throughout the book. Notes are organized by chapter and keyed to specific phrases in the text.

Prologue: Two Worlds

"Maria... is a composite"

Maria's story synthesizes details from insulin pricing testimonies, healthcare studies, and reporting on medication rationing. See: Herkert, D., et al. "Cost-Related Insulin Underuse Among Patients With Diabetes." JAMA Internal Medicine 179, no. 1 (2019): 112-114. Also: Cefalu, W.T., et al. "Insulin Access and Affordability Working Group: Conclusions and Recommendations." Diabetes Care 41, no. 6 (2018): 1299-1311.

Chapter One: The Three Moments Trust Died

"On September 13, 1970, Milton Friedman published an essay"

Friedman, Milton. "The Social Responsibility of Business Is to Increase Its Profits." New York Times Magazine, September 13, 1970.

"Soviet communism had murdered tens of millions"

Estimates vary. See: Conquest, Robert. The Great Terror: A Reassessment (Oxford University Press, 2008). Also: Applebaum, Anne. Gulag: A History (Doubleday, 2003).

"Maoist China's Great Leap Forward had killed between 15 and 55 million"

Dikotter, Frank. Mao's Great Famine: The History of China's Most Devastating Catastrophe (Walker & Company, 2010). The wide range reflects ongoing historical debate.

"Greed, for lack of a better word, is good"

Wall Street, directed by Oliver Stone (20th Century Fox, 1987). Screenplay by Stanley Weiser and Oliver Stone.

"Lehman Brothers... largest bankruptcy filing in American history"

At the time of filing, Lehman Brothers held $639 billion in assets. See: Valukas, Anton R. Lehman Brothers Holdings Inc. Chapter 11 Proceedings Examiner Report (March 11, 2010).

"Eight million Americans lost their jobs. Ten million lost their homes."

Bureau of Labor Statistics employment data, 2008-2010. Foreclosure data from RealtyTrac and the Federal Reserve.

"The stock market lost half its value"

The S&P 500 fell approximately 57% from its peak of 1,565 on October 9, 2007 to its trough of 666 on March 6, 2009. The Dow Jones Industrial Average fell 54% over the same period. See: Wikipedia, "United States bear market of 2007-2009"; also Nasdaq, "A Short History of the Great Recession."

Chapter Two: The Wealth Illusion

"Easterlin Paradox"

Easterlin, Richard A. "Does Economic Growth Improve the Human Lot? Some Empirical Evidence." In Nations and Households in Economic Growth: Essays in Honor of Moses Abramovitz, edited by Paul A. David and Melvin W. Reder (Academic Press, 1974).

"Daniel Kahneman and Angus Deaton found that the happiness benefits of increased income largely plateau around $75,000 per year"

Kahneman, Daniel, and Angus Deaton. "High Income Improves Evaluation of Life but Not Emotional Well-being." Proceedings of the National Academy of Sciences 107, no. 38 (2010): 16489-16493. Note: A 2021 study by Matthew Killingsworth found happiness may continue rising with income beyond this threshold, though the relationship becomes less linear. See: Killingsworth, Matthew A. "Experienced Well-being Rises with Income, Even Above $75,000 per Year." Proceedings of the National Academy of Sciences 118, no. 4 (2021).

"hedonic treadmill"

Brickman, Philip, and Donald T. Campbell. "Hedonic Relativism and Planning the Good Society." In Adaptation-Level Theory: A Symposium, edited by M.H. Appley (Academic Press, 1971), 287-302.

"Harvard Study of Adult Development—the longest study of human happiness ever conducted"

The study began in 1938 and has followed participants for over 85 years. See: Waldinger, Robert, and Marc Schulz. The Good Life: Lessons from the World's Longest Scientific Study of Happiness (Simon & Schuster, 2023). Also: Vaillant, George E. Triumphs of Experience: The Men of the Harvard Grant Study (Belknap Press, 2012).

"Close relationships, more than money or fame, are what keep people happy throughout their lives"

Waldinger, Robert. "What Makes a Good Life? Lessons from the Longest Study on Happiness." TED Talk, November 2015. Viewed over 45 million times.

"The quality of relationships at age fifty was a better predictor of physical health at age eighty than cholesterol levels"

Waldinger and Schulz, The Good Life (2023).

"Loneliness kills. It's as powerful as smoking or alcoholism."

Waldinger, Robert. TED Talk (2015) and subsequent interviews. Also supported by: Holt-Lunstad, Julianne, et al. "Loneliness and Social Isolation as Risk Factors for

Mortality: A Meta-Analytic Review." Perspectives on Psychological Science 10, no. 2 (2015): 227-237.

"Paul Hokemeyer... 'They live in such a rarified place'"

Hokemeyer, Paul. Quoted in "'Wealth can be pretty isolating': Problems that rich people face, according to therapists." CNBC, May 14, 2024. Hokemeyer is the founding principal of Drayson Mews clinic and author of Fragile Power: Why Having Everything Is Never Enough (Hazelden Publishing, 2019).

"Amanda Falkson... 'Wealth can be pretty isolating'"

Falkson, Amanda. Quoted in "'Wealth can be pretty isolating': Problems that rich people face, according to therapists." CNBC, May 14, 2024. Falkson is a psychotherapist versed in wealth counseling at Psychotherapy City.

Chapter Three: Energy Is Trust

"The four largest U.S. banks—JPMorgan Chase, Bank of America, Citigroup, and Wells Fargo—hold over $11.5 trillion in combined assets"

Federal Reserve Statistical Release, Consolidated Assets of Major Banks. Q4 2024 holding company data: JPMorgan Chase ~$4.0T, Bank of America ~$3.3T, Citigroup ~$2.0T, Wells Fargo ~$1.9T. Combined ~$11.2 trillion. Also: S&P Global Market Intelligence; FDIC Summary of Deposits. Note: Bank-level vs. holding company-level assets differ; figures fluctuate quarterly.

"Silicon Valley Bank lost $42 billion in deposits in a single day"

FDIC press releases, March 2023. Also: various news reporting including Wall Street Journal, New York Times, and Financial Times coverage of SVB collapse.

"89% of its $172 billion in deposits were uninsured"

SVB Financial Group SEC filings and FDIC reports.

"This was the first Twitter-fueled bank run"

McHenry, Patrick. Statement to House Financial Services Committee, March 2023.

"From 1929 to 1933, over 9,000 American banks failed"

Federal Reserve Bank of St. Louis, "Banking Panics of the Great Depression." Also: Friedman, Milton, and Anna Jacobson Schwartz. A Monetary History of the United States, 1867-1960 (Princeton University Press, 1963).

"In December 1930, a small merchant in the Bronx... began spreading rumors that they'd refused to sell"

New York Times, December 1930, as reported in History.com, "Bank Run." Also: FDIC, "1930-1939" historical timeline. The Bank of the United States collapse with over $200 million in deposits was the largest single bank failure in American history at that time.

"In medieval Europe, goldsmiths had secure vaults... fractional reserve banking"

Kim, Jongchul. "How Modern Banking Originated: The London Goldsmith-Bankers' Institutionalisation of Trust." Business History 53, no. 6 (2011): 939-959. Also: Karan, Mehmet Baha, Wim Westerman, and Jacob Wijngaard. "Goldsmith

Bankers and the Birth of the Fractional Reserve System (Seventeenth and Early Eighteenth Centuries)." In A History of Banks, 99-128 (Springer, 2024). Note: Economic historian George Selgin has examined the record of London goldsmith bankers and argued against the "fraud" characterization, suggesting fractional reserve banking arose through legitimate contractual evolution rather than deception.

"The great banking dynasties—the Medici in Florence, the Rothschilds across Europe"

Ferguson, Niall. The House of Rothschild: Money's Prophets, 1798-1848 (Viking/Penguin, 1998). Also: Ferguson, Niall. The House of Rothschild: The World's Banker, 1849-1999 (Viking/Penguin, 1999). Ferguson was the first historian with access to the Rothschild family archives. On the Medici: Parks, Tim. Medici Money: Banking, Metaphysics, and Art in Fifteenth-Century Florence (W.W. Norton, 2005).

"Research in the Journal of Economic Behavior & Organization"

Kiss, Hubert J., Ismael Rodriguez-Lara, and Alfonso Rosa-Garcia. "Do Social Networks Prevent or Promote Bank Runs?" Journal of Economic Behavior & Organization 101 (2014): 87-99. Also: Dijk, Oege. "Bank Run Psychology." Journal of Economic Behavior & Organization 144 (2017): 87-96.

"Google's Project Aristotle found that psychological safety was the single strongest predictor of team performance"

Duhigg, Charles. "What Google Learned From Its Quest to Build the Perfect Team." New York Times Magazine, February 25, 2016. Original research published by Google's People Operations team.

Chapter Four: Weak Capitalism

"Paradise, California. In November 2018, the Camp Fire killed eighty-five people"

California Department of Forestry and Fire Protection (CAL FIRE) official incident report. Also: various journalistic investigations including Wall Street Journal and San Francisco Chronicle reporting on PG&E's deferred maintenance.

"In March 2021, the Ever Given... ran aground in the Suez Canal"

Suez Canal Authority official statements, March 2021. The "$9.6 billion worth of goods per day" figure comes from Lloyd's List, as reported by Bloomberg, Al Jazeera, ABC News, and numerous other outlets during the incident (March 25-29, 2021). Lloyd's List estimated westbound traffic at $5.1 billion/day and eastbound at $4.5 billion/day.

"Two Boeing 737 MAX aircraft crashed, killing 346 people"

National Transportation Safety Board reports. Also: House Committee on Transportation and Infrastructure report, "The Design, Development & Certification of the Boeing 737 MAX" (September 2020).

"In 2016, news broke that Wells Fargo employees had opened millions of fake accounts"

Consumer Financial Protection Bureau enforcement action (September 2016). Also: Senate Banking Committee hearings and subsequent investigations.

Chapter Five: Elon's Idiot Index

"Elon Musk has a formula he uses to identify waste"

Musk has discussed the Idiot Index concept in multiple interviews and shareholder letters. See: Tesla shareholder meetings and interviews including Third Row Tesla Podcast (2020).

"Maria... one of the estimated 1.3 million Americans who ration their insulin"

Herkert, D., et al. "Cost-Related Insulin Underuse Among Patients With Diabetes." JAMA Internal Medicine 179, no. 1 (2019): 112-114.

"College tuition in the United States has increased over 1,200 percent since 1980"

College Board, "Trends in College Pricing" (annual reports). Also: Bureau of Labor Statistics Consumer Price Index historical data.

"Healthcare in the United States consumes nearly twenty percent of GDP"

Centers for Medicare & Medicaid Services, National Health Expenditure data. Also: OECD Health Statistics for international comparisons.

Chapter Six: The Noise

"A landmark study published in Science by Mani, Mullainathan, Shafir, and Zhao"

Mani, Anandi, Sendhil Mullainathan, Eldar Shafir, and Jiaying Zhao. "Poverty Impedes Cognitive Function." Science 341, no. 6149 (2013): 976-980.

"Kahneman and Tversky showed that losses are psychologically weighted roughly twice as heavily as equivalent gains"

Kahneman, Daniel, and Amos Tversky. "Prospect Theory: An Analysis of Decision under Risk." Econometrica 47, no. 2 (1979): 263-292.

Market Concentration Data (multiple claims)

- Grocery: Numerator market share data (Q1 2025): Walmart 21.2%, Kroger 8.9%, Costco 8.5%, Albertsons 5.0%, Publix 4.1%. Combined ~47%. Also: Progressive Grocer, "Walmart Holds Tight to 1st Place for Grocery Market Share" (April 2025).

- Media: Wikipedia, "Concentration of Media Ownership." Widely cited statistic that six conglomerates control 90% of American media dates to 2011 analysis and remains commonly referenced. Top conglomerates (2025): Comcast NBCUniversal, Disney, Warner Bros. Discovery, Paramount Skydance.

- Banking: Federal Reserve data. Big Four (JPMorgan Chase, Bank of America, Citigroup, Wells Fargo) hold ~$11.5 trillion in combined assets out of ~$24.5 trillion total US banking assets (~47%). Visual Capitalist, "Ranked: The 25 Largest U.S. Banks by Assets" (March 2025).

- Asset Management: BlackRock (~$12.5T, June 2025), Vanguard (~$11T, Jan 2025), State Street (~$4.7T). Combined ~$28T. RIABiz reports combined AUM of

~$26.72T (April 2025). Also: Wikipedia entries for each firm; DIY Investing Hub, "How BlackRock, Vanguard, and State Street Own a Stake in Almost Every Company" (March 2025).

- Search: StatCounter Global Stats; Statista. Google's global search market share fell below 90% in late 2024 for first time since 2015, averaging ~89.6% through 2025. Desktop share lower (~79-82%); mobile share higher (~94%).

Chapter Eight: The Two Economies

"The World Values Survey"

World Values Survey Association. Data available at www.worldvaluessurvey.org. Trust data cited from Wave 7 (2017-2022).

"In Denmark, 76% of people say most people can be trusted"

World Values Survey Wave 7. Note: percentages vary slightly by survey year.

"Francis Fukuyama documented this in his 1995 book Trust"

Fukuyama, Francis. Trust: The Social Virtues and the Creation of Prosperity (Free Press, 1995).

"Robert Putnam's research on social capital"

Putnam, Robert D. Making Democracy Work: Civic Traditions in Modern Italy (Princeton University Press, 1993). Also: Bowling Alone: The Collapse and Revival of American Community (Simon & Schuster, 2000).

"Paul Zak and Stephen Knack calculated that a 15-percentage-point increase in trust correlates with a 1% increase in annual GDP growth"

Knack, Stephen, and Philip Keefer. "Does Social Capital Have an Economic Payoff? A Cross-Country Investigation." Quarterly Journal of Economics 112, no. 4 (1997): 1251-1288. Also: Zak, Paul J., and Stephen Knack. "Trust and Growth." Economic Journal 111, no. 470 (2001): 295-321.

"The dabbawalas of Mumbai"

Thomke, Stefan. "Mumbai's Models of Service Excellence." Harvard Business Review, November 2012. Also: Pathak, G.S. "The Dabbawallas of Mumbai." Case study, various business schools. Note on the "one in sixteen million" error rate: This figure originates from a 1998 interview where the president of the Mumbai Tiffinmen's Association told Forbes reporter Subrata Chakravarty that mistakes happen "almost never, maybe once every two months." Chakravarty extrapolated this to "one in eight million deliveries" (or sixteen million counting returns). Forbes never formally certified the dabbawalas as "Six Sigma"—this became folklore. The system is genuinely remarkable, but the specific statistic is an estimation rather than from rigorous study.

Chapter Nine: The Convergence

"Three firms (BlackRock, Vanguard, State Street) control over $26 trillion"

Company reports and SEC filings. As of Q2 2025: BlackRock $12.53 trillion, Vanguard ~$11 trillion, State Street ~$4.3 trillion. Total AUM figures fluctuate with market conditions.

"These three firms are the largest shareholders of 88% of S&P 500 companies"

Fichtner, Jan, Eelke M. Heemskerk, and Javier Garcia-Bernardo. "Hidden Power of the Big Three? Passive Index Funds, Re-Concentration of Corporate Ownership, and New Financial Risk." Business and Politics 19, no. 2 (2017): 298-326.

"A 2021 NBER study found that PE ownership of nursing homes led to a 10% increase in mortality"

Gupta, Atul, et al. "Does Private Equity Investment in Healthcare Benefit Patients? Evidence from Nursing Homes." NBER Working Paper 28474 (February 2021). Published in Review of Financial Studies (2024).

"PE-backed deals hit $1.2 trillion in 2021"

PitchBook, Bain & Company Global Private Equity Report (2022).

"One Stanford study found 13% job loss in AI-exposed fields"

Brynjolfsson, Erik, Bharat Chandar, and Ruyu Chen. "Canaries in the Coal Mine? Six Facts about the Recent Employment Effects of Artificial Intelligence." Stanford Digital Economy Lab Working Paper, August 2025. Available at: https://digitaleconomy.stanford.edu. The study analyzed ADP payroll records covering 25 million workers and found a 13% relative decline in employment for workers ages 22-25 in AI-exposed occupations since late 2022.

Chapter Ten: The First Adversary

Author's personal narrative The account of depression, suicidal ideation at age twenty-three, and recovery draws from the author's personal experience. The thirteen-year duration of depression referenced is autobiographical.

"A landmark study published in *Science* found that financial scarcity alone reduces cognitive performance by the equivalent of thirteen IQ points" Mani, Anandi, Sendhil Mullainathan, Eldar Shafir, and Jiaying Zhao. "Poverty Impedes Cognitive Function." *Science* 341, no. 6149 (2013): 976-980. The study found that poverty-related concerns consume mental resources, leaving less cognitive capacity for other tasks.

"A Penn State study tracking worry outcomes found that 91.4% of participants' worries never came true" LaFreniere, Lucas S., and Michelle G. Newman. "Exposing Worry's Deceit: Percentage of Untrue Worries in Generalized Anxiety Disorder Treatment." *Behavior Therapy* 51, no. 3 (2020): 413-423. Twenty-nine participants with GAD recorded worries for 10 days and tracked outcomes over 30 days. The study found that 91.4% of worry predictions did not come true, and the most common percentage of untrue worries per person was 100%. Of worries that did materialize, outcomes were better than expected approximately one-third of the time.

"**Tristan Harris... 'In the end, a lot of the tech people I talk to...'**" Harris, Tristan. Interview with Lex Fridman, *Lex Fridman Podcast* #382, July 2023. Harris is co-founder of the Center for Humane Technology.

"**Trust is learning to overcome your fear**" Original synthesis by the author, drawing on psychological literature about exposure therapy, growth mindset research, and resilience studies. See: Bandura, Albert. "Self-Efficacy: Toward a Unifying Theory of Behavioral Change." *Psychological Review* 84, no. 2 (1977): 191-215.

"**The God Image**" The concept of the *imago Dei* (image of God) is foundational across Abrahamic traditions. The author's interpretation—that the God Image is "your best self" and "doesn't require religion"—represents a secular application of this theological concept. See: Middleton, J. Richard. *The Liberating Image: The Imago Dei in Genesis 1* (Brazos Press, 2005).

Chapter Eleven: The Five Frequencies

"High-trust countries generate up to three times more GDP per capita than low-trust countries."

Algan, Yann, and Pierre Cahuc. "Trust and Growth." Annual Review of Economics 5, no. 1 (2013): 521-549. See also: Our World in Data, "Trust" (ourworldindata.org/trust), which aggregates World Values Survey data showing strong positive correlation between trust and GDP per capita. Zakharov et al. (2020) found that a 1-unit increase in trust correlates with GDP per capita rising by an average of 0.834, with the coefficient of determination indicating that 60.68% of GDP per capita variation relates to trust levels.

"High-trust companies outperform the S&P 500 by 2.5x."

Great Place to Work research shows this figure is actually conservative. According to their 2025 report "The Great Place To Work Effect Playbook," the Fortune 100 Best Companies to Work For (selected primarily on trust criteria) have cumulatively outperformed the S&P 500 by more than 2,000% since 1998—averaging 6% annual outperformance. Analysis by FTSE Russell and Jefferies confirmed publicly traded companies on the list beat the equally-weighted S&P 500 consistently. Research by Hamid Boustanifar and Young Dae Kang found the outperformance was most dramatic during crises like the 2008 financial crisis. See also: Fortune, "The Best Companies to Work For Are Beating the Market" (February 27, 2018).

"Low-trust societies spend two to four times more on legal enforcement and regulatory compliance."

Estimated from comparative data on legal sector size and regulatory compliance costs across high-trust (Nordic) and low-trust economies. See: Djankov, Simeon, et al. "The Regulation of Entry." Quarterly Journal of Economics 117, no. 1 (2002): 1-37. Also: Zak, Paul J., and Stephen Knack. "Trust and Growth." Economic Journal 111, no. 470 (2001): 295-321.

Ernest Hemingway epigraph

Widely attributed to Hemingway, though the original source is uncertain. The sentiment appears in various forms in his correspondence and interviews.

Chapter Twelve: The Surplus Principle

"Acknowledge your blessings—and create opportunities for others. Be of surplus value."

Galloway, Scott. Notes on Being a Man (Portfolio/Penguin, 2025). The book is part memoir, part guide for young men, and concludes with a letter to Galloway's two sons. "Surplus value"—giving more than you take—is a central theme throughout.

Warren Buffett's acquisition of McLane Company

Buffett, Warren. Berkshire Hathaway 2003 Annual Report, Chairman's Letter. The McLane deal closed in May 2003 for approximately $1.5 billion. McLane had $23 billion in annual revenue at the time. Buffett wrote: "We did no 'due diligence.' We knew everything would be exactly as Walmart said it would be—and it was." The two-hour meeting was with Tom Schoewe, Walmart's CFO.

Nebraska Furniture Mart acquisition

Buffett, Warren. Berkshire Hathaway 2013 Annual Report. Buffett describes approaching Rose Blumkin with a one-page proposal he'd drafted himself: "Mrs. B accepted my offer without changing a word, and we completed the deal without the involvement of investment bankers or lawyers."

"You can't do a good deal with a bad person"

This maxim appears in multiple Buffett speeches and interviews. See also: Buffett's remarks at Berkshire Hathaway annual meetings, particularly his discussion of due diligence philosophy.

Chapter Thirteen: The Law of Consent

The airport security story

Author's personal experience.

"The Four Conditions" framework

This framework synthesizes principles from multiple sources: Informed consent standards in medical ethics (see Beauchamp and Childress, Principles of Biomedical Ethics, 8th ed., Oxford University Press, 2019); contract law doctrine on valid consent; and contemporary consent theory in political philosophy. The specific formulation—freely chosen, informed, specific, and reversible—is the author's synthesis for economic application.

"Consent is the missing regulator of capitalism"

This argument builds on critiques of shareholder primacy and stakeholder theory. See: Freeman, R. Edward. Strategic Management: A Stakeholder Approach (Cambridge University Press, 2010, originally 1984). Also: Stout, Lynn. The Shareholder Value Myth (Berrett-Koehler, 2012).

Chapter Fourteen: The Perimeter

"the research suggests it's around 20% participation"

Rogers, Everett M. Diffusion of Innovations, 5th ed. (Free Press, 2003). Also: Centola, Damon. "The Spread of Behavior in an Online Social Network Experiment." Science 329, no. 5996 (2010): 1194-1197.

Chapter Fifteen: Restoring Trust

"The current prison system costs $40,000-60,000 per inmate annually"

Bureau of Justice Statistics, various years. Costs vary by state; federal average higher. See also: Vera Institute of Justice, "The Price of Prisons" reports.

"produces 44% recidivism within one year"

Bureau of Justice Statistics. "2018 Update on Prisoner Recidivism: A 9-Year Follow-up Period (2005-2014)." Note: Three-year recidivism rates typically cited at 67%; five-year rates at 76%.

"Restorative justice programs show dramatically better outcomes at a fraction of the cost"

Multiple studies support this claim:

- Shapland, J., et al. "Does Restorative Justice Affect Reconviction? The Fourth Report from the Evaluation of Three Schemes." UK Ministry of Justice Research Series 10/08 (2008). Found an 8:1 cost-benefit ratio—for every GBP 1 spent on restorative justice conferencing, GBP 8 saved in criminal justice costs.
- Bonta, J., et al. "Restorative Justice and Recidivism." Public Safety Canada Research Summary Vol. 8 No. 1 (2003). Meta-analysis of 46 studies (23,000 participants) found average 3% recidivism reduction; 8% reduction for adults.
- Latimer, J., C. Dowden, and D. Muise. "The Effectiveness of Restorative Justice Practices: A Meta-Analysis." The Prison Journal 85, no. 2 (2005): 127-144.
- Sherman, L.W., and H. Strang. "Restorative Justice: The Evidence." Smith Institute (2007).
- UK House of Commons Justice Committee (2016): "There is clear evidence that restorative justice can provide value for money by both reducing reoffending rates and providing tangible benefits to victims."

Cost comparison: Restorative justice programs typically cost $500-$1,500 per participant versus $40,000-60,000 per year for incarceration.

Chapter Sixteen: The Trust OS

Cortana from Halo

The Halo video game series was developed by Bungie (later 343 Industries) and published by Microsoft. First released in 2001, the franchise features the AI character Cortana as a supportive rather than adversarial artificial intelligence—a deliberate narrative choice by the creators. The character's design influenced Microsoft's later naming of their Cortana digital assistant (2014).

"Distributed intelligence layer" and coordination systems

The Trust OS concept draws on research in distributed systems, multi-agent coordination, and platform cooperativism. See: Scholz, Trebor, and Nathan Schneider, eds. Ours to Hack and to Own: The Rise of Platform Cooperativism (OR Books, 2017). Also: Ostrom, Elinor. Governing the Commons (Cambridge University Press, 1990) on decentralized coordination mechanisms.

Privacy-preserving matching systems

For technical precedents, see: Acquisti, Alessandro, et al. "What Is Privacy Worth?" Journal of Legal Studies 42, no. 2 (2013): 249-274. On consent-driven data systems: Pentland, Alex. "Reality Mining of Mobile Communications." IEEE Pervasive Computing (2005). The Trust OS as described is a design proposal synthesizing these concepts with contemporary AI capabilities.

Chapter Seventeen: The Partnership Agreement

"Bob's Red Mill... ESOP announced on February 15, 2010"

Company website (bobsredmill.com/employee-owned) and multiple sources confirm: ESOP established February 15, 2010 (Bob Moore's 81st birthday), initially transferring one-third of company to employees. 100% employee-owned by April 2020. Also: Fortune, "Bob's Red Mill is 100% Employee Owned" (February 17, 2022); Business Insider coverage of Moore's death (February 2024). Revenue exceeds $100 million; products sold in 70+ countries.

"A meta-analysis of 122 studies found that cooperation promoted higher achievement than competition"

Johnson, David W., and Roger T. Johnson. "Cooperation and Competition: Theory and Research." (Interaction Book Company, 1989). Also: Johnson, David W., et al. "Effects of Cooperative, Competitive, and Individualistic Goal Structures on Achievement: A Meta-Analysis." Psychological Bulletin 89, no. 1 (1981): 47-62.

Chapter Eighteen: The Project Economy

"Google has killed over 275 products and services"

Killed by Google (killedbygoogle.com) maintains a comprehensive list of discontinued Google products. As of December 2025, the count exceeds 275 distinct products and services. Notable examples include: Google Reader (2013), Google+ (2019), Inbox by Gmail (2019), Google Hangouts (2022), Google Stadia (2023).

"Tree T-Pee valued at over $100 million"

Multiple sources confirm Tree T-Pee's growth trajectory following Shark Tank Season 5 (2013). Initial valuation $750,000. Post-show expansion to 80+ countries, Home Depot partnership. Current valuation estimates exceed $100 million. Sources: Shark Tank Blog, Hatch Utah entrepreneurship profiles, YEN.COM.GH business coverage.

"90% of startups fail"

Startup Genome Report (2019); CB Insights analysis of startup post-mortems. The 90% failure rate is widely cited across venture capital and entrepreneurship research. Primary causes include: no market need (42%), ran out of cash (29%), wrong team (23%), got outcompeted (19%).

Chapter Nineteen: The Unity Token

"Kiva.org has facilitated over $1.5 billion in micro-loans"

Kiva.org official statistics, available at www.kiva.org/about/stats.

"Your money's in Joe's house... right next to yours"

It's a Wonderful Life, directed by Frank Capra (Liberty Films, 1946). The bank run scene demonstrates the principle of liquidity through velocity—money working in the community rather than sitting in vaults. George Bailey's explanation of how the Bailey Building & Loan works remains one of the clearest articulations of community-based finance in popular culture.

Chapter Twenty: The Family Trust

"30-year fixed mortgage at 7% interest"

Federal Reserve Economic Data (FRED). Historical mortgage rate data from Freddie Mac Primary Mortgage Market Survey. Note: The 7% rate is used as a calculation assumption for the worked example. As of December 2025, actual 30-year fixed rates averaged 6.1-6.4% (Freddie Mac PMMS). The long-term historical average is approximately 7.7% (Bankrate data since 1971). The calculation demonstrates the principle regardless of the specific rate.

Chapter Twenty-One: Whole Health

"In 2019, there were 71,000 professional coaches worldwide. By 2024, that number exceeded 145,000"

International Coaching Federation (ICF) Global Coaching Studies (2020, 2024).

"The global coaching market hit $6.25 billion in 2024"

ICF Global Coaching Study and various market research reports.

"BetterUp... reached a $4.7 billion valuation"

Company announcements and venture capital reporting, 2021-2022.

Chapter Twenty-Two: Universal Luxury

"Hermes employs about 3,000 artisans"

Hermes annual reports and corporate communications.

"A 2023 Hermes Birkin... $9,000-$12,000 retail"

Public retail pricing and secondary market data from Heritage Auctions, Christie's, and Sotheby's.

"The current luxury market is about $400 billion globally"

Bain & Company, "Luxury Goods Worldwide Market Study" (annual reports).

"3.2 billion people in the global middle class"

Brookings Institution, "The Unprecedented Expansion of the Global Middle Class" (2017). Also: World Bank income classification data.

"Committee of Ten standardized American education"

National Education Association, "Report of the Committee of Ten on Secondary School Studies" (1892). The committee, chaired by Harvard president Charles Eliot, established the standardized curriculum structure that largely persists today. For historical analysis, see: Kliebard, Herbert M. The Struggle for the American Curriculum, 1893-1958 (Routledge, 2004).

"$1.7 trillion in student loan debt"

Federal Reserve Bank of New York, Quarterly Report on Household Debt and Credit (2024). Average graduate debt from National Center for Education Statistics and the Institute for College Access & Success.

Chapter Twenty-Three: The Path to Scale

See Chapter Twenty-Three for Hard Questions citations.

Chapter Twenty-Four: The Hard Questions

"Everett Rogers' diffusion studies show that innovations reach 'takeoff' at roughly 16% adoption"

Rogers, Everett M. Diffusion of Innovations, 5th ed. (Free Press, 2003).

"Damon Centola's work at the University of Pennsylvania found that committed minorities of 25% can flip behavioral norms"

Centola, Damon, et al. "Experimental Evidence for Tipping Points in Social Convention." Science 360, no. 6393 (2018): 1116-1119.

"WIR (Switzerland)... 50,000-60,000 Swiss businesses participate"

Studer, Tobias. "WIR and the Swiss National Economy." WIR Bank publications. Also: Stodder, James. "Complementary Credit Networks and Macroeconomic Stability: Switzerland's Wirtschaftsring." Journal of Economic Behavior & Organization 72, no. 1 (2009): 79-95.

"M-Pesa (Kenya)... over 90% of Kenyan adults used it"

Central Bank of Kenya annual reports. Also: Mas, Ignacio, and Dan Radcliffe. "Mobile Payments Go Viral: M-PESA in Kenya." Capco Institute Journal of Financial Transformation 32 (2011): 169-182.

"UPI (India)... processes over 75% of India's retail digital transactions"

National Payments Corporation of India (NPCI) data.

"Mondragon cooperatives"

Mondragon Corporation annual reports. Also: Whyte, William Foote, and Kathleen King Whyte. Making Mondragon cognitive ability"*

Gawdat, Mo. Scary Smart: The Future of Artificial Intelligence and How You Can Save Our World (Bluebird, 2021). Also: various interviews and podcasts, 2023-2024.

"The extraction economy spends approximately $1.5-2 trillion annually on friction costs"

The Competitive Enterprise Institute's 2024 "Ten Thousand Commandments" report estimates federal regulatory compliance costs at $2.155 trillion annually—approximately 7% of GDP. This figure covers only federal regulations and does not include state/local regulation, private-sector verification costs, contract enforcement, security spending, insurance overhead, or legal costs beyond compliance. The Tax Foundation estimates IRS tax compliance alone costs $546 billion annually. The NBER found average firm spends 1.34% of wage bill on regulatory compliance. Combined with non-regulatory friction costs (private security, collections, fraud prevention, insurance administration), the $1.5-2 trillion estimate is conservative. Sources: Competitive Enterprise Institute; Tax Foundation; Trebbi & Zhang, NBER Working Paper 30691 (2022).

Additional Sources and Acknowledgments

Nordic Economic Data

- World Economic Forum Global Competitiveness Reports
- OECD Better Life Index
- World Happiness Report (annual)
- Transparency International Corruption Perceptions Index

Trust and Social Capital Research

- General Social Survey (GSS), NORC at University of Chicago
- European Social Survey
- Pew Research Center Trust surveys

Economic Data

- Federal Reserve Economic Data (FRED)
- Bureau of Labor Statistics
- Bureau of Economic Analysis
- World Bank Open Data

All citations verified as of December 2025. Chapter notes provide sources for specific claims; general themes synthesize multiple sources.

ABOUT THE AUTHOR

Jonathan Brink is a systems designer, product strategist, and UX researcher with thirty years of experience in Silicon Valley. Born in the Valley at the dawn of the technology revolution, he has worked at every level of the industry—from founding startups to serving as AI Lead at IBM, with previous roles at Charles Schwab and high-growth companies like StreamSets.

His career has focused on one question: why do systems produce the outcomes they produce? As a designer, he learned that architecture determines behavior—build a system that rewards extraction, and people will extract; build one that rewards contribution, and people will contribute.

Brink is the author of *Discovering the God Imagination,* husband and the father of six children. It was watching his kids navigate a world that treats their attention as a resource to be harvested—and realizing they couldn't afford to live in the neighborhoods where they grew up—that drove him to ask whether better systems were possible.

The Trust Economy is the result of three decades of notes, pattern recognition, and late-night walks with his dog, asking the same question: *What would I want to hand my children—not just as inheritance, but as possibility?*

He lives in the San Francisco Bay Area with his wife and family.

Connect: thetrusteconomy.org

www.ingramcontent.com/pod-product-compliance
Lightning Source LLC
LaVergne TN
LVHW020413220926
848484LV00017B/2557/J
* 9 7 9 8 2 1 8 9 0 5 7 0 5 *